A Random Walk Down Wall Street

COLLEGE EDITION REVISED

A Random Walk Down Wall Street

COLLEGE EDITION REVISED

BURTON G. MALKIEL

W · W · NORTON & COMPANY · INC ·

NEW YORK

Published simultaneously in Canada
by George J. McLeod Limited, Toronto

This book was designed by Robert Freese.
The types are Bulmer and Baskerville.
The book was manufactured by Vail-Ballou Press, Inc.

PRINTED IN THE UNITED STATES OF AMERICA

3 4 5 6 7 8 9 0

To Jonathan

without whom this book would
have been finished a year earlier.

Contents

Contents

7

Preface to the College Edition Revised

The revised edition of *Random Walk* differs from the first in two major respects. First, the book has been thoroughly revised and updated. It would not seem that much could change in less than a year and a half, but during this time financial markets have been characterized by unprecedented upheaval and by extraordinary innovations that create opportunities for individual investors. For example, by 1974 the availability of several liquid-asset mutual funds and floating-rate notes had created superior alternatives to savings accounts for the liquid funds of many investors. Such innovations required the addition of much new material.

Second, I have included a new chapter (Eight) that I believe is required reading for every serious student of financial markets. The chapter covers in a non-technical manner the major theoretical and empirical findings of the "capital-asset pricing model," probably the major subject for academic research in finance over the past decade. Edgar Bunce of Prudential Insurance provided some of the data used in that chapter.

Thanks are due to many of the same people who helped with the first edition for reading over the new materials and offering valuable advice. Paul Brenner, my research assistant during the summer of 1974, was invaluable in updating tables and collecting material for new exhibits. Sherry Ahrens, Phyllis Byrd, Annmarie Ritz, and Helen Talar faithfully transformed my scribbling into legible drafts. Donald Lamm and Robert Kehoe of W. W. Norton's College Department were extremely helpful in many ways. Finally, I want to thank the many thoughtful people who took the trouble to write me with their most useful suggestions for revisions.

Burton G. Malkiel

Princeton, New Jersey
August 1974

Acknowledgments

My debts of gratitude to people and institutions who have helped me with this book are enormous in both number and degree. My academic colleagues and friends in the financial community who have contributed to various drafts of chapters are too numerous to mention. I must acknowledge explicitly, however, the many who have read through the entire manuscript and offered extremely valuable suggestions and criticisms. These include Peter Asch, Leo Bailey, Jeffrey Balash, William Baumol, G. Gordon Biggar, Jr., Lester Chandler, Barry Feldman, William Grant, Sol Malkiel, Richard Quandt, Michael Rothschild, H. Barton Thomas, and Robert Zenowich. It is particularly appropriate that I emphasize the usual *caveat* that the above-named individuals are blameless for any errors of fact or judgment in these pages. Many have warned me patiently and repeatedly about the madness of my heresies, and the above list includes several who disagree sharply with my position.

Many research assistants have labored long in compiling information for this book. Especially useful contributions were made by Barry Feldman, Paul Messaris, Barry Schwartz, Greg Smolarek, Ray Soldavin, and Elizabeth Woods. Helen Talar and Phyllis Durepos not only faithfully and accurately typed several drafts of the manuscript, but also offered extremely valuable research assistance as well. Elvira Giaimo provided most helpful computer programming. Many of the supporting studies for this book were conducted at Princeton's Financial Research Center.

A vital contribution was made by Patricia Taylor, a professional writer and editor. She read through two complete drafts of the book and made innumerable contributions to the style, organization, and content of the manuscript. She deserves much of the credit for whatever lucid writing can be found in these pages.

I am also grateful to Arthur Lipper Corporation for permission to use their mutual fund rankings, Wiesenberger Investment Services for the use of their data in many of my tables, Moody's Investors Service for permission to reproduce several of their stock charts, Consumers Union for their estimates of life insurance costs, College Retirement Equities Fund for making available to me James Farrell's performance studies, and Smith, Barney & Co., Inc. for allowing me the run of their investment library.

My association with W. W. Norton & Company has been an extremely pleasant one, and I am particularly grateful to my editor, Starling Lawrence, for his invaluable help.

Finally, the contribution of my wife, Judith Malkiel, was of inestimable importance. No perfunctory uxorial reference of "cheerful encouragement" can do justice to her contribution. She painstakingly edited every page of the manuscript and was helpful in every phase of this undertaking. This acknowledgment of my debt to her is the largest understatement of all.

Burton G. Malkiel

Princeton, New Jersey
April 1973

PART ONE

Stocks and Their Value

CHAPTER ONE

Firm Foundations and Castles in the Air

> What is a cynic? A man who knows the price of everything, and the value of nothing.—Oscar Wilde, *Lady Windermere's Fan*

Any book about common stocks can tell of the excitement and warn of the pitfalls. But how many show you how to determine what stocks are really worth, why they fluctuate so erratically, or how professional investors operate in the market? How many really show what sensible investment strategies are open to the person who has no connections?

In this book I will take you on a random walk down Wall Street, providing a guided tour of the complex world of finance and practical advice on investment opportunities and strategies. Many people say that the individual investor has scarcely a chance today against Wall Street's pros. Nothing could be further from the truth. You can do just as well as the experts—perhaps even better. Later on I'll even show you how you can buy shares in professionally managed portfolios for 75¢ on the dollar.

A Guided Random Walk

"Random walk" is a real obscenity on Wall Street. It is an epithet that the academic world insultingly hurls at the professional soothsayers. In essence, the random walk theory espouses the belief that future stock prices cannot be predicted. It says that a blindfolded monkey throwing darts at the newspaper's financial pages could select a portfolio that would do just as well as one carefully selected by the experts. Therefore investment advisory services, earnings predictions, and complicated chart patterns are useless. Obviously, Wall Street does not view this conclusion favorably. The market professionals retort that the academics are so immersed in equations and Greek symbols (to say nothing of excruciatingly stuffy prose) that they couldn't tell a bear from a bull even in a china shop. You can see there's a tremendous battle going on, and it's fought with deadly intent. That's why I think you'll enjoy this random walk down Wall Street. It has all the ingredients of high drama—fortunes made and lost—and classical arguments about the cause.

But before we begin, perhaps I should introduce myself and state my qualifications as guide. In writing this book I have drawn on three aspects of my background; each provides a different perspective on the stock market.

First is my employment more than a decade ago as a market professional with one of Wall Street's leading investment firms. It takes one, after all, to know one. In a sense, I remain a market professional in that I currently sit on the finance committee of a $2½ billion common-stock fund. This perspective has been indispensable to me. Some things in life can never fully be appreciated or understood by a virgin. The same might be said of the stock market.

Second is my current position as an economist at a leading university. Specializing in securities markets and investment behavior, I have acquired detailed knowledge of academic research and findings on investment opportunities. I have relied on many new research findings in framing recommendations for you.

Last, and certainly not least, I have been a lifelong investor and successful participant in the market. How successful I cannot say, for it is a peculiarity of the academic world that a professor is not supposed to make money. A professor may inherit lots of money, he may marry lots of money, and he may spend lots of money, but he is never, never supposed to earn lots of money: it's unacademic. Anyway, teachers are supposed to be "dedicated," or so politicians and administrators often say—especially when trying to justify the low academic pay scales. Academics are supposed to be seekers of knowledge, not of financial reward. It is in the former sense, therefore, that I shall tell you of my victories on Wall Street.

This book has a lot of facts and figures. Don't let that worry you. It is specifically intended for the financial layman —and offers practical, tested investment advice. You need no prior knowledge to follow it. All you need is the interest and the desire to have the stock market work for you.

What Do All the Numbers on the Page Mean?

As I started to say back under point three, I have had a lifelong fascination with the stock market. It started when, as a small boy, I grabbed my father's newspaper as he walked in the door to see if Captain Marvel escaped from his deadly trap and to check on Ted Williams' latest batting average. As I leafed through the newsprint spread out on the living room floor I could hear my father say, "Aren't you even going to say hello?" I stopped where I was—a pageful of numbers from the financial section—and quickly said hello. To demonstrate even further my filial affection, I even asked him a question: "Dad, what's all those figures?" And that's as good a fictional account as any of how my thirst for knowledge of the financial world started.

The numbers were prices—the amount of money buyers had paid sellers for particular common stocks. There were thousands of stocks and thousands of prices. Quite a lot for a small boy to digest. I started at the very beginning.

Technically, I learned, a common stock represents a certificate of part ownership of a corporation. If you own, for example, one share of stock in a company that has issued 100 shares, you are entitled to $\frac{1}{100}$ of the net assets of the company if it happens to dissolve, and one vote out of 100 in any corporate election. The latter generally means that each year you may vote on whether to accept management's recommendation that the firm's public accountants and auditors be retained for another year. Similarly, you are entitled to vote yes or no on management's slate of directors. Unless you own more than a small percentage of a company's stock, however, management normally can control the electoral process from which its powers nominally derive. Indeed, one company mails out the proxy form for electing the board of directors on the back of a dividend check. The stockholder who endorses the check has also voted to retain management in power. Thus the idea of a stockholder of General Motors being the boss of the president is really only a public relations gimmick.

To be honest, the niceties of just what rights a common stock conveyed didn't excite me very much. I almost went back to Captain Marvel. But then I learned that one could make a lot of money on these certificates. That intrigued me —intellectually, of course. These profits come in two forms: (1) through dividends; and (2) through selling the stock at a higher price than you bought it, and thereby realizing a capital gain. Both forms are unreliable in that they are dependent on future events. Dividends, after all, can be eliminated by the company's management, and stock prices can fall. That's what makes the fascination of investing—it's a gamble whose success depends on an ability to predict the future. When you are successful, you get not only psychic rewards but large monetary ones as well. It's an addicting combination of possibilities and beats Captain Marvel's adventures any day of the week.

Of the two forms of profit, capital gains have the greatest potential, but are also the most undependable. Thus it's crucial to understand how stocks are valued by buyers and sellers and what determines future prices. Stock valuation then boils down to a matter of predicting. To make sensible decisions in the stock market you must predict not only future dividends but future stock prices as well.

How to predict future stock prices? That is the investment question for both amateurs and professionals in the market. It concerns the brokers who execute your buy and sell orders and give you advice on stock selection, and also the professional money managers who invest the billion-dollar pension and retirement funds as well as the popular mutual funds.

Generally the pros take their pick of two approaches to stock valuation. I call one the "firm-foundation theory" and the other the "castle-in-the-air theory." Millions have been gained and lost on these theories. To add to the drama, they appear to be mutually exclusive. Analysts debate their merits from coast to coast. Given their hold on the financial community, it is necessary to examine each in some detail. An understanding of these two approaches is essential to enable you to take your walk down Wall Street, to interpret much financial news, and to appraise your broker's advice. It is also a prerequisite for keeping you safe from serious blunders in the market and for comprehending the specific investment strategy I will recommend later in the book.

The Firm-Foundation Theory

The firm-foundation theory argues that each common stock has a firm anchor of something called intrinsic value, which can be determined by careful analysis of the company's present position and future prospects. When market prices fall below this firm foundation of intrinsic value a buying opportunity arises, because this fluctuation will eventually be corrected, or so the theory goes. Similarly, should the price of a stock rise considerably above its intrinsic value, the stock is then recommended as a candidate for sale. Investing then becomes a dull but straightforward matter of comparing a stock's actual price with its firm foundation of value.

It is difficult to ascribe to any one individual the credit for originating the firm-foundation theory. S. Eliot Guild is often given this distinction, but the classic development of the technique and particularly the nuances associated with it was worked out by John B. Williams.

In *The Theory of Investment Value,* Williams presented an actual formula for determining the intrinsic value of stock. Williams based his approach on dividend income. In a fiendishly clever attempt to keep things from being simple, he introduced the concept of "discounting" into the process. Discounting basically involves looking at income backwards. Rather than seeing how much money you will have next year (say $1.05 if you put $1 in a savings bank at 5 percent interest), you look at money expected in the future and see how much less it is currently worth (thus, next year's $1 today is worth only about 95¢, which could be invested at 5 percent to produce $1 at that time).

Williams was actually serious about this. He went on to argue that the intrinsic value of a stock was equal to the present (or discounted) value of all its future dividends. Investors were advised to "discount" the value of moneys received later. Because so few people understood it, the term caught on and "discounting" now enjoys popular usage among investment people. It received a further boost under the aegis of Professor Irving Fisher of Yale, a distinguished economist and investor.

The logic of the firm-foundation theory is quite respectable. Wrapped in staid, conservative language, it stresses that stock value ought to consist of the earnings a firm will be able to distribute in the future. But it is here that the tricky little factor of future expectations sneaks in. It stands to reason that a company whose dividends are expected to increase is worth more than one whose dividends are likely to remain static. Thus, security analysts must estimate long-term growth rates. And not only that—they must also try to figure out how long an extraordinary growth rate can be maintained. When the market gets overly enthusiastic about how far in the future growth can continue, it is popularly held on Wall Street that "stocks are discounting not only the future but perhaps even the hereafter."

The point is that the firm-foundation theory relies on some tricky forecasts of the extent and duration of future growth. The mathematical precision with which most intrinsic-value formulas are presented makes it seem easy to specify the worth of a share. Forecasting the future is inherently a very treacherous occupation. Consequently, the anchor of intrinsic value may be a less dependable one than is claimed.

The firm-foundation theory is not confined to economists alone. Thanks to a very influential book, Graham and Dodd's *Security Analysis,* first published in 1934, a whole generation of Wall Street security analysts was converted to the fold. Sound investment management, the practicing analysts learned, simply consisted of buying securities whose prices were temporarily below intrinsic value and selling ones whose prices were temporarily too high. It was that easy. Of course, instructions for determining intrinsic value were furnished and any analyst worth his salt could calculate it with one whisk of the slipstick.

Recently, economists have further enhanced the firm-foundation theory in creating valuation formulas with an additional wrinkle to include an allowance for the risk or quality of the shares. This mathematical legerdemain comes with the spiffy title of capital-asset pricing model. The figures, calculations, and exotic symbols are both impressive and unreadable even for many professional economists. Nevertheless, the *Journal of Finance*—the pinnacle of magazine publishing for the financial economist—continues to sprout pages with terms such as quadratic programming, Riemann surfaces, and bordered Hessian matrices. I do not recommend it for bedtime reading, except to cure insomnia.

The Castle-in-the-Air Theory

The castle-in-the-air theory of stock prices has nothing to do with intrinsic values. It concentrates on psychic values. Lord Keynes, a famous economist and outstandingly successful investor, enunciated the theory most lucidly in 1936. Keynes felt that intrinsic values—depending as they do on forecasts of the future—are too difficult to determine. It was his opinion that professional investors prefer to devote their energies to an analysis of how the crowd of investors is likely to behave in the future and how during periods of optimism they tend to build their hopes into castles in the air. The successful investor tries to beat the gun by estimating what investment situations are most susceptible to public castle-building and then buying before the crowd.

According to Keynes, the firm-foundation theory involved too much work and was of doubtful value. Keynes practiced what he preached. While London's financial men toiled many weary hours in darkened rooms, he played the market from his bed for half an hour each morning. This leisurely method of investing earned him several million pounds for his own account and a tenfold increase in the market value of the endowment of his college, King's College, Cambridge.

In the depression years in which Keynes gained his fame, most people concentrated on his ideas for stimulating the economy. It was hard for anyone to build castles in the air or to dream that others would do so. Nevertheless, in his book,

General Theory of Employment, Interest and Money, he devoted an entire chapter to the stock market and to the importance of investor expectations.

Keynes noted the pitfalls of predicting future dividends. No one knows for sure what will influence future earnings prospects and dividend payments. As a result, Keynes says, most persons are "largely concerned, not with making superior long-term forecasts of the probable yield of an investment over its whole life, but with foreseeing changes in the conventional basis of valuation a short time ahead of the general public." Keynes, in other words, applied psychological principles rather than financial evaluation to the study of the stock market.

> [Most persons] are concerned, not with what an investment is really worth to a man who buys it "for keeps," but with what the market will value it at, under the influence of mass psychology, three months or a year hence. . . . For it is not sensible to pay 25 for an investment of which you believe the prospective yield to justify a value of 30, if you also believe that the market will value it at 20 three months hence.

Keynes describes the playing of the stock market in terms readily understandable to his fellow Englishmen: it is analogous to entering a newspaper beauty-judging contest in which you have to select the six prettiest faces out of 100 photographs. The prize goes to the person whose selections most nearly conform to those of the group as a whole.

The smart player recognizes that his personal criteria of beauty are irrelevant in determining the contest winner. A better strategy is to select those faces the other players are likely to fancy. This logic tends to snowball. After all, the other contestants are no fools and they are likely to play the game with at least as keen a perception. Thus the optimal strategy is not to pick those faces the player thinks are prettiest, or even those he may believe the other players are likely to fancy, but rather to predict what the average opinion is

likely to think the average opinion will be or to proceed even
further along this sequence. So much for British beauty con-
tests.

But trying to divine what others will think we think also
implies work. Might predicting future dividends be easier
after all? Keynes did not think so: "Investment based on
genuine long-term expectation is so difficult today as to be
scarcely practicable." Besides, trying to predict long-run
intrinsic values was terribly boring to Keynes.

> Life is not long enough—human nature desires quick re-
> sults, there is a peculiar zest in making money quickly, and
> remoter gains are discounted by the average man at a very high
> rate. The game of professional investment is intolerably bor-
> ing and over-exacting to anyone who is entirely exempt from
> the gambling instinct; whilst he who has it must pay this pro-
> pensity the appropriate toll.

The newspaper-contest analogy represents the ultimate
form of a castle-in-the-air theory of price determination. A
share of stock is worth one price to a buyer because he expects to sell it to someone else at a higher price. The stock,
in other words, holds itself up by its own bootstraps. The new
buyer in turn anticipates that future buyers will assign still
higher value to the shares.

In this kind of world, there is a sucker born every minute
—and he exists to buy your shares at a higher price than you
paid for them. Any price will do as long as others may be willing to pay more. There is no reason, only mass psychology.
All the smart investor has to do is beat the gun—get in at the
very beginning. This theory might less charitably be called
the "greater-fool theory." It's perfectly all right to pay three
times what a stock is worth as long as later on you can find
some innocent to pay five times what it's worth.

The castle-in-the-air theory has many advocates, both in
the financial and academic communities. Keynes' newspaper
contest is the same game played by "Adam Smith" in *The*

Money Game. Mr. Smith also espouses the same view of stock price determination. On the academic side, Oskar Morgenstern has been a leading champion. The views he expresses in *The Theory of Games and Economic Behavior,* of which he is coauthor, have had a significant impact not only on economic theory but also on national security decisions and strategic corporate planning. In 1970 he coauthored another book, *The Determination of Stock Prices.* In this book he and his colleague, Clive Granger, argue that the search for intrinsic value in stocks is a search for the will-o'-the-wisp. In an exchange economy the value of any asset depends on an actual or prospective transaction. Morgenstern believes that every investor should post the following Latin maxim above his desk:

Res tantum valet quantum vendi potest.
(A thing is worth only what somone else will pay for it.)

How the Random Walk Is to Be Conducted

With this short introduction out of the way, come join me for a random walk down Wall Street. My first task will be to acquaint you with the historical patterns of security pricing and how they bear on these two different theories of stock prices. It was Santayana who warned that if we did not learn the lessons of the past we would be doomed to repeat the same errors. Therefore, in the pages to come I will describe some spectacular crazes—both long past and recently past. Some readers may pooh-pooh the mad public rush to buy tulip bulbs in seventeenth-century Holland and the eighteenth-century South Sea Bubble in England. But no one can disregard the new-issue mania of 1960–61, the conglomerate wave of the middle 1960s, and the boom and bust of the so-called concept stocks during the 1969–70 period—all involving the savvy institutions and investment pros. All too many

investors are lazy and careless—a terrifying combination
when greed gets control of the market and everyone wants
to cash in on the latest craze or fad.

Then I throw in my own 2¢ worth of experience. Even in
the midst of a period of speculation I believe it is possible to
find a logical basis for security prices. In Chapter Four I
present a detailed analysis of the decade of the 1960s and
early 1970s that should be helpful in giving investors a sense
of value and in protecting you from the horrible blunders
made by many professional investment managers.

Theories are fine in their place, but it's important to look
behind them and see how professional investment people
actually practice their calling. In Part Two I rely on My Wall
Street experience and current academic research to analyze
various systems used by market professionals in their attempt
to beat the market.

The pros use two general methods: fundamental and
technical analysis. Fundamental analysis is the technique
used by those believing in the firm-foundation theory. It
involves a study of the fundamental valuation factors—earnings growth, dividend payments, risk—upon which the firm-
foundation theory is built. Technical analysis is more often
used by those subscribing to the castle-in-the-air view of the
market. It involves an attempt to measure the psychology of
the crowd and its propensity to build castles in the air. Unfortunately, both types of analysts have feet of clay. Using
these methods, the Street has touted such sure winners as
Four Seasons Nursing Centers of America, which sold at over
$90 per share in 1968 and recently traded at 2¢. The sad fact
is that you are likely to be just as well off picking stocks by
letting your fingers take a random walk down the Wall Street
stock pages as by following their advice. I'll back that statement up, too.

Finally, in Part Three, I shall attempt to make order out
of chaos. I will show that the lessons of history and the record
of professionals do suggest answers to the questions of what

you should do with your money and what sound investment strategies are available to you. Even in a random-walk market there are important opportunities available to increase your returns from the market.

While my recommendations are often substantially different from the conventional wisdom, they are presented in easy-to-follow, step-by-step fashion, in the tradition of the many how-to-do-it books. This is the golden age of the how-to-do-it book. For a judicious investment of a dollar or two at the corner paperback bookstore, one can purchase a detailed guide on how to overhaul automobile engines, paint with the skill of a Rembrandt, eat anything you want and lose weight, and even become a sensuous man or woman. Admittedly, this volume promises less than books of the genre *How I Made a Million Dollars in the Stock Market in My Spare Time and Found God*. Nevertheless, it is intended to develop sensible rules to guide the conduct of individual investors. I think you will find our walk both enjoyable and profitable.

CHAPTER TWO

The Madness of Crowds

October. This is one of the peculiarly dangerous months to speculate in stocks in. The others are July, January, September, April, November, May, March, June, December, August and February.—Mark Twain, *Pudd'nhead Wilson*

Greed run amok has been an essential feature of every spectacular boom in history. In their frenzy for money, market participants throw over firm foundations of value for the dubious but thrilling assumption that they too can make a killing by building castles in the air. Such thinking can, and has, enveloped entire nations.

The psychology of speculation is a veritable theater of the absurd. Three of its plays are presented in this chapter. The castles that were built during the performances were based on Dutch tulip bulbs, English "bubbles," and good old American blue-chip stocks. In each case, some of the people made some money some of the time, but only a very few emerged unscathed.

History, in this instance, does teach a lesson: While the castle-in-the-air theory can well explain such speculative binges, outguessing the reactions of a fickle crowd is a most dangerous game. It is a lesson that needs to be cried out. Sky-rocketing markets that depend on purely psychic support have invariably succumbed to the financial laws of gravity. Unsustainable prices may persist for years, but eventually they reverse themselves. Such reversals come with the sudden-ness of an earthquake; and the bigger the binge, the greater the resulting hangover. Few of the reckless builders of castles in the air have been nimble enough to anticipate these re-versals perfectly and escape without losing a great deal of money when everything came tumbling down.

The Tulip-Bulb Craze

What would you say if someone offered to sell you a single tulip bulb for the "ridiculously low price" of $7,000? The idea of paying as much for a tulip bulb as for a Mercedes seems inconceivable. And yet, if you thought that in a few months you might be able to trade your tulip bulb for two Mercedes, might you not be tempted? That was the specula-tive psychology behind the tulip-bulb craze.

It all began rather unspectacularly around the middle of the sixteenth century. It was at that time that the tulip made its European debut, having been imported from Constan-tinople, where it had long been a favorite. The Dutch took to the flower, and it became a sign of good taste for any man of means to have a collection. While the prices of bulbs were high relative to those of other flowers, the tulip's first eighty years in Holland were marked by a prosperous tranquillity.

But then a slowly creeping bulbomania set in. By the early 1630s, the tulip had become a much-sought-after fad. One year a certain color was "in"; the next, a particular species. Since the "in" tulip commanded the highest prices, it seemed perfectly natural for merchants to try predicting what varieties would be popular in the coming year—just as department store buyers try to gauge the public fancy in color and hemlines for the next season. The next step in the tulip-bulb craze was for several smart Dutchmen to ask: "Why stop at simply trying to obtain a normal inventory of salable merchandise? Why not buy up an extra-large stock-pile before the prices go up?" That's how you beat others to the gun. And that's how speculative crazes are born!

So many people tried to beat the gun that it finally went off. Tulip-bulb prices began to rise wildly. As people saw that big profits were being made, they rushed into the market like lemmings into the sea. Charles Mackay, who chronicled these events in his book *Extraordinary Popular Delusions,* noted that the ordinary industry of the country was dropped in favor of speculation in tulip bulbs. "Nobles, citizens, farmers, mechanics, seamen, footmen, maid-servants, even chimney sweeps and old clotheswomen dabbled in tulips." Everyone imagined that the passion for tulips would last forever, and buyers from all over the world would come to Holland and pay whatever prices were asked for them.

The whole affair seems absurd. But we are all emotional human beings, not mechanical value calculators, and none of us is immune to the temptation to jump into the speculative stream. The hardest time to resist being sucked into investing in overpriced commodities—be they tulips or securities—is precisely when the speculative frenzy is at its height. This is the time of greatest optimism. As potential investors compare market prices at the peak of the boom with prices that prevailed earlier, there is a feeling of pain at having missed the boat. Since everyone else is so optimistic, it is so easy to convince yourself: "I'll jump on board now and join in what must be one of the greatest profit opportunities of my lifetime." And there lies the route to disaster. This is why a historical perspective can be so useful to investors.

The last years of the tulip-bulb orgy—1634 to 1638—took on an almost pathological hue. People from all walks of life converted property into cash to play the tulip market. Not content with simply investing their funds in the market, they developed a method to gain greater profits from the "inevitable" rise in prices.

Part of the genius of financial markets is that, when there is a real demand for a method to enhance speculative opportunities, the market will surely provide it. The instruments that enabled tulip speculators to get the most action for their money were "call options" similar to those popular today in the stock market.

A call option conferred on the holder the right to buy tulip bulbs (call for their delivery) at a fixed price (usually approximating the current market price) during a specified period. He was charged an amount called the option premium, which might run 15 to 20 percent of the current market price. An option on a tulip bulb currently worth 100 guilders, for example, would cost the buyer only about 20 guilders. If the price moved up to 200 guilders, the option holder would exercise his right; he would buy at 100 and simultaneously sell at the then current price of 200. He then had a profit of 80 guilders (the 100 guilders' appreciation less the 20 guilders he paid for the option). Thus he enjoyed a fourfold increase in his money, whereas an outright purchase would only have doubled his money. By using the call option it was possible to play the market with a much smaller stake as well as get more action out of any money invested. The call is one way to leverage one's investment. Leveraging is any technique that increases the potential rewards (and risks) of an investment. Such devices helped to insure broad participation in the market. The same is true today.

Prices of bulbs rose to unbelievable heights. A single bulb of the Harlaem species was exchanged for twelve acres of building ground. After all, it's easier to build a castle in the air than on the ground. Another variety fetched 4,600 florins, a new carriage, and two gray horses, plus a complete set of harnesses. A bulb of the Viceroy species commanded the sum of all the following items in exchange: seventeen bushels of wheat, thirty-four bushels of rye, four fat oxen, eight fat swine, twelve fat sheep, two hogsheads of wine, four tuns of beer, two tons of butter, 1,000 pounds of cheese, a complete bed, a suit of clothes, and a silver drinking cup thrown in for good measure.

The history of the period was filled with many tragicomic episodes. For example, one incident concerned a returning sailor who brought news to a wealthy merchant of the arrival of a shipment of new goods. The merchant rewarded him with a breakfast of fine red herring. Seeing what he thought was an onion on the merchant's counter, and no doubt thinking it very much out of place amidst silks and velvets, he proceeded to take it as a relish for his herring. Little did he dream that the "onion" would have fed a whole ship's crew for a year. It was a costly Semper Augustus tulip bulb. The sailor paid dearly for his relish—his no longer grateful host had him imprisoned for several months on a felony charge.

At last some of the smart Dutchmen who had earlier decided to build up inventories started to wonder what tulip bulbs were actually "worth" and ultimately began to ask more questions. They wondered if public enthusiasm could last forever. Could tulip prices really go any higher, or even stay at current inflated levels? Should they get out now while they were ahead? The answers to such questions usually convinced the owners of tulip bulbs to sell. Prices plummeted and panic reigned.

Government ministers stated officially that there was no reason for tulip bulbs to fall in price—but no one listened. Dealers went bankrupt and refused to honor their commitments to buy tulip bulbs. A government plan to settle all contracts at 10 percent of their face value was frustrated when bulbs fell even below this mark. And prices continued to decline. Down and down they went until the tulip bulb became almost worthless.

And what of the smart Dutchmen—the ones who had asked the right questions at the right time? In the end, they too were engulfed by the tulip craze. For the final chapter of this bizarre story is that the shock generated by the boom and collapse led to a prolonged depression in Holland. No one was spared.

The South Sea Bubble

Suppose your broker called you and recommended that you invest in a new company with no sales or earnings—just great prospects. "What business?" you say. "I'm sorry," your broker explains, "no one must know what the business is, but I can promise you enormous riches." A con game, you say. Right you are, but 200 years ago in England this was one of the hottest new issues of the period. And, just as you guessed, investors got very badly burned. The story illustrates how fraud can make greedy people even more eager to part with their money.

At the time of the South Sea Bubble, the British were ripe for throwing away money. A long period of English prosperity had resulted in fat savings and thin investment outlets. The South Sea Company, which obligingly filled the need for investment vehicles, had been formed in 1711 to restore faith in the government's ability to meet its obligations. The company took on a government IOU of £10 million. As a reward, it was given a monopoly over all trade to the South Seas. The public believed there were immense riches in such trade, and regarded the stock with distinct favor. The directors, an avaricious lot, decided in 1719 to capitalize—both literally and figuratively—on their reputation by offering to fund the entire national debt. That was boldness indeed. The public loved it.

In 1720, when a bill to that effect was brought before Parliament, the company's stock promptly rose from £130 to £300. Favorable rumors (purposely and widely spread by the directors) intoxicated the country with the thought of instant wealth. Visions of glory danced in investors' heads when they heard England might be granted the right of free trade with all of Spain's colonies. Mexicans supposedly were waiting for the opportunity to empty their gold mines in return for England's abundant supply of cotton and woolen goods. This was free enterprise at its finest.

On April 12, 1720, five days after the bill became law, the South Sea Company sold a new issue of stock at 300. Fights broke out among investors surging to buy it. The price had to go up—and the eager buyers were right. It advanced to 340 within a few days. To ease the public appetite, the South Sea directors announced another new issue—this one at £400. But the public was ravenous. Within a month the stock was at 550. In a span of only four days it must have set some kind of record because it is reported to have shot from 550 to 890.

Then June, and a small sense of sanity, dawned. Reality, in such skyrocketing conditions, could be a cold bath indeed: in one day the stock fell from 890 to 640. And here is where the knavish nature of the directors really became apparent. They gave their agents orders to buy, thus stabilizing the price, and then—through a combination of manipulation and rumor—drove the price all the way up to 1,000. The speculative craze was in full bloom.

Not even the South Sea Company was capable of handling the demands of all the fools who wanted to be parted from their money. Investors looked for other new ventures where they could get in on the ground floor. Just as speculators today search for the next Xerox and the next IBM, so in England in the early 1800s they looked for the next South Sea Company. Promoters obliged by organizing and bringing to the market a flood of new issues to meet the insatiable craving for investment. Even the Prince of Wales wanted his castle. He became governor of one company and was rumored to have made £40,000 on his speculation.

As the days passed, new financing proposals ranged from

ingenious to absurd—from importing a large number of jackasses from Spain to making salt water fresh. Increasingly the promotions involved some element of fraud, such as making boards out of sawdust. There were nearly one hundred different projects, each more extravagant and deceptive than the other, but each offering the hope of immense gain. They soon received the name of "bubbles," as appropriate a name as could be devised. Like bubbles, they popped quickly —usually within a week or so.

The public, it seemed, would buy anything. New companies seeking financing during this period were organized for such purposes as: the building of ships against pirates; encouraging the breeding of horses in England (there were two issues for this purpose); trading in human hair; building of hospitals for bastard children; extracting of silver from lead; and even for a wheel of perpetual motion.

The prize, however, must surely go to the unknown soul who started "A Company for carrying on an undertaking of great advantage, but nobody to know what it is." The prospectus promised unheard-of rewards. At nine o'clock in the morning, when the subscription books opened, crowds of people from all walks of life practically beat down the door in an effort to subscribe. Within five hours a thousand investors handed over their money for shares in the company. Not being greedy himself, the promoter promptly closed up shop and set off for the Continent. He was never heard from again.

Not all investors in the bubble companies believed in the feasibility of the schemes to which they subscribed. People were "too sensible" for that. They did believe, however, in the "greater-fool" theory—that prices would rise, that buyers would be found, and that they would make money. Thus, most investors considered their actions the height of rationality as, at least for a while, they could sell their shares at a premium in the "after market," that is, the trading market in the shares after their initial issue.

Whom the gods would destroy, they first ridicule. Signs

that the end was near were demonstrated with the issuance of a pack of South Sea playing cards. Each card contained a caricature of a bubble company, with an appropriate verse inscribed underneath. One of these, the Puckle Machine Company, was supposed to produce machines discharging both round and square cannonballs and bullets. Puckle modestly claimed that his machine would make a total revolution in the art of war. The eight of spades described it as follows:

> A rare invention to destroy the crowd
> Of fools at home instead of fools abroad.
> Fear not, my friends, this terrible machine,
> They're only wounded who have shares therein.

Many individual bubbles had been pricked without dampening the speculative enthusiasm, but the deluge came in August with an irreparable puncture to the South Sea Company. This was self-administered by its directors and officers. Realizing that the price of the shares in the market bore no relationship to the real prospects of the company, they sold out in the summer.

The news leaked and so did the stock. By September of 1720 the price had fallen to 700. Since the directors had already made their profits, they decided there was no need for action on their part. When the public heard this, the price immediately fell to 504, and in the next few days to 400. Soon the shares were at 150, and panic reigned. Government officials tried in vain to restore confidence and a complete collapse of the public credit was barely averted.

"Thus," *The Parliamentary History of England* states, "were seen in the space of eight months, the rise, progress, and fall of that mighty fabric, which being wound up by mysterious springs to a wonderful height, had fixed the eyes and expectations of all Europe, but whose foundation, being fraud, illusion, credulity, and infatuation, fell to the ground as soon as the artful management of its directors was discovered." So much for castles in the air.

Wall Street Lays an Egg

The bulbs and bubbles are, admittedly, ancient history. Could the same sort of thing happen on sophisticated Wall Street? Let's turn to more familiar and recent events from our own past and see. America, the land of opportunity, had its turn in the late 1920s. And given our emphasis on freedom and growth, we produced one of the most spectacular booms and one of the loudest crashes civilization has ever known.

Conditions could not have been more favorable for a speculative craze. The country had experienced almost a decade of unrivaled prosperity. One could not but have faith in American business and, as Calvin Coolidge said, "The business of America is business." Businessmen were likened to religious missionaries and almost deified. Such analogies were even made in the opposite direction. Bruce Barton, of Batten, Barton, Durstine and Osborn, the New York advertising agency, wrote in *The Man Nobody Knows* that Jesus was "the first businessman," whose parables were "the most powerful advertisements of all time."

While the euphoric mood of optimism and faith in business that prevailed in the twenties led to a widespread enthusiasm about the stock market, much of the increase in stock prices from 1923 through 1927 could be justified in terms of intrinsic-value considerations. Dividends and earnings had increased considerably during this period, and the foundation of value undergirding the stock market was certainly much stronger.

Beginning in 1928, however, speculation accelerated to boost prices well beyond supportable levels. From early March 1928 through early September 1929 the market's percentage increase equaled that of the entire period from 1923 through early 1928. The price rises for the major industrial corporations sometimes reached 10 or 15 points per day. The extent of the rise is illustrated in the following table.

Not "everybody" was speculating in the market, as was

Security	Opening Price March 3, 1928	High Price September 3, 1929 *	Percentage Gain in 18 Months
American Telephone & Telegraph	179½	335⅝	87.0
Bethlehem Steel	56⅞	140⅜	146.8
General Electric	128¾	396¼	207.8
Montgomery Ward	132¾	466½	251.4
National Cash Register	50¾	127½	151.2
Radio Corporation of America	94½	505	434.5

* Adjusted for stock splits and the value of rights received subsequent to March 31, 1928.

commonly assumed. Borrowing to buy stocks (buying on margin) did increase from only $1 billion in 1921 to almost $9 billion in 1929. Nevertheless, only about a million persons owned stocks on margin in 1929. Still, the speculative spirit was at least as widespread as in the previous crazes and was certainly unrivaled in its intensity. More important, stock-market speculation was central to the culture. John Brooks, in *Once in Golconda,** recounted the remarks of a British correspondent newly arrived in New York: "You could talk about Prohibition, or Hemingway, or air conditioning, or music, or horses, but in the end you had to talk about the stock market, and that was when the conversation became serious."

Unfortunately, there were hundreds of smiling operators only too glad to help the public construct castles in the air.

* Golconda, now in ruins, was a city in India. According to legend, everyone who passed through it became rich.

Manipulation on the stock exchange set new records for un-
scrupulousness. No better example can be found than the
operation of investment pools. One such undertaking raised
the price of RCA stock 61 points in four days. Let me explain
how the pools could manipulate the price of a stock.

An investment pool required close cooperation on the
one hand and complete disdain for the public on the other.
Generally such operations began when a number of traders
banded together to manipulate a particular stock. They ap-
pointed a pool manager (who justifiably was considered something of an artist) and promised not to doublecross each other
through private operations.

The pool manager accumulated a large block of stock
through inconspicuous buying over a period of weeks. If
possible, he obtained an option to buy a substantial block of
stock at the current market price within a stated period of,
say, three or six months. Next he tried to enlist the stock's
specialist on the exchange floor as an ally.

Pool members were in the swim with the specialist on
their side. A stock-exchange specialist functions as a broker's
broker. If a stock was trading at $50 a share and you gave
your broker an order to buy at $45, the broker typically left
that order with the specialist. If and when the stock fell to
$45, the specialist then executed the order. All such orders
to buy below the market price or sell above it were kept in
the specialist's supposedly private "book." Now you see why
the specialist could be so valuable to the pool manager. The
book gave information about the extent of existing orders to
buy and sell at prices below and above the current market.
It was always helpful to know as many of the cards of the
public players as possible. Now the real fun was ready to
begin.

Generally, at this point the pool manager had members
of the pool trade between themselves. For example, Haskell
sells 200 shares to Sidney at 40, and Sidney sells them back at
40⅛. The process is repeated with 400 shares at prices of

40¼ and 40½. Next comes the sale of a 1,000-share block at 40⅝, followed by another at 40¾. These sales were recorded on ticker tapes across the country and the illusion of activity was conveyed to the thousands of tape watchers who crowded into the brokerage offices of the country. Such activity, generated by so-called "wash sales," created the impression that something big was afoot.

Now, tipsheet writers and market commentators under the control of the pool manager would tell of exciting developments in the offing. The pool manager also tried to insure that the flow of news from the company's management was increasingly favorable—assuming the company management was involved in the operation. If all went well, and in the speculative atmosphere of the 1928–29 period it could hardly miss, the combination of tape activity and managed news would bring the public in.

Once the public came in the free-for-all started and it was time discreetly to "pull the plug." Since the public was doing the buying, the pool did the selling. The pool manager began feeding stock into the market, first slowly and then in larger and larger blocks before the public could collect its senses. At the end of the roller-coaster ride the pool members had netted large profits and the public was left holding the suddenly deflated stock.

But people didn't have to band together to defraud the public. Many individuals, particularly corporate officers and directors, did quite well on their own. Take Albert Wiggin, the head of Chase, the nation's second largest bank at the time. In July 1929 Mr. Wiggin became apprehensive about the dizzy heights to which stocks had climbed and no longer felt comfortable speculating on the bull side of the market. (He is rumored to have made millions in a pool boosting the price of his own bank.) Believing that the prospects for his own bank's stock were particularly dim (perhaps because of his previous speculation), he sold short over 42,000 shares of Chase stock. Selling short is a way to make money if stock prices fall. It involves selling stock you do not presently own in the expectation of buying it back later at a lower price. It's like hoping to buy low and sell high, but in reverse order.

Wiggin's timing was perfect. Immediately after the short sale the price of Chase stock began to fall, and when the crash came in the fall the stock dropped precipitously. When the account was closed in November, Mr. Wiggin had netted a profit of over $84 million from the operation. Conflicts of interest apparently did not trouble Mr. Wiggin. Usually corporate officers are encouraged to own the stock of their company so that they will have an added incentive to put out their best efforts. Wiggin, on the other hand, had provided himself with an incentive (and a very large one at that) to encourage the deterioration of the shares of the financial institution he headed.

There's a sequel to this story. When Wiggin retired in 1932, the Chase Executive Committee thanked him warmly for his many services to the bank and unanimously voted him a life pension of $100,000 per year.

On September 3, 1929 the market averages reached a peak that was not to be surpassed for a quarter of a century. The "endless chain of prosperity" was soon to break; general business activity had already turned down months before. Prices drifted for the next day, and on the following day, September 5, the market suffered a sharp decline known as the "Babson Break."

This was named in honor of Roger Babson, a frail, goateed, pixyish-looking financial adviser from Wellesley, Massachusetts. At a financial luncheon that day he had said, "I repeat what I said at this time last year and the year before, that sooner or later a crash is coming." Wall Street professionals greeted the new pronouncements from the "sage of Wellesley," as he was known, with their usual derision.

As Babson implied in his statement, he had been predicting the crash for several years and he had yet to be proven right. Nevertheless, at two o'clock in the afternoon, when

Babson's words were quoted on the "broad" tape (the Dow-Jones financial-news ticker, which is an essential part of the furniture in every brokerage house across the country), the market went into a nosedive. In the last frantic hour of trading, two million shares changed hands—Telephone went down 6 points, Westinghouse 7, and U.S. Steel 9 points. It was a prophetic episode, and after the Babson Break the possibility of a crash, which was entirely unthinkable a month before, suddenly became a common subject for discussion.

Confidence faltered. September had many more bad than good days. At times the market fell sharply. Bankers and government officials assured the country that there was no cause for concern. Professor Irving Fisher of Yale, one of the progenitors of the intrinsic-value theory, offered his soon-to-be-immortal opinion that stocks had reached what looked like a "permanently high plateau."

By Monday, October 21, the stage was set for a classic stock market break. The declines in stock prices had led to calls for more collateral from margin customers. Unable or unwilling to meet the calls, these customers were forced to sell their holdings. This depressed prices and led to more margin calls and finally to a self-sustaining selling wave.

The volume of sales on October 21 zoomed to over 6 million shares. The ticker fell way behind, to the dismay of the tens of thousands of individuals watching the tape from brokerage houses around the country. Nearly an hour and forty minutes had elapsed after the close of the market before the last transaction was actually recorded on the stock ticker.

The indomitable Fisher dismissed the decline as a "shaking out of the lunatic fringe that attempts to speculate on margin." He went on to say that prices of stocks during the boom had not caught up with their real value and would go higher. Among other things, the professor believed that the market had not yet reflected the beneficient effects of Prohibition, which had made the American worker "more productive and dependable."

On October 24, later called "Black Thursday," the market volume reached almost 13 million shares. Prices sometimes fell $5 and $10 on each trade. Many issues dropped 40 and 50 points during a couple of hours. On the next day, Herbert Hoover offered his famous diagnosis, "The fundamental business of the country . . . is on a sound and prosperous basis."

Tuesday, October 29, was the most catastrophic day in the history of the New York Stock Exchange. Over 16.4 million shares were traded. (A 16-million-share day in 1929 would be equivalent to something like a 250-million-share day in 1974 because of the greater number of shares now listed on the New York Stock Exchange.) Prices fell almost perpendicularly, and kept on falling, as is illustrated by the following table, which shows the extent of the decline during the autumn of 1929 and over the next three years.

Security	High Price September 3, 1929	Low Price November 13, 1929	Low Price for Year 1932
American Telephone & Telegraph	304	197¼	70¼
Bethlehem Steel	140⅜	78¼	7¼
General Electric	396¼	168⅛	8½
Montgomery Ward	137⅞	49¼	3½
National Cash Register	127½	59	6¼
Radio Corporation of America	101	28	2½

Perhaps the best summary of the debacle was given by *Variety,* the show-business weekly, which headlined the story, "Wall Street Lays an Egg." The speculative boom was dead and billions of dollars of share values—as well as the dreams

of millions—were wiped out. The crash in the stock market
was followed by the most devastating depression in the history of the country.

An Afterword

Why are memories so short? Why do such speculative crazes
seem so isolated from the lessons of history? I have no
apt answer to offer, but I am convinced that Bernard Baruch
was correct in suggesting that a study of these events can help
equip investors for survival. The consistent losers in the
market, from my personal experience, are those who are unable to resist being swept up in some kind of tulip-bulb
craze. It is not hard, really, to make money in the market. As
we shall see later, investors who select stocks by throwing
darts at the stock listings in the *Wall Street Journal* can make
fairly handsome long-run returns. What is hard to avoid is
the alluring temptation to throw your money away on short,
get-rich-quick speculative binges.

And yet the melody lingers on. I have a good friend who
once built a modest stake into a small fortune. Then along
came a stock called Alphanumeric. In addition to offering an
exciting name, it also promised to revolutionize the method
of feeding data into computers. My friend was hooked.

I begged him to investigate first whether the huge future
earnings that were already reflected in the price could possibly be achieved given the likely size of the market. (Of
course, the company had no *current* earnings.) He thanked
me for my advice but dismissed it by saying that stock prices
weren't based on "fundamentals" like earnings and dividends. "They are based on hope and dreams," he said. "The
history of stock valuation bears me out. This Alphanumeric
story will have all the tape watchers drooling with excitement
and conjuring up visions of castles in the air. Any delay in

buying would be self-defeating." And so my friend had to rush in before the crowd could bid up the price.

And rush in he did, buying at $80, which was close to the peak of a craze in that particular stock. The stock plunged to $2, and with it my friend's fortune—which is now much more modest than what he originally started out with. The ability to avoid such horrendous mistakes is probably the most important factor in preserving one's capital and allowing it to grow. The lesson is so obvious and yet so easy to ignore.

CHAPTER THREE

Stock Valuation in the Swinging Sixties

Everything's got a moral if only you can find it.—Lewis Carroll, Alice's Adventures in Wonderland

The madness of the crowd, as we have just seen, can be truly spectacular. The examples I have just cited, plus a host of others, have convinced more and more people to put their money under the care of a professional—someone who knows what makes the market tick and who can be trusted to act prudently. Thus most of us find that at least a part (and often all) of our investable funds are in the hands of institutional portfolio managers—those who run the large pension and retirement funds, mutual funds, investment counseling organizations and the like. While the crowd may be mad, the institution is above all that. The institution is, to borrow a phrase from Tennyson, "of loyal nature and of noble mind." Very well, let us then take a look at the sanity of institutions.

The Sanity of Institutions

By 1960, institutions and other professional investors accounted for almost half of the total shares traded on the New York Stock Exchange; in 1969, they had taken a commanding position with a volume of 66 percent. Results of more recent samples of trading activity suggest that institutions accounted for approximately 70 percent of stock exchange volume. Surely, in a market where professional investors dominate trading, the game must have changed. The hard-headed, sharp-penciled reasoning of the pros ought to be a guarantee that the extravagant excesses of the past will be avoided.

And yet in 1969 a company with annual sales of only $16 million was "valued" by the market at $1 billion—the latter value being obtained by multiplying the number of shares outstanding by the price per share. Throughout the past twenty years of institutional domination of the market, prices often gyrated more rapidly and by much greater amounts than could plausibly be explained by apparent changes in their anticipated intrinsic values.

In 1955, for example, General Electric announced that its scientists had created exact duplicates of the diamond. The market became entranced at once, despite the public acknowledgment that these diamonds were not suitable for sale as gems and that they could not be manufactured cheaply enough for industrial use. Within twenty-four hours, the shares of G.E. rose 4¼ points. This increased the total market value of all G.E. shares by almost $400 million, approximately twice the then current value of total worldwide diamond sales and six times the value of all industrial diamond sales. Clearly, the price rise was not due to the worth of the discovery to the company, but rather to the castle-building potential this would hold for prospective buyers. Indeed, speculators rushed in so fast to beat the gun that the entire price rise was accomplished in the first minutes of trading during the day following the announcement.

Of course, we should not generalize from isolated instances. Professional investors, however, did participate in three distinct speculative movements during the decade of the 1960s. These were the growth-stock and new-issue craze of the 1959–61 period, the conglomerate boom of the mid-1960s, and the performance cult of the late 1960s, which led to the worship of "concept" stocks. In each case, professional institutions bid actively for stocks not because they felt such stocks were undervalued under the firm-foundation principle, but because they anticipated that some greater fools would take the shares off their hands at even more inflated prices. It's true these speculative movements were somewhat less dramatic than those I covered in the preceding chapter. But the parallels are obvious and, particularly since they relate to present-day markets, I think you'll find this tour through the decade of the sixties especially useful.

The New "New Era": The Growth Stock/New Issue Craze

In the 1959–61 period, growth was the magic word. It was the corollary to the "Soaring Sixties," the wonderful decade to come. Growth stocks (those issues for which an extraordinary rate of earnings growth was expected), especially those associated with glamorous new technologies like Texas Instruments and Varian Associates, far outdistanced the standard blue-chip stocks. Wall Street was eager to pay good money for space travel, transistors, klystron tubes, optical scanners, and other esoteric things. Backed by this strong enthusiasm, the price of securities in these businesses rose wildly.

By 1959 the traditional rule that stocks should sell at a multiple of 10 to 15 times their earnings has been supplanted by multiples of 50 to 100 times earnings, or even more for the most glamorous issues. For example, at the peak of the craze in 1961 Control Data, a new computer company, sold for over 200 times its previous year's earnings. Farrington, a handbag manufacturer that had consistently lost money but hoped to manufacture a new electronics device, rose rapidly in the over-the-counter market. The stock later plummeted to 2 and eventually the company went bankrupt. Even large, well-established growth companies with a technological basis rose to unprecedented heights, as the following table illustrates.

	1961		1962	
Security	High Price	Price Earnings Multiple *	Low Price	Price Earnings Multiple *
IBM	607	80.7	300	34.4
Texas Instruments	206¾	87.6	49	23.0
Microwave Associates	60⅜	85.0	8	12.7
Fairchild Camera	88¼	42.0	31	13.1
Perkin-Elmer	83½	67.3	25	16.7

* Price divided by earnings per share for the year.

Growth took on an almost mystical significance, and questioning the propriety of such valuations became, as in the generation past, almost heretical. These prices could not be justified on firm-foundation principles. But investors firmly believed that later in the wonderful decade of the sixties, buyers would eagerly come forward to pay even higher prices. Lord Keynes must have smiled quietly from wherever it is that economists go when they die.

To be sure, many professionals viewed the market with incredulity. One New York investment manager noted: "I think this market is crazy, just plain crazy. There are still good stocks around, companies selling at 10 to 20 times earnings and with good earnings prospects. But people seem to want to buy stocks selling at 60 or 80 times a company's earnings. I don't know why. This just isn't a thinking man's market."

I had just gone to work on Wall Street during the boom and recall vividly one of the senior partners of my firm shaking his head and admitting that he knew of no one over forty, with any recollection of the 1929–32 crash, who would buy and hold the high-priced growth stocks. But the young Turks held sway. The sky was the limit and the growth stocks were the ones that were going up. *Newsweek* quoted one broker as saying that speculators have the idea that anything they buy "will double overnight. The horrible thing is, it has happened."

But more was to come. Promoters, eager to satisfy the insatiable thirst of investors for the space-age stocks of the soaring sixties, created new offerings by the dozens. A new-issue craze (more were offered in this 1959–62 period than at any other time in history) developed as investors—both individual and institutional—whipped themselves into a speculative frenzy. The new-issue mania of the period rivaled the South Sea Bubble in its intensity and also, regrettably, in the fraudulent practices that were revealed.

It was called the "tronics boom," since the stock offerings often included some garbled version of the word "electronics" in their title even if the companies had nothing to do with the electronics industry. Buyers of these issues didn't really care what the companies made—so long as it sounded electronic, with a suggestion of the esoteric. For example, American Music Guild, whose business consisted entirely of the door-to-door sale of phonograph records and players, changed its name to Space-Tone before "going public." The shares were sold to the public at 2, and within a few weeks rose to 14.

The name was the game. There were a host of "trons" such as Astron, Dutron, Vulcatron, and Transitron, and a

number of "onics" such as Circuitronics, Supronics, Video-
tronics, and several Electrosonics companies. Leaving nothing to chance, one group put together the winning combination Powertron Ultrasonics. The prices commanded in the
market by these companies were unbelievable.

Jack Dreyfus, of Dreyfus and Company, commented on
the mania as follows:

> Take a nice little company that's been making shoelaces for
> 40 years and sells at a respectable six times earnings ratio.
> Change the name from Shoelaces, Inc. to Electronics and
> Silicon Furth-Burners. In today's market, the words "elec-
> tronics" and "silicon" are worth 15 times earnings. How-
> ever, the real play comes from the word "furth-burners,"
> which no one understands. A word that no one understands
> entitles you to double your entire score. Therefore, we have
> six times earnings for the shoelace business and 15 times
> earnings for electronic and silicon, or a total of 21 times
> earnings. Multiply this by two for furth-burners and we now
> have a score of 42 times earnings for the new company.

In a later investigation of the new-issue phenomenon, the
Securities and Exchange Commission uncovered considerable
evidence of fraudulence and market manipulation. For example, some investment bankers, especially those who underwrote the smaller new issues, would often hold a substantial
volume of securities off the market. This made the market so
"thin" at the start that the price would rise quickly in the
after market.

In one "hot issue" that almost doubled in price on the
first day of trading, the SEC found that a considerable portion of the entire offering was sold to broker-dealers, many of
whom held on to their allotments for a period until the
shares could be sold at much higher prices. The SEC also
found that many underwriters allocated large portions of hot
issues to insiders of the firms such as partners, relatives,
officers, and other securities dealers to whom a favor was

owed. In one instance, 87 percent of a new issue was allocated to "insiders," rather than to the general public, as was proper.

Another trick was for the underwriter to allocate stock to brokers only on the condition that they trade the stock at rising prices. The investor, in turn, was allowed to purchase some stock at the original offering price only if he would buy more in the market after the initial offering, thus swelling the demand for the shares in the after market.

The following table shows some representative new issues of this period and records their price movements after the shares were issued. At least for a while, the new-issue buyers did very well indeed. Large advances over their already in-

Security	Offering Date	Offering Price	Bid Price First Day of Trading	High Bid Price 1961	Low Bid Price 1962
Boonton Electronics Corp.	March 6, 1961	5½ *	12¼ *	24½ *	1⅝ *
Bristol Dynamics	March 20, 1961	7	16	23	3⅛
Geophysics Corp. of America	December 8, 1960	14	27	58	9
Hydro-Space Technology	July 19, 1960	3	7	7	1
Mother's Cookie Corp.	March 8, 1961	15	23	25	7
Seaboard Electronic	July 5, 1961	5½	8¾	15½	2¼
Universal Electronic Labs	November 25, 1961	4	4½	18	1⅜

* Per unit of 1 share and 1 warrant

flated initial offering prices were scored for such companies as Boonton Electronics and Geophysics Corporation of America. The speculative fever was so great that even Mother's Cookie could count on a sizable gain. Think of the glory they could have achieved if they had called themselves "Mothertron's Cookitronics." Ten years later, the shares of most of these companies were almost worthless.

Many underwriters wore a smug smile during this period. They not only received a handsome underwriting fee for their role but also usually received warrants from the company to purchase additional shares of stock at very low prices. The small investment banking firm of Michael A. Lomasney & Co., for example, underwrote an issue of 100,000 shares of B.B.M. Photocopy, which it sold for $3 a share. In addition to an underwriting fee of approximately $20,000 Lomasney also received 20,000 warrants, each warrant entitling him to buy one share of stock at a price of one cent. Within a short period B.B.M. was selling at $40 per share, which gave the warrants a paper value of approximately $800,000. Thus Lomasney was close to a million dollars richer for his efforts, while the company received $280,000—the $300,000 from the issue of its shares less the $20,000 underwriting commission.

But the public had done well with new issues and many believed they represented a sure road to wealth. The 1961 price gain in the table above told them so and reinforced their general mood of optimism. Speculation in these securities and in space-age stocks was the closest the bull market of the early sixties came to the speculative fever of 1929.

New issues became standard cocktail party chatter, and women's clubs abandoned lectures on art or other cultural pursuits for discussions of the stock market. Tips and rumors were ubiquitous. Brokers reported record crowds in their offices, and the general volume of trading soared dramatically. The jargon and speculative spirit of Wall Street spread to other markets as well—such as the art market.

Robert Sobel, author of *The Big Board,* noted that the

Art Market Guide and Forecaster urged the purchase of paintings as follows:

32 ARTISTS TO *TRIPLE* IN PRICE

With the Art Market for paintings up 975% since the war— and 65% in the last year alone—you can lose immense profits by failing to keep informed of the *monetary* values of art, present and future. Among the 500 painters whose price trends are under regular study by our organization, many have gone down in price as well as up—ranging from *gains* up to 61,900% to *losses* of 87% (compared to the 975% gain for the whole market as measured by the new *AMG 500-Painters Average*).

Where was the Securities and Exchange Commission all this time? Hadn't it changed the rule from "Let the buyer beware" to "Let the seller beware"? Aren't new issuers required to register their offering with the SEC? Can't they (and their underwriters) be punished for false and misleading statements?

Yes to all these questions and yes, the SEC was there, but by law it had to stand by quietly. As long as a company has prepared (and distributed to investors) an adequate prospectus, the SEC can do nothing to save buyers from themselves. For example, many of the prospectuses of the period contained the following type of warning in bold letters on the cover.

WARNING: THIS COMPANY HAS NO ASSETS OR EARNINGS AND WILL BE UNABLE TO PAY DIVIDENDS IN THE FORESEEABLE FUTURE. THE SHARES ARE HIGHLY RISKY.

But just as the warnings on packs of cigarettes do not prevent many people from smoking, so the warning that this investment may be dangerous to your wealth cannot block a speculator from forking over his money if he is hell-bent on doing so. The SEC can warn a fool but it cannot prevent him from parting with his money. And the buyers of new issues were so convinced the stocks would rise in price (no matter what the company's assets or past record) that the underwriter's problem was not how he could sell the shares but how to allocate them among the frenzied purchasers.

Fraudulence and market manipulation are different matters. Here the SEC can take and has taken strong action. Indeed, many of the little-known brokerage houses on the fringes of respectability, which were responsible for most of the new issues and for manipulation of their prices, were suspended for a variety of peculations.

The staff of the SEC is limited, however; the major problem is the attitude of the general public. When investors are infused with a get-rich-quick attitude and are willing to snap up any piece of bait, anything can happen—and usually does. Without public greed, the manipulators would not stand a chance.

The tronics boom came back to earth in 1962. The tailspin started early in the year and exploded in a horrendous selling wave five months later. On Monday, May 28, the worst day of the decline, the Dow-Jones averages of thirty leading industrial stocks fell 34.95 points (this was second only to the drop of 38.33 recorded in 1929). On that single day, the decline in the market value of all stocks listed on the New York Stock Exchange amounted to $20.8 billion. Even on October 28, 1929 only $9.6 billion evaporated, because the total value of listed stocks was smaller on that day. "Something like an earthquake hit the stock market," editorialized the *New York Times*. Growth stocks, even the highest-quality ones, took the brunt of the decline, falling much further than the general market. Yesterday's hot issue became today's cold turkey.

Many professionals refused to accept the fact that they had speculated recklessly. Rather they blamed the decline on President Kennedy's tough stand with the steel industry, which led to a rollback of announced price hikes. Former President Eisenhower blamed the decline on Kennedy's "reckless spending programs," and Walter Lippmann chastised Kennedy for not fulfilling his "promise to bring about something near to the full employment of capital and labor and a rising rate of economic growth."

Others did recognize the speculative mania and said simply that the market, and growth stocks in particular, were "too high" in 1961. As far as steel prices were concerned, with strong foreign competition in steel the price rises would probably have been rescinded anyway. Very few pointed out that it is always easy to look back and say when prices were too high or too low. Fewer still said that no one seems to know the proper price for a stock at any given time.

Synergy Generates Energy: The Conglomerate Boom

The market shook off its losses and settled down to ponder its next move. It was not too long in coming.

I've said before that part of the genius of the financial market is that if a product is demanded, it is produced. The product that all investors desired was expected growth in earnings per share. And if growth wasn't to be found in a name, it was only to be expected that someone would find another way to produce it. By the mid-sixties, creative entrepreneurs had discovered that growth was a word and that the word was *synergism*.

Synergism is the quality of having 2 plus 2 equal 5. Thus, it seemed quite plausible that two separate companies with an earning power of $2 million each might produce combined earnings of $5 million if the businesses were consolidated. This magical, mystical, surefire profitable new creation was called a conglomerate.

While antitrust laws kept large companies from purchasing firms in the same industry, it was possible for a while to purchase firms in other industries without interference from the Justice Department. The consolidations were carried out in the name of synergism. Ostensibly, mergers would allow the conglomerate to achieve greater financial strength (and thus greater borrowing capabilities at lower rates); to enhance marketing capabilities through the distribution of complementary product lines; to give greater scope to superior managerial talents; and to consolidate, and thus make more efficient, operating services such as personnel and accounting departments. All this led to synergism—a stimulation of sales and earnings for the combined operation that would have been impossible for the independent entities alone.

In fact, the major impetus for the conglomerate wave of the 1960s was that the acquisition process itself could be made to produce growth in earnings per share. Indeed, the managers of conglomerates tended to possess financial expertise rather than the operating skills required to improve the profitability of the acquired companies. By an easy bit of legerdemain, they could put together a group of companies with no basic potential at all and produce steadily rising per-share earnings. The following example shows how this monkey business was performed.

Suppose we have two companies—the Able Circuit Smasher Company, an electronics firm, and Baker Typewriter Company, which makes typewriters. Each has 200,000 shares outstanding. It's 1965 and both companies have earnings of $1 million a year, or $5 per share. Let's assume neither business is growing and that, with or without merger activity, earnings would just continue along at the same level.

The two firms sell at different prices, however. Since Able Circuit Smasher Company is in the electronics business, the market awards it a price-earnings multiple of 20 which, multiplied by its $5 earnings per share, gives it a market price of $100. Baker Typewriter Company, in a less glamorous business, has its earnings multiplied at only 10 times and, consequently, its $5 per share earnings command a market price of only $50.

The management of Able Circuit would like to become a

conglomerate. It offers to absorb Baker by swapping stock at
the rate of two for three. The holders of Baker shares would
get two shares of Able stock—which have a market value of
$200—for every three shares of Baker stock—with a total
market value of $150. Clearly this is a tempting proposal, and
the stockholders of Baker are likely to accept cheerfully. The
merger is approved.

We have a budding conglomerate, newly named Synergon, Inc., which now has 333,333 shares * outstanding and
total earnings of $2 million to put against them, or $6 per
share. Thus, by 1966 when the merger has been completed,
we find that earnings have risen by 20 percent, from $5 to $6,
and this growth seems to justify Able's former price-earnings
multiple of 20. Consequently, the shares of Synergon (née
Able) rise from $100 to $120, everybody's judgment is con-
firmed, and all go home rich and happy. In addition, the
shareholders of Baker who were bought out need not pay
any taxes on their profits until they sell their shares of the
combined company. The top three lines of the table on the
following page illustrate the transaction thus far.

A year later, Synergon finds Charlie Company, which earns
$10 per share or $1 million with 100,000 shares outstanding.
Charlie Company is in the relatively risky military-hardware
business so its shares command a multiple of only 10 and sell
at $100. Synergon offers to absorb Charlie Company on a
share-for-share exchange basis. Charlie's shareholders are de-
lighted to exchange their $100 shares for the conglomerate's
$120 shares. By the end of 1967, the combined company has
earnings of $3 million, shares outstanding of 433,333, and
earnings per share of $6.92.

Here we have a case where the conglomerate has literally
manufactured growth. Neither Able, Baker, nor Charlie was
growing at all; yet simply by virtue of the fact of their

* There are 200,000 original shares of Able plus an extra 133,333, which
get printed up to exchange for Baker's 200,000 shares according to
the terms of the merger.

	Company	Earnings Levels	Number of Shares Outstanding	Earnings per Share	Price-Earnings Multiple	Price
Before Merger 1965	Able	$1,000,000	200,000	$5.00	20	$100
	Baker	1,000,000	200,000	5.00	10	50
After First Merger 1966	Synergon (Able and Baker Combined)	2,000,000	333,333	6.00	20	120
	Charlie	1,000,000	100,000	10.00	10	100
After Second Merger 1967	Synergon (Able, Baker, and Charlie Combined)	3,000,000	433,333	6.92	20	138⅜

merger, the unwary investor who may finger his *Stock Guide* to see the past record of our conglomerate will find the following figures:

Earnings per Share

	1965	1966	1967
Synergon, Inc.	$5.00	$6.00	$6.92

Clearly, Synergon is a growth stock and its record of extraordinary performance appears to have earned it a high and possibly even an increasing multiple of earnings.

The trick that makes the game work is the ability of the electronics company to swap its high-multiple stock for the stock of another company with a lower multiple. The typewriter company can only "sell" its earnings at a multiple of 10. But when these earnings are packaged with the electronics company, the total earnings (including those from selling typewriters) could be sold at a multiple of 20. And the more acquisitions Synergon could make, the faster earnings per share would grow and thus the more attractive the stock would look to justify its high multiple.

The whole thing was like a chain letter—no one would get hurt as long as the growth of acquisitions proceeded exponentially. Of course the process could not continue for long, but the possibilities were mind-boggling for those who got in at the start. It seems difficult to believe that Wall Street professionals could be so myopic as to fall for the conglomerate con game, but accept it they did for periods of several years. Or perhaps, as subscribers to the castle-in-the-air theory, they only believed that other people would fall for it.

The story of Synergon describes the standard conglomerate earnings "growth" gambit. There were a lot of other monkeyshines practiced. Convertible bonds (or convertible preferred stocks) were often used as a substitute for shares in paying for acquisitions. A convertible bond is an IOU of the company, paying a fixed interest rate, that is convertible at the option of the holder into shares of the firm's common stock. As long as the earnings of the newly acquired subsidiary were greater than the relatively low interest rate that was placed on the convertible bond, it was possible to show even more sharply rising earnings per share than those in the previous illustration. This is because no new common stocks at all had to be issued to consummate the merger, and thus the combined earnings could be divided by a smaller number of shares.

One company was truly creative in financing its acquisition program. It used a convertible preferred stock that paid no cash dividend at all.* Instead, the conversion rate of the security was to be adjusted annually to provide that the

* Convertible preferred stock is similar to a convertible bond in that the preferred dividend is a fixed obligation of the company. But neither the principal nor the preferred dividend is considered a *debt,* so your company can usually skip a payment with greater freedom. Of course, in the example above, the stock paid no cash dividend at all.

preferred stock be convertible into more common shares each year. The older pros in Wall Street shook their heads in disbelief over these shenanigans.

It is hard to believe that investors did not count the dilution potential of the new common stock that would be issued if the bondholders or preferred stockholders were to convert their securities into common stock. Indeed, as a result of such manipulations, corporations are now required to report their earnings on a "fully diluted" basis, to account for the new common shares that must be set aside for potential conversions. But most investors in the middle 1960s ignored such niceties and were satisfied only to see steadily and rapidly rising earnings.

Automatic Sprinkler Corporation (now called A-T-O Inc.) is a good example of how the game of manufacturing growth was actually played during the 1960s. Between 1963 and 1968, the company's sales volume rose by over 1400 percent. This phenomenal record was due solely to acquisitions. In the middle of 1967, four mergers were completed in a twenty-five day period. These newly acquired companies were all selling at relatively low price-earnings multiples, and thus helped to produce a sharp growth in earnings per share. The market responded to this "growth" by bidding up the price-earnings multiple to over 50 times earnings in 1967. This boosted the price of the company's stock from about $8 per share in 1963 to $73⅝ in 1967.

Mr. Figgie, the president of Automatic Sprinkler, performed the public relations job necessary to help Wall Street build its castle in the air. He automatically sprinkled his conversations with talismanic phrases about the synergy of the free-form company and its interface with change and technology. He was always ready to talk about the "bottom line" of the income statement (where you get down to what the company earned) and insisted on emphasizing "earnings per share." He did not hesitate to project growth five to ten years out in the future. (After all, who'll remember in ten years what your forecast was?) He was careful to point out that he looked at twenty to thirty deals for each one he bought. Wall Street loved every word of it.

Mr. Figgie was not alone in conning Wall Street. Managers of other conglomerates almost invented a new language in the process of dazzling the investment community. They talked about market matrices, core technology fulcrums, modular building blocks, and the nucleus theory of growth. No one from Wall Street really knew what the words meant, but they all got the nice, warm feeling of being in the technological mainstream.

Conglomerate managers also found a new way of describing the businesses they had bought. Their shipbuilding businesses became "marine systems." Zinc mining became the "space minerals division." Steel fabrication plants became the "materials technology division." A lighting fixture or a lock company became part of the "protective services division." And if one of the "ungentlemanly" security analysts (somebody from CCNY rather than Harvard Business School) had the nerve to ask how you can get 15 to 20 percent growth from a foundry or a meat packer, the typical conglomerate manager suggested that his efficiency experts had isolated millions of dollars of excess costs; that his marketing research staff had found several fresh, uninhabited markets; and that the target of tripling profit margins could be easily realized within two years. To this add talk of breakfast and Sunday meetings with your staff, and the image of the hardworking, competent, go-go atmosphere is complete.

Instead of going down with merger activity, the price-earnings multiples of conglomerate stocks rose higher and higher. Even Textron, which generally disdained gimmickry and retained its terribly maladroit name indicating the company's association with the beleaguered textile industry, finally got its multiple up to 25 times earnings. Prices and multiples for a selection of conglomerates in 1967 are shown in the following table.

| | 1967 | | 1969 | |
Security	High Price	Price-Earnings Multiple	Low Price	Price-Earnings Multiple
Automatic Sprinkler (A-T-O Inc.)	73⅝	51.0	10⅞	13.4
Litton Industries	120⅜	44.1	35	14.4
Teledyne Inc.	71½ [a]	53.8	28¼	14.2
Textron, Inc.	55	24.9	23¼	10.1

[a] Adjusted for subsequent split.

The music slowed drastically for the conglomerates on January 19, 1968. On that day, the granddaddy of the conglomerates, Litton Industries, announced that earnings for the second quarter of that year would be substantially less than had been forecast. It had recorded 20 percent yearly increases for almost an entire decade. The market had so thoroughly come to believe in alchemy that the announcement was treated with disbelief and shock. In the selling wave that followed, conglomerate stocks declined by roughly 40 percent before a feeble recovery set in.

Worse was to come. In July, the Federal Trade Commission announced it would make an in-depth investigation of the conglomerate merger movement. Again the stocks went tumbling down. The Securities and Exchange Commission and the accounting profession finally made their move and began to make attempts to clarify the reporting techniques for mergers and acquisitions.

In January 1969, Litton again announced lower earnings. If that company—believed to be the best managed of the group—was unable to maintain earnings growth, how could the others continue to do so? Perhaps weak parts do not a strong whole make. The sell orders came flooding in. These were closely followed by new announcements from the SEC and the Assistant Attorney General in charge of antitrust, indicating a strong concern about the accelerating pace of the merger movement.

It should be quite a while before the conglomerate castle rises again, although given the propensity of institutions to run in packs after any concept suggesting growth one can't be quite that sure. The aftermath of this speculative phase revealed two disturbing factors. First, conglomerates were mortal and were not always able to control their far-flung empires. Indeed, investors became disenchanted with the conglomerate's new math; 2 plus 2 certainly did not equal 5 and some investors wondered if it even equaled 4. Second, the government and the accounting profession expressed real concern about the pace of mergers and about possible abuses. These two worries on the part of investors reduced—and in many cases eliminated—the premium multiples that had been paid for the anticipation of earnings from the acquisition process alone. This in itself makes the alchemy game almost impossible, for the acquiring company has to have an earnings multiple larger than the acquired company if the ploy is to work at all.

The combination of lower earnings and flattened price-earnings multiples implied a drastic decline in the prices of conglomerates. The preceding table indicates the depths to which stock prices sank in 1969 as the players in the game all rushed to grab their seats. Even greater declines were suffered in the 1970 bear market.

Interestingly enough, it was the professional investors who were hurt the most in the wild scramble for chairs. Few mutual or pension funds were without large holdings of conglomerate stocks. Castles in the air are not reserved as the sole prerogative of individuals; institutional investors can build them too.

Performance Comes to the Market:
The Bubble in Concept Stocks

Despite the prolonged death rattle of the conglomerate, new life stirred elsewhere on Wall Street. It probably came into being during the mid-sixties when there was heightened competition among mutual funds for the customer's dollar. This new golden calf was called *performance*. It meant that a fund performing better than the others (that is, the value of the stocks in its portfolio went up faster than the stocks in its competitors' portfolios) was a far easier fund to sell to the public than one with a less lustrous record.

Some fund managers even suggested that the performance funds were safer. One mutual fund manager suggested, "The safest way to preserve capital is by doubling it." The customers said amen and never bothered to ask why tripling wouldn't be safer still. And not only that: since performance funds tended to distribute capital gains rather than dividends, the tax bite was lower (only half of these gains were subject to tax and the maximum rate was a flat 25 percent). So, with the public buying, mutual fund salesmen began to clamor for even greater performance.

And perform the funds did—at least over short periods of time. Fred Carr's highly publicized Enterprise Fund racked up a 117 percent total return (including both dividends and capital gains) in 1967 and followed this with a 44 percent return in 1968. The corresponding figures for the Standard & Poor's 500 Stock Index were 25 percent and 11 percent respectively. This performance brought large amounts of new money into the fund, and into other funds that could boast glamorous performances. The public no longer bet on the horse but rather on the jockey.

How did these jockeys do it? They concentrated the portfolio in dynamic stocks. Take the Dreyfus Fund and the growth-oriented Fidelity Funds. Jack Dreyfus, a high-stakes bridge player, got a running start on the performance record

by investing heavily in Polaroid during that company's most
rapid growth stage. Fidelity, run by Edward Johnson and
Gerald Tsai, also held large blocks of stock in a relatively
few rapidly growing companies. Johnson and Tsai were not
faithful to these companies, however. At the sign of a better
story, they would quickly switch. Both funds chalked up impressive successes in the mid-sixties and this led to many
imitators. The camp followers were quickly given the accolade "go-go" funds, and the fund managers were often called
"the youthful gunslingers." "Nothing succeeds so well as success," Talleyrand once observed, and this was certainly true
for the performance funds in their early years—the customers' dollars flowed in.

The fickleness of men like Gerry Tsai extended even to
their own relationships. Feeling he could make a better story
on his own, Tsai left Fidelity in February 1966. In retrospect
his ambitions were modest: he felt he would be able to raise
$25 million in an initial offering for his own fund, the Man-
hattan Fund. His underwriters, Bache & Co., agreed and
opened their subscription books for orders. Both found out
that Gerry didn't know his own multiple. $274 million was
subscribed on the first day. Within a year, Gerry Tsai had
more than $400 million to manage. Tsai became the first
superstar of the performance game and brokers could sound
wise by watching the ticker tape and saying, "Ah, Gerry is
buying again."

The performance game was not limited to mutual funds.
It spread to all kinds of investing institutions. Businessmen
who had to make constantly larger contributions to their
workers' pension funds to meet retirement obligations
began to ask pointedly whether they might be able to reduce
their current expenses by switching more of the fund from
fixed-income bonds into common stocks with exciting growth
possibilities. Even university endowment-fund managers were
pressured to strive for performance. McGeorge Bundy of the

Ford Foundation chided the portfolio managers of universities:

> It is far from clear that trustees have reason to be proud of
> their performance in making money for their colleges. We
> recognize the risks of unconventional investing, but the true
> test of performance in the handling of money is the record
> of achievement, not the opinion of the respectable. We have
> the preliminary impression that over the long run caution
> has cost our colleges and universities much more than im-
> prudence or excessive risk-taking.

And so performance investing took hold of Wall Street
in the late 1960s. The commandments for fund managers
were simple: Concentrate your holdings in a relatively few
stocks and don't hesitate to switch the portfolio around if a
more desirable investment appears. And because near-term
performance was especially important (investment services
began to publish monthly records of mutual fund performance) it would be best to buy stocks with an exciting concept
and a compelling story. You had to be sure the market would
recognize the beauty of your stock now—not far into the future. Hence, the birth of the so-called concept stock.

Xerox was a classic example of a concept stock. The concept was that of a new industry where machines would make
dry copies by electrostatic transference. The company, Xerox,
with its patent protection and it running head start, could
look forward to several years of increased earnings. It was a
true story—a believable story, one that would quicken the
pulse of any good performance-fund manager.

But even if the story were not totally believable, as long
as the investment manager was convinced that the average
opinion would think that the average opinion would believe
the story, that's all that was needed. The youthful gunslingers
became disenchanted with normal security analysts who
could tell you how many railroad ties Penn Central had, but

couldn't tell you when the company was about to go bankrupt. "I don't want to listen to that kind of security analyst,"
one of Wall Street's gunslingers told me. "I just want a good
story or a good concept."

According to Martin Mayer, an investment manager who
ran one of 1968's hottest mutual funds had a framed sign in
Gothic lettering hanging on the wall of his office: "Invest
Then Investigate." This was the reverse of the stock exchange's long-established slogan and was as apt a symbol as
any for the atmosphere of the day. The gunslingers would
buy thousands of shares of any security on any good story,
and it became perfectly respectable to adopt a concept approach. Mayer quotes another fund manager as saying, "Since
we hear stories early, we can figure enough people will be
hearing it in the next few days to give the stock a bounce,
even if the story doesn't prove out." Many Wall Streeters
looked on this as a radical new investment strategy, but Lord
Keynes had it all spotted in 1936.

Eventually, it reached a point where any concept would
do. Enter Cortess W. Randell. His concept was a youth company for the youth market. He became founder, president,
and major stockholder of National Student Marketing. Randell's motto, if he had one, appears to have been borrowed
from Shakespeare: "Nothing can seem foul to those that
win." First, he sold an image—one of affluence and success.
He owned a personal white Lear Jet named Snoopy, an apartment in New York's Waldorf Towers, a $600,000 castle with
a mock dungeon in Virginia, and a 55-foot yacht that slept
twelve. Adding to his image was an expensive set of golf
clubs propped up by his office door. Apparently the only
time the clubs were used was at night when the office clean-
up crew drove wads of paper along the carpet.

He spent most of his time visiting the financial community or calling them on the sky phone from his Lear, and
sold the concept of NSM in the tradition of a South Sea
Bubble promoter. Randell's real métier was evangelism.

When he told meetings of security analysts that NSM was well on its way toward becoming a $700 million marketing organization, they listened with faith, respect, and awe.

The concept that Wall Street bought from Randell was that a single company could specialize in servicing the needs of young people. NSM built its early growth via the merger route, just as the ordinary conglomerates of the 1960s had done. The difference was that each of the constituent companies had something to do with the college-age youth market. Subsidiary companies sold magazine subscriptions, books and records, posters, paper dresses, guidebooks for summer jobs, student directories, a computer dating service, youth air-fare cards, sweatshirts, live entertainment programs, and a variety of consumer staples. What could be more appealing to a youthful gunslinger than a youth-oriented concept stock —a full-service company to exploit the youth subculture. Youth was in—this one couldn't miss.

Randell kept up his whirlwind promotional pace, making new converts as he went along. Glowing press releases issued forth from company headquarters and Randell's earnings projections for the company became increasingly optimistic.

While there were some thistles among such roses (the earnings growth was produced by the old conglomerate gambit with the generous support of some creative accounting), the "concept" investors bought heavily in the company and blithely ignored all questions. When Gerry Tsai's Manhattan Fund bought 120,000 shares for $5 million, it became clear that Randell had obtained the imprimatur of Wall Street's performance investors. Even some of the most august and conservative firms, including Bankers Trust, Morgan Guaranty, and Boston's venerable State Street Fund, bought stock. Pension funds, including General Mills, bought heavily; and United States Trust Company (the country's largest trust company) bought the stock for many of its accounts. University endowment fund managers, heeding the words of McGeorge Bundy, also bought in the mad scramble for performance. Blocks of NSM were bought by Harvard, Cornell, and the University of Chicago. Bundy himself practiced what he preached, and the previously conservatively managed Ford Foundation Fund also bought a large block.

The following table shows the high prices and enormous price-earnings multiples for National Student Marketing and for a small group of other concept stocks. The number of institutional holders (probably understated) for each security is also shown. Clearly, institutional investors are at least as adept as the general public at building castles in the air.

Security	High Price 1968–69	Price-Earnings Multiple at High	Number of Institutional Holders Year-end 1969	Low Price 1970	Percentage Decline
Four Seasons Nursing Centers of America	90¾	113.4	24	0.20	99
National Environ-ment Corp.	27	103.8	8	⅜	99
National Student Marketing	35¾ [a]	111.7	21	⅞	98
Performance Systems	23	∞	13	⅛	99

[a] Adjusted for subsequent stock split.

There were other concepts. Health care, for example, attracted quite a few adherents. Given the increasing numbers of older people and the spread of federal and private health insurance plans, someone was bound to make lots of money. Four Seasons Nursing Centers of America looked just like that someone. The biggest and most aggressive mutual funds bought in. At one point in 1969, institutions owned close to 50 percent of the company's stock.

The company expanded at a feverish pace, financing itself largely through the issuance of debt. These borrowings were sweetened, however, with so-called "equity kickers."

This meant that attached to each bond were warrants to buy common stock of Four Seasons at fixed prices. Thus, if the stock price continued to go up, the bondholders could exercise their warrants and make additional profits.

These issues were so popular that customers would swear at their underwriters if they were not given a chance to buy. The institutional buyers who flocked in were not only Americans—even the "shrewd" European bankers bought heavily. European purchasers included such illustrious names as Banque Rothschild, Kreditbank Luxembourgeoise, Crédit Commercial de France, and the European operations of such U.S. firms as American Express Securities, S.A.; Bache & Co.; Burnham & Co.; and Merrill Lynch, Ltd. Four Seasons president Jack L. Clark boasted, "Without the institutions, we couldn't have grown nearly this fast."

As the debt mounted up no one seemed to worry much about the old ideas of prudent debt ratios, for this was a new concept and the rules of the game had changed. On June 26, 1970 the company filed a petition for reorganization under Chapter X of the Bankruptcy Act.

National Environment demonstrates the benefits of a new name. It started out in life as a prosaic construction company. I once asked one of the performance fund managers why a home builder was worth over 100 times earnings. He answered, "You are obviously not into the environment concept. This stock is 'hea-vy.' It gives me good vibrations."

Once National Environment got its price-earnings multiple up, it started an acquisition program, turning itself into a junior conglomerate. For example, in 1968 it bought a firm called "Uncle John's Restaurants" and promptly changed its name to "Envirofood, Inc." It also added nursing homes, insurance, soft drinks, and wholesale liquor operations, just to be sure it didn't miss any of the current fads. This company was really with it.

Minnie Pearl's concept is our last example of the period. Minnie Pearl was a fast-food franchising firm that was as

accommodating as all get out. To please the financial community, Minnie Pearl's chickens became "Performance Systems." After all, what better name could be chosen for performance-oriented investors? On Wall Street a rose by any
other name does not smell as sweet. The ∞ shown in the
table under "price-earnings multiple" indicates that the
multiple was infinity. Performance Systems had no earnings
at all to divide into the stock's price at the time it reached its
high in 1968. As the table indicates, Minnie Pearl laid an egg
—and a bad one at that. The subsequent performance for
this and the other stocks listed was indeed truly remarkable
—although not quite what their buyers had anticipated.

Why did the stocks actually perform so badly? One general answer was that their price-earnings multiples were inflated beyond reason. If a multiple of 100 drops to the more
normal multiple of 15 for the market as a whole, you have
lost 85 percent of your investment right there. But in addition most of the concept companies of the time ran into severe operating difficulties. The reasons were varied: too
rapid expansion, too much debt, loss of management control,
etc. These companies were run by men who were primarily
promoters, not sharp-penciled operating managers. In addition, fraudulent practices were common. For example, Performance Systems reported profits of $3.2 million in 1969.
The SEC claimed that this report was "false and misleading." In 1972 Performance Systems issued a revision of the
1969 report. Apparently a loss of $1.3 million more accu-
rately reflected 1969 operations.

And so when the 1969–71 bear market came, these concept stocks went down just as fast as they went up. In the end
it was the pros who were conned most of all. While there is
nothing wrong with seeking good performance, the mad
rush to outgun the competition week by week had disastrous
consequences. The cult of performance and the concept of
"concept" stocks were henceforth greeted with disdain when
mentioned in Wall Street.

CHAPTER FOUR

The Firm-Foundation Theory of Stock Prices

The greatest of all gifts is the power to estimate things at their true worth.—La Rochefoucauld, *Reflexions; ou sentences et maximes morales*

We have seen that the stock market at times conforms well to the castle-in-the-air theory, and styles and fads often play a critical role in security pricing. For this reason, the game of investing can be extremely dangerous. When the market favors some particular characteristic in a stock, financial entrepreneurs usually find some way of manufacturing it—or at least a close substitute. The public inevitably pays dearly for such creativity.

Investors can and should learn vicariously from the stock market. And I hope this historical review has provided sufficient warning to save you from the traps that ensnare builders of castles in the air. Autopsies should be as useful in the practice of investment as in medicine. At the same time, to be forewarned is not to be forearmed in the investment world. Investors also need a sense of justification for market prices—a standard, even if only a very loose one, with which to compare current market prices. Is there such a thing? I happen to think so—though I believe it neither rests on a firm foundation nor floats like a castle in the air.

The firm-foundation theorists, who include many of Wall Street's most prosperous and highly paid security analysts, know full well that purely psychic support for market valuations has proved a most undependable pillar, and skyrocketing markets have invariably succumbed to the financial laws of gravity. Therefore, many security analysts devote their energies to estimating a stock's firm foundation of value. Let's see what lies behind such estimates.

The "Fundamental" Determinants of Stock Prices

What is it that determines the real or intrinsic value of a share? What are the so-called fundamentals that security analysts look at in estimating a security's firm foundation of value?

I said in the first chapter that firm-foundation theorists view the worth of any share as the present value of all dollar benefits the investor expects to receive from it. Remember that the word "present" indicates that a distinction must be made between dollars expected immediately and those anticipated later on, which must be "discounted." All future income is worth less than money in hand; for if you had the money now you could be earning interest on it. In a very real sense, time is money.

In arriving at their value estimates, firm-foundation theorists usually take the standpoint of a very long-term investor who buys his shares "for keeps." The only benefits such an investor receives will come to him if the company pays out some part of its earnings in cash dividends. Thus the worth of a share to a long-term investor will be the present or discounted value of all the future dividends the firm is expected to pay.

Of course, the flow of future dividends is dependent on a number of factors. I will now describe four determinants affecting future dividends and then give four broad rules for applying these to determine the present (or firm-foundation) value of the stocks you are considering. If you follow these rules consistently, firm-foundation theorists suggest you will find yourself safe from the speculative crazes I have just described.

Determinant 1: The expected growth rate Most people don't realize the implications of compound growth on financial decisions. It is often said that the Indian who sold Manhattan Island in 1626 for $24 was rooked by the white man. In fact, he may have been an extremely sharp salesman. Had he put his $24 away at 6 percent interest, compounded semi-annually, it would now be worth approximately $20 billion, and with it he could buy back much of the now-improved land. Such is the magic of compound growth!

Similarly, the implications of various growth rates on the size of future dividends may be surprising to many readers. As the table below shows, growth at a 15 percent rate means that dividends will double every five years.* Alternate rates are also presented.

Growth Rate of Dividends	Present Dividend	Dividend in Five Years	Dividend in Ten Years	Dividend in Twenty-Five Years
5 percent	$1.00	$1.28	$1.68	$ 3.39
15 percent	1.00	2.01	4.05	32.92
25 percent	1.00	3.05	9.31	264.70

* A handy rule for calculating how many years it takes dividends to double is to divide 70 by the long-term growth rate. Thus, if dividends grow at 15 percent per year they will double in a bit less than five years (70 ÷ 15).

The catch (and doesn't there always have to be at least one, if not twenty-two?) is that dividend growth does not go on forever. Corporations and industries have life cycles similar to most living things. There is, for corporations in particular, a high mortality rate at birth. Survivors can look forward to rapid growth, maturity, and then a period of stability. Later in the life cycle, companies eventually decline and either perish or undergo a substantial metamorphosis. Consider the leading corporations in the United States 100 years ago. Such names as Eastern Buggy Whip Company, La Crosse and Minnesota Steam Packet Company, Lobdell Car Wheel Company, Savanna and St. Paul Steamboat Line, and Hazard Powder Company, the already mature enterprises of the time, would have ranked high in a *"Fortune Top 500"* list of that era. All are now deceased.

Look at the industry record. Railroads, the most dynamic growth industry a century ago, finally matured and enjoyed a long period of prosperity before entering their present period of decline. The paper and aluminum industries provide more recent examples of the cessation of rapid growth and the start of a more stable, mature period in the life cycle. These industries were the most rapidly growing in the United States during the 1940s and early 1950s. By the 1960s they were no longer able to grow any faster than the economy as a whole. Similarly, the most rapidly growing industry of the late 1950s and 1960s, the electronics industry, had slowed to a crawl by the 1970s.

And even if the natural life cycle doesn't get a company, there's always the fact that it gets harder and harder to grow at the same percentage rate. A company earning $1 million need increase its earnings by only $100,000 to achieve a 10 percent growth rate, whereas a company starting from a base of $10 million in earnings needs $1 million in additional earnings to produce the same record.

The nonsense of relying on very high long-term growth rates is nicely illustrated by working with population projections for the United States. If the populations of the nation and of California continue to grow at their recent rates, 120 percent of the United States population will live in California by the year 2035! Using similar kinds of projections, it can be estimated that at the same time 240 percent of the people in the country with venereal disease will live in California. As one Californian put it on hearing these forecasts, "Only the former projections make the latter one seem at all plausible."

As hazardous as projections may be, share prices must reflect differences in growth prospects if any sense is to be made of market valuations. Also, the probable length of the growth phase is very important. If one company expects to enjoy a rapid 20 percent growth rate for ten years, and another growth company expects to sustain the same rate for only five years, the former company is, other things being equal, more valuable to the investor than the latter. The point is that growth rates are general rather than gospel truths. And this brings us to the firm-foundation theorists' first rule for evaluating securities:

> *Rule 1: A rational investor should be willing to pay a higher price for a share, the larger the growth rate of dividends.*

To this is added an important corollary:

> *Corollary to Rule 1: A rational investor should be willing to pay a higher price for a share the longer the growth rate is expected to last.*

Determinant 2: The expected dividend payout The amount of dividends you receive at each payout—as contrasted to their growth rate—is readily understandable as being an important factor in determining stock price. The higher the dividend payout, other things being equal, the greater the value of the stock. The catch here is the phrase *other things being equal.* Stocks that pay out a high percentage of earnings in dividends may be poor investments if their growth prospects are unfavorable. Conversely, many companies in their most dynamic growth phase often pay out little or none of their earnings in dividends. But for two companies whose expected growth rates are the same, you are better off with the one whose dividend payout is higher.

Beware of the stock dividend. This provides no benefits whatever. The practice is employed on the pretext that the firm is preserving cash for expansion while providing dividends in the form of additional shares. Stockholders presumably like to receive new pieces of paper—it gives them a warm feeling that the firm's managers are interested in their welfare. Some even think that by some alchemy the stock dividend increases the worth of their holdings.

In actuality, only the printer profits from the stock dividend. To distribute a 100 percent stock dividend, a firm must print one additional share for each share outstanding. But with twice as many shares outstanding, each share represents only half the interest in the company that it formerly did. Earnings per share and all other relevant per-share statistics about the company are now halved. This unit change is the only result of a stock dividend. When Great Britain replaced one shilling with five new pence, the English, being a sensible people, did not celebrate. Neither should stockholders greet with any joy the declaration of stock splits or dividends—unless these are accompanied by higher cash dividends or news of higher earnings.

The only conceivable advantage of a stock split (or large stock dividend) is that lowering the price level of the shares might induce more public investors to purchase them. People like to buy in 100-share lots, and if a stock's price is very high many investors will feel excluded. But 2 and 3 percent stock dividends, which are so commonly declared, do no good at all.

The distribution of new certificates for stock dividends

brings up the whole concept of actual certificates of ownership. This is an incredibly cumbersome and archaic system
and should be eliminated. Records of ownership could
easily be kept on the memory disks of large computers. If
stockholders could rid themselves of their atavistic longing
for pretty embossed certificates, Wall Street's current paperwork dilemma could be made manageable, commission rates
might be reduced, and my wife and other environmentalists
could congratulate themselves on another victory.

Now that I've got that off my chest, let's sum up by printing the second rule:

> *Rule 2: A rational investor should be willing to
> pay a higher price for a share, other things being
> equal, the larger the proportion of a company's
> earnings that is paid out in cash dividends.*

Determinant 3: The degree of risk   Risk plays an important
role in the stock market, no matter what your overeager
mutual fund salesman may tell you. There is always a risk—
and that's what makes it so fascinating. Risk also affects the
valuation of a stock.

The more respectable a stock is—that is, the less risk it
has—the higher its quality. Stocks of the so-called blue-chip
companies, for example, are said to deserve a quality premium. (Why high-quality stocks are given an appellation
derived from the poker tables is a fact known only to Wall
Street.) Most investors prefer less risky stocks and, therefore,
these stocks can command higher price-earnings multiples
than their risky, low-quality counterparts.

Measuring risk is well-nigh impossible, but this has not
daunted the economist. Being a resourceful sort, he has come
up with a method that seems simple indeed. Economists say,
the bigger the swings in the company's stock prices (or in its
total yearly returns, including dividends), the greater the
risk. For example, a nonswinger such as AT&T gets the *Good
Housekeeping* seal of approval for "widows and orphans."

That's because its earnings do not decline much if at all during recessions, and its dividend has never been cut. Therefore, when the market goes down 20 percent, AT&T usually trails with perhaps only a 10 percent decline. Control Data, on the other hand, has a very volatile past record and it characteristically falls by 40 percent or more when the market declines by 20 percent. It is called a "flyer," or an investment that is a "businessman's risk." The investor gambles in owning stock in such a company; particularly if he may be forced to sell out during a time of unfavorable market conditions.

When business is good and the market mounts a sustained upward drive, however, Control Data can be expected to outdistance AT&T. But if you are like most investors, you value stable returns over speculative hopes, freedom from worry about your portfolio over sleepless nights, and limited loss exposure over the possibility of a downhill roller coaster ride. You will prefer the more stable security, other things being the same. This leads to a third basic rule of security valuation.

> Rule 3: A rational (and risk-averse) investor should
> be willing to pay a higher price for a share, other
> things being equal, the less volatile are movements
> in the company's share prices.

Determinant 4: The level of market interest rates The stock market, no matter how much it may think so, does not exist as a world unto itself. Investors should consider how much profit they can obtain elsewhere. Interest rates, if they are high enough, can offer a stable, profitable alternative to the stock market.

Consider a year such as 1974, when interest rates on *prime* quality corporate bonds, such as those of AT&T and its affiliates, were close to 10 percent. Bonds of somewhat lower quality were being offered at well over 11 percent. The expected returns from stock prices could not match these bond rates; money flowed into bonds while stock prices fell sharply. Finally, stock prices reached such a low level that a sufficient number of investors were attracted to stem the decline. To put it another way, in order to attract investors from high-yielding bonds, stock must offer bargain-basement prices.* Thus, the last rule for the firm-foundation theory is:

> *Rule 4: A rational investor should be willing to pay a higher price for a share, other things being equal, the lower are interest rates.*

Two Important Caveats

The four valuation rules imply that a security's firm-foundation value (and its price-earnings multiple) will be higher the larger the company's growth rate and the longer its duration; the larger the dividend payout for the firm; the lower the general level of interest rates; and the more stable (less volatile) the company's stock-price movements.

As I indicated earlier, economists have taken rules such as these and expressed in a mathematical formula the exact price (present value) at which shares should sell. In principle, such theories are very useful in suggesting a rational basis for stock prices and in giving investors some standard of value. Of course, the rules must be compared with the facts to see if they conform at all to reality, and I will get to that in a moment. But before we even think of using and testing these rules in a very precise way, there are two important caveats to bear in mind.

Caveat 1: Expectations about the future cannot be proven in the present. Remember, not even Jeane Dixon can ac-

---

* The point can be made another way by noting that since higher interest rates enable us to earn more now, any deferred income should be "discounted" more heavily. Thus the present value of any flow of future dividend returns will be lower when current interest rates are relatively high.

curately predict all of the future. Yet some people have absolute faith in security analysts' estimates of the long-term
growth prospects of a company and the duration of that
growth.

Predicting future earnings and dividends is a most hazardous occupation. It requires not only the knowledge and
skill of an economist, but also the acumen of a psychologist.
On top of that, it is extremely difficult to be objective; wild
optimism and extreme pessimism constantly battle for top
place. During 1960, when the economy and the world situation were relatively stable, investors had no trouble convincing themselves that the coming decade would be soaring and
prosperous. As a result, very high growth rates were pro-
jected for a large number of corporations. Ten years later,
in 1970, the economy was stagnant and student unrest appeared to indicate an unstable situation. The best investors
could do that year was to project modest growth rates for
most corporations.

The point to remember is that no matter what formula
you use for predicting the future, it always rests in part on an
indeterminate premise. Although many Wall Streeters claim
to see into the future, they are just as fallible as the rest of us.

*Caveat 2: Precise figures cannot be calculated from unde-
termined data.*   It stands to reason that you can't obtain
precise figures by using indefinite factors. Yet to achieve
desired ends, investors and security analysts do this all the
time. Here's how it's done.

Take a company that you've heard lots of good things
about. You study the company's prospects, and suppose you
conclude that it can maintain a high growth rate for a long
period. How long? Well, why not ten years?

You then calculate what the stock should be "worth" on
the basis of the current dividend payout, the expected future
growth rate of dividends, and the general level of interest
rates, perhaps making an allowance for the riskiness of the

shares.* It turns out to your chagrin that the price the stock is worth is just slightly less than its present market price.

You now have two alternatives. You could regard the stock as overpriced and refuse to buy it or, you could say, "Perhaps this stock could maintain a high growth rate for eleven years rather than ten. After all, the ten was only a guess in the first place, so why not eleven years?" And so you go back to your slide rule and lo and behold you now come up with a worth for the shares that is larger than the current market price. Armed with this "precise" knowledge, you make your sound purchase.

The reason the game worked is that the longer one projects growth, the greater is the stream of future dividends. Thus, the present value of a share is at the discretion of the calculator. If eleven years was not enough to do the trick, twelve or thirteen might well have sufficed. There is always some combination of growth rate and growth period that will produce any specific price. In this sense it is intrinsically impossible, given human nature, to calculate the intrinsic value of a share.

J. Peter Williamson, author of an excellent textbook for financial analysts entitled *Investments,* provides another example. In the book, Williamson estimated the present (or firm-foundation) value of IBM shares by using the same general principle of valuation I have described above; that is, by estimating how fast IBM's dividends would grow and for how long. Williamson first made the sensible assumption that IBM would grow at a fairly high rate for some number of years before falling into a much smaller mature growth

---

* If you actually want to do the calculation, just write out your estimates for the future flow of dividends expected, get hold of a set of "present value" tables to "discount" the dividends to their present worth, and then sit down at an adding machine to get the total. Now they even make vest-pocket computers that enable you to do away with the tables and perform the whole operation while riding in on the train from Princeton.

rate. In 1968, when he made his estimate, IBM was selling
at $320 per share.

> I began by forecasting growth in earnings per share at 16%.
> This was a little under the average for the previous ten
> years . . . I forecast a 16% growth rate for 10 years, fol-
> lowed by indefinite growth at . . . 2% . . . When I put
> all these numbers into the formula I got an intrinsic value
> of $172.94, about half of the current market value.

Since the intrinsic value and market value of IBM stock
were so far apart, Williamson decided that perhaps his estimates of the future might not be accurate. He experi-
mented further:

> It doesn't really seem sensible to predict only 10 years of
> above average growth for IBM, so I extended my 16%
> growth forecast to 20 years. Now the intrinsic value came to
> $432.66, well above the market.

Had Williamson opted for thirty years of above-average
growth, he would be projecting IBM to generate a future
sales volume about one half the then current U.S. national
income. With all due respect to IBM, such a growth rate
does not seem possible.

The point to remember from such examples is that the
mathematical precision of the firm-foundation value formulas is based on treacherous ground: forecasting the future.
The major fundamentals for these calculations are never
known with certainty; they are only relatively crude estimates—perhaps one should say guesses—about what might
happen in the future. And depending on what guesses you
make, you can convince yourself to pay any price you want
to for a stock.

There is, I believe, a fundamental indeterminateness
about the value of common shares even in principle. God
Almighty does not know the proper price-earnings multiple
for a common stock.

Testing the Rules

With the rules and caveats in mind, let us take a closer look at stock prices and examine whether the rules seem to conform to actual practice. Let's start with Rule 1—the larger the anticipated growth rate, the higher the price of a share.

To begin, we'll reformulate the question in terms of price-earnings (P/E) multiples rather than the market prices themselves. This provides a good yardstick for comparing stocks—which have different prices and earnings—against one another. A stock selling at $100 per share with earnings of $5 per share would have the same P/E ratio (20) as a stock selling at $40 with earnings of $2 per share. It is the P/E multiple, not the dollar price, that really tells you how a stock is valued in the market.

Our reformulated question now reads: Are actual price-earnings multiples higher for stocks where a high growth rate is anticipated? A major study by Princeton's Financial Research Center strongly indicates the answer is yes.

It was easy to collect the first half of the data required. P/E multiples are printed daily in papers such as the *New York Times* and the *Wall Street Journal.* To obtain information on expected long-term growth rates, the Center surveyed eighteen leading investment firms whose business it is to produce the forecasts upon which buy and sell recommendations are made. (I'll describe later how they make these forecasts.) Estimates were obtained from each firm of the five-year growth rates anticipated for a large sample of stocks.

I will not bore you with the details of the actual statistical study that was performed.* The results are illustrated, however, for a few representative securities in the chart below. It is clear that, just as Rule 1 asserts, high P/E ratios are associated with high expected growth rates. This general pattern has held up in every year since 1961, when the Center began its study.

* It is listed among the references for this chapter.

Price   Expected Long-Term
Earnings   Growth Rate
Multiple

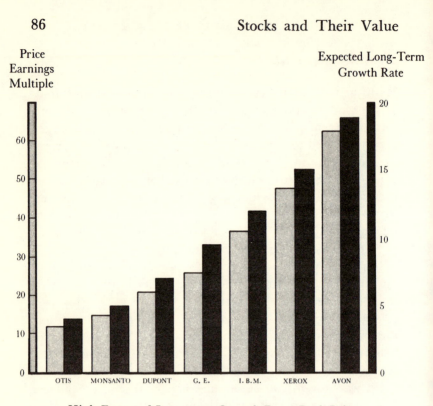

High Expected Long-term Growth Rates Push Price-
Earnings Multiples Up
Data for January, 1973

   In addition to demonstrating how the market values different growth rates, the chart can also be used as a practical
investment guide. Suppose you were considering the purchase of a stock with an anticipated 10 percent growth rate
and you knew that, on average, stocks with 10 percent
growth sold, like IBM, at 37 times earnings. If the stock you
were considering sold at a price-earnings multiple of 50, you
might reject the idea of buying the stock in favor of one
more reasonably priced in terms of current market norms.
If, on the other hand, your stock sold at a multiple below
the average in the market for that growth rate, the security

is said to represent good value for your money. I'll return to the practical use of such techniques, as well as the pitfalls, at several later points.

How about Rules 2, 3, and 4? Just as we were able to test for a relationship between earnings multiples and anticipated growth rates, it was also possible to collect the necessary data and find the way in which not only growth, but dividend payout, interest rates, and risk (price volatility) influence price-earnings multiples in the market. The particular techniques used need not concern us. What is important to realize is that there does seem to be a logic to market valuations. Market prices seem to behave just as the four rules developed by the firm-foundation theorists would lead us to expect. It is comforting to know that at least to this extent there is an underlying rationality to the stock market.

One More Caveat

So market prices do seem to have an inherent logic. In each year for over a decade, stock prices have been closely related to differential patterns of expected growth as well as to the other "fundamental" valuation influences so important to proponents of the firm-foundation theory. Yes, Virginia, it looks like there may be a firm foundation of value after all, and some jokers in Wall Street actually think you can make money knowing what it is.

Caveat 3: What's growth for the goose is not always growth for the gander.   The difficulty comes with the value the market puts on specific fundamentals. It is always true that the market values growth, and that higher growth rates and larger multiples go hand in hand. But the crucial question is: How much more should you pay for higher growth?

There is no consistent answer. In some periods, as in the

early 1960s and 1970s, when growth was thought to be especially desirable, the market has been willing to pay an
enormous price for stocks exhibiting high growth rates. At
other times, high-growth stocks commanded only a modest
premium over the multiples of common stocks in general.

The point is illustrated in the following table. IBM has
consistently sold at a much higher multiple than the market.
But the differential in multiples has been quite volatile.
IBM's multiple was over three times that of the market in
December 1961. Five months later it was not even two times
as great.

Price-Earnings Multiples for IBM and for
the Market in General *

| | P/E Multiples | | Premium—IBM P/E |
	IBM	S & P Index	as a % of S & P P/E
Market Peak 1961	64	20	320%
Market Low 1962	29	16	181%
Market Peak 1968	50	18	278%
Market Low 1970	25	16	156%
Market Peak 1972	44	17	259%

* As measured by the Standard & Poor's 425-Stock Index.

A similar way of looking at the changing premiums paid
for growth stocks since 1955 is shown in the following chart,
which graphs the percentage premiums for an average of ten
leading growth stocks compared with the Standard & Poor's
425-Stock Index. Care was taken to insure that the stocks in
the average retained roughly the same growth prospects in
the eyes of the Wall Street pros. The chart tells a disappointing story for anyone looking for a consistent long-term
valuation relationship. Growth can be as fashionable as tulip
bulbs, as investors in growth stocks painfully learned in 1962.

The Premium Paid for Growth

rnings Multiple of Growth Stocks
Relative to S & P 425 Index

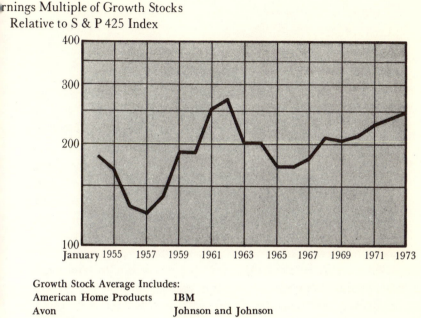

Growth Stock Average Includes:

American Home Products	**IBM**
Avon	Johnson and Johnson
Coca Cola	Eli Lilly
Disney *	Marriott *
Eastman Kodak	Xerox

* Disney and Marriott since 1969. Prior thereto Hewlett Packard and Minnesota Mining and Manufacturing were included.

Source: William W. Helman, "The Economic Outlook for 1973 and 1974," Smith, Barney & Co., 1973.

From a practical standpoint, the rapid changes in market valuations that have occurred suggest that it would be very dangerous to use any one year's valuation relationships as an indication of market norms. However, by comparing how growth stocks are currently valued with historical precedent, investors should at least be able to isolate those periods when a touch of the tulip bug has smitten investors. The chart also illustrates that in early 1973, the well-known growth stocks

seemed to be quite richly priced in the market and did not
offer the values they had for some years after the 1962 cor-
rection. I'll return to this point later.

What's Left of the Firm Foundation?

A renowned rabbi, whose fame for adjudicating disputes had
earned him the reputation of a modern-day Solomon, was
asked to settle a long-standing argument between two philosophers. The rabbi listened intently as the first disputant vig-
orously presented his case. The rabbi reflected on the argument and finally pronounced, "Yes, you are correct." Then
the second philosopher presented his case with equal vigor
and persuasion and argued eloquently that the first philosopher could not be correct. The rabbi nodded his approval
and indicated, "You are correct." A bystander, somewhat con-
fused by this performance, accosted the rabbi to complain,
"You told both philosophers they were right, but their arguments were totally contradictory. They both can't be correct."
The rabbi needed only a moment to formulate his response:
"Yes, you are indeed correct."

In adjudicating the dispute between the firm-foundation
theorists and those who take a castle-in-the-air view of the
stock market, I feel a little like the accommodating rabbi. It
seems clear that so-called "fundamental" considerations do
have a profound influence on market prices. We have seen
that price-earnings multiples in the market are influenced by
expected growth, dividend payout, risk, and the rate of interest. Higher anticipations of earnings growth and higher
dividend payouts tend to increase price-earnings multiples.
Higher risk and higher interest rates tend to pull them down.
There is a logic to the stock market, just as the firm founda-
tionists assert.

Thus, when all is said and done, it appears that there is a
yardstick for value, but one that is a most flexible and unde-

pendable instrument. To change the metaphor, stock prices are in a sense anchored to certain "fundamentals" but the anchor is easily pulled up and then dropped in another place. For the standards of value, we have found, are not the fixed and immutable standards that characterize the laws of physics, but rather the more flexible and fickle relationships that are consistent with a marketplace heavily influenced by mass psychology.

Not only does the market change the values it puts on the various fundamental determinants of stock prices, but the most important of these fundamentals are themselves liable to change depending on the state of market psychology. Stocks are bought on expectations—not on facts.

The most important fundamental influence on stock prices is the level and duration of the future growth of corporate earnings and dividends. But, as I pointed out earlier, future earnings growth is not easily estimated, even by market professionals. In times of great optimism it is very easy for investors to convince themselves that their favorite corporations can enjoy substantial and persistent growth over an extended period of time. By raising his estimates of growth, even the most sober firm-foundation theorist can convince himself to pay any price whatever for a share.

During periods of extreme pessimism, many security analysts will not project any growth that is not "visible" to them over the very short run and hence will estimate only the most modest of growth rates for the corporations they follow. But if expected growth rates themselves and the price the market is willing to pay for this growth can both change rapidly on the basis of market psychology, then it is clear that the concept of a *firm* intrinsic value for shares must be an elusive will-o'-the-wisp. As an old Wall Street proverb runs: No price is too high for a bull or too low for a bear.

Dreams of castles in the air, of getting rich quick, may therefore play an important role in determining actual stock prices. And even investors who believe in the firm-foundation theory might buy a security on the anticipation that eventually the average opinion would expect a larger growth rate for the stock in the future. After all, investors who want to reap extraordinary profits may find that the most profitable course of action is to beat the gun and anticipate future changes in the intrinsic value of shares.

Still, this analysis suggests that the stock market will not be a perpetual tulip-bulb craze. The existence of some generally accepted principles of valuation does serve as a kind of balance wheel. For the castle-in-the-air investor might well consider that if prices get too far out of line with normal valuation standards, the average opinion may soon expect that others will anticipate a reaction. To be sure, these standards of value are extremely loose ones and difficult to estimate. But sooner or later in a skyrocketing market, some investors may begin to compare the growth rates that are implicit in current prices with more reasonable and dispassionate estimates of the growth likely to be achieved.

It seems eminently sensible to me that both views of security pricing tell us something about actual market behavior. But the important investment question is how you can use the theories to develop practically useful investment strategies. More about this in Part Two, where we take a closer look at how the professionals use the two theories in their own investing.

How the Pros Play the Biggest Game in Town

CHAPTER FIVE

Technical and Fundamental Analysis

A picture is worth ten thousand words.—Old Chinese proverb

On one hot summer day in 1971, 31 million shares with a value of over $1½ billion were traded on the New York Stock Exchange. Professional investment analysts and counselors are involved in what has been called the biggest game in town. Exchanges of shares valued at $1 billion are now considered routine daily volumes on the big board, and this is only part of the story. A large volume of trading is carried out on the American Stock Exchange, on the over-the-counter markets, and on a variety of regional exchanges across the country.

If the stakes are high, so are the rewards. Margin clerks routinely draw salaries of $20,000 per year. Security analysts and successful salesmen, euphemistically called "account executives," make considerably more. At the top of the salary scale are the money managers themselves—the men who run the large mutual, pension, and trust funds. "Adam Smith," after writing *The Money Game,* the number-one best seller of 1968, boasted that he would make a quarter of a million dollars from his book. His Wall Street friends retorted, "You're only going to make as much as a second-rate institutional salesman." Admittedly, the depression that hit Wall Street during the early 1970s made such talk appear particularly overstated. Still, it is fair to conclude that while not the oldest, the profession of high finance is certainly one of the most generously compensated.

Part Two of this book concentrates on the methods and results of the professionals of Wall Street, State Street, Montgomery Street, and the various road-town financial centers. How do they cope with the basic uncertainty in determining the fair value for any security? How do they attempt to measure the psychological reactions of the crowd and to predict its future behavior? What tools do they use in selecting securities to buy and in managing other people's money? And how good are they at performing their job? What value should we put on professional investment advice?

Technical versus Fundamental Analysis

The attempt to predict accurately the future course of stock prices and thus the appropriate time to buy or sell a stock must rank as one of man's most persistent endeavors. This search for the golden egg has spawned a variety of methods ranging from the scientific to the occult. There are people today who forecast future stock prices by measuring sunspots, looking at the phases of the moon, or measuring the vibrations along the San Andreas Fault. Most, however, opt for one of two methods: technical or fundamental analysis.

The alternative techniques used by the investment pros are related to the two theories of the stock market I covered in Part One. Technical analysis is the method of predicting the appropriate time to buy or sell a stock used by those believing in the castle-in-the-air view of stock pricing. Fun-

damental analysis is the technique of applying the tenets of
the firm-foundation theory to the selection of individual
stocks.

Technical analysis is essentially the making and interpreting of stock charts. Thus its practitioners, a small but ab-
normally dedicated cult, are called chartists. They study the
past—both the movements of common stock prices and the
volume of trading—for a clue to the direction of future
change. Most chartists believe that the market is only 10 percent logical and 90 percent psychological. They generally
subscribe to the castle-in-the-air school and view the investment game as one of anticipating how the other players will
behave. Charts, of course, tell only what the other players
have been doing in the past. The chartist's hope, however, is
that a careful study of what the other players are doing will
shed light on what the crowd is likely to do in the future.

Fundamental analysts take the opposite tack, believing
the market to be 90 percent logical and only 10 percent psychological. Caring little about the particular pattern of past
price movement, fundamentalists seek to determine an issue's proper value. Value in this case is related to growth,
dividend payout, and risk, according to the rules of the firm-
foundation theory outlined in the last chapter. By estimating
such factors as growth for each company, the fundamentalist
arrives at an estimate of a security's intrinsic value. If this is
below the market price, then the investor is advised to buy.
Fundamentalists believe that eventually the market will reflect accurately the security's real worth. Perhaps 90 percent
of the Wall Street security analysts consider themselves fundamentalists. Many would argue that chartists are lacking in
dignity and professionalism.

What Can Charts Tell You?

The first principle of technical analysis is that all information
about earnings, dividends, and the future performance of a

company is automatically reflected in the company's past market prices. A chart showing these prices and the volume of trading already comprises all the fundamental information, good or bad, that the security analyst can hope to know. The second principle is that prices tend to move in trends: a stock that is rising tends to keep on rising, whereas a stock at rest tends to remain at rest.

A true chartist doesn't even care to know what business or industry a company is in, as long as he can study its stock chart. A chart shaped in the form of an "inverted bowl" or "pennant" means the same for Control Data as it does for IBM. Fundamental information on earnings and dividends is considered at best to be useless—and at worst a positive distraction. It is either of inconsequential importance for the pricing of the stock or, if it is important, it has already been reflected in the market days, weeks, or even months before the news has become public. For this reason, many chartists will not even read the newspaper except to follow the daily price quotations.

One of the most prominent chartists, John Magee, operates from a small office in Springfield, Massachusetts, where even the windows are boarded up to prevent any outside influences from distracting his analysis. Magee was once quoted as saying, "When I come into this office I leave the rest of the world outside to concentrate entirely on my charts. This room is exactly the same in the blizzard as on a moonlit June evening. In here I can't possibly do myself and my clients the disservice of saying 'buy' simply because the sun is out or 'sell' because it is raining."

As shown in the figure below, you can easily construct a chart. You simply draw a vertical line whose bottom is the stock's low for the day and whose top is the high. This line is crossed to indicate the closing price for the day. In the figure, the stock had a range of quotations that day between 20 and 21 and closed at 20½. The process can be repeated for each trading day. It can be used for individual stocks or for one of the stock averages that you see in the financial pages of most newspapers. Often the chartist will also indicate the volume of shares of stock traded during the day by another vertical line at the bottom of the chart. Gradually, the highs and lows on the chart of the stock in question jiggle up and down sufficiently to produce patterns. To the chartist, these patterns have the same significance as X-ray plates to a surgeon.

One of the first things the chartist looks for is a trend. The figure below shows one in the making. It is the record of price changes for a stock over a number of days—and the prices are obviously on the way up. The chartist draws two lines connecting the tops and bottoms, creating a "channel" to delineate the uptrend. Since the presumption is that momentum in the market will tend to perpetuate itself, the chartist interprets such a pattern as a bullish augury—the stock can be expected to continue to rise. As Magee has written in the bible of charting, *Technical Analysis of Stock Trends,* "Prices move in trends, and trends tend to continue until something happens to change the supply-demand balance."

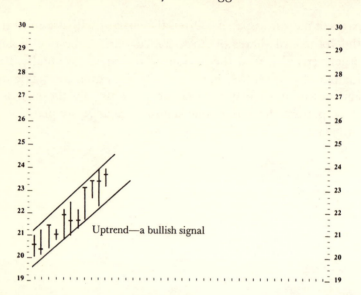

Uptrend—a bullish signal

Suppose, however, that at about 24, the stock finally runs into trouble and is unable to gain any further ground. This is called a resistance level. The stock may wiggle around a bit and then turn downward. One pattern, which chartists claim reveals a clear signal that the market has topped out, is a head and shoulders formation. This is shown in the figure below.

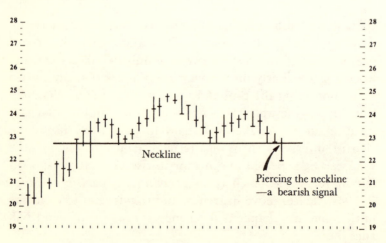

Neckline

Piercing the neckline
—a bearish signal

The stock first rises and then falls slightly, forming a rounded shoulder. It rises again, going slightly higher, before once more receding, forming a head. Finally the right shoulder is formed, and chartists wait with bated breath for the sell signal, which sounds loud and clear when the stock "pierces the neckline." With the glee of Count Dracula surveying one of his victims, the chartists are off and selling, anticipating that a prolonged downtrend will follow as it allegedly has in the past. Of course, sometimes the market surprises the chartist. For example, the stock may make an end run up to 30 right after giving a bear signal. This is called a bear trap or, to the chartist, the exception that proves the rule.

It follows from the technique that the chartist is a trader, not a long-term investor. The chartist buys when the auguries look favorable and sells on bad omens. He flirts with stocks just as some flirt with women, and his scores are successful

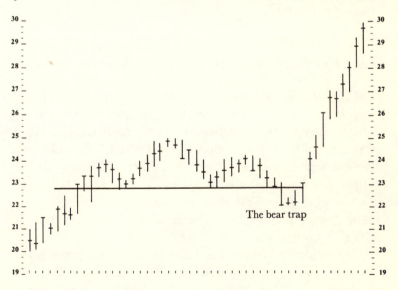

The bear trap

in-and-out trades, not rewarding long-term commitments. Indeed, the psychiatrist Dr. Don D. Jackson, author with Albert Haas, Jr. of *Bulls, Bears and Dr. Freud,* has suggested that such an individual may be playing a game with overt sexual overtones.

When the chartist chooses a stock for potential investment there is typically a period of observation and flirtation before he commits himself, since for the chartist—as in romance and sexual conquest—timing is essential. There is mounting excitement as the stock penetrates the base formation and rises higher. Finally, if the affair has gone well, there is the moment of fulfillment—profit-taking, and the release and afterglow that follow. The chartist's vocabulary features such terms as double bottoms, breakthrough, violating the lows, firmed up, big play, ascending peaks, and buying climax. And all this takes place under the pennant of that great symbol of sexuality: the bull.

The Rationale for the Charting Method

Probably the hardest question to answer is: Why is charting supposed to work? Some of my best friends are chartists and I have listened very carefully to their explanations, but I have yet really to understand them. Indeed, many chartists freely admit *they* don't know why charting should work— history just has a habit of repeating itself. Even Magee, the chartist seer, goes so far as to say that we can never hope to know "why" the market behaves as it does, we can only aspire to understand "how."

According to Magee, the situation in the stock market is analogous to that of a pig in a barn. The barn is all closed up on the ground floor, but it has a hayloft above with a large open door. The pig has a harness around his body to which is attached a long pole, the top of which is visible through the hayloft door. Of course, when the pig moves about, so will the pole. Magee supposes that we are perched in a nearby tree observing the motions of the top of the pole, which is all we can see. We must deduce from the pole's movement what is happening below, just as market participants must deduce what is happening in the market from the price movements they can observe. Magee goes on to say that it is not important to know the color or size of the pig . . . or even whether it is a pig at all; it is only important to be able to make predictions about the next movement of the pole.

> Some of the watchers who are not comfortable with highly abstract symbols will assign "meanings" to the pole's movements. They will try to "interpret" these movements as corresponding to various assimilative, combative, copulative, etc., actions of the pig. Others, [like Magee, the author] who might consider themselves "pure technicians," will watch the pole, and work entirely on the basis of what the pole has done, is doing, or might be expected to do according to trends, repetitive motions, extrapolations, etc.

Yet it is in our nature to ask why. To me, the following explanations of technical analysis appear to be the most plausible. Trends might tend to perpetuate themselves for either of two reasons. First, it has been argued that the crowd instinct of mass psychology makes it so. When investors see the price of a speculative favorite going higher and higher, they want to jump on the bandwagon and join the rise. Indeed, the price rise itself helps fuel the enthusiasm in a self-fulfilling prophecy. Each rise in price just whets the appetite and makes investors expect a further rise.

Second, there may be unequal access to fundamental information about a company. When some favorable piece of news occurs, such as the discovery of a rich mineral deposit, it is alleged that the insiders are the first to know and they act, buying the stock and causing its price to rise. The insiders then tell their friends, who act next. Then the professionals find out the news and the big institutions put blocks of the shares in their portfolios. Finally, the poor slobs like you and me get the information and buy, pushing the price still higher. This process is supposed to result in a rather gradual increase in the price of the stock when the news is good and a decrease when the news is bad. Chartists claim that this scenario is somewhat close to what actually happened in the Texas Gulf Sulphur case, and even if they do not have access to this inside information, observation of price movements alone enables them to pick up the scent of the "smart money" and permits them to get in long before the general public.

Chartists believe that another reason their techniques have validity is that people have a nasty habit of remembering what they paid for a stock, or the price they *wish* they had paid. For example, suppose a stock sold for about $50 a share for a long period of time, during which a number of investors bought in. Suppose then that the price drops to $40.

The chartists claim that the public will be anxious to sell out the shares when they rise back to the price at which they were bought, and thus break even on the trade. Consequently, the price of $50 at which the stock sold initially becomes a "resistance area." Each time the resistance area is reached and the stock turns down again, the theory holds that the resistance level becomes even harder to cross, because more and more investors get the idea that the market or the individual stock in question cannot go any higher.

A similar argument lies behind the notion of "support levels." Chartists say that many investors who failed to buy when the market fluctuated around a relatively low price level will feel they have missed the boat when prices rise. Presumably such investors will jump at the chance to buy when prices drop back to the original low level.

Chartists also believe that investors who sold shares when the market was low and then saw prices rise will be anxious to buy those shares back if they can get them again at the price for which they sold. The argument then is that the

original low price level becomes a "support area," since investors will believe that prices will again rise above that level.
In chart theory, a "support area" that holds on successive
declines becomes stronger and stronger. So if a stock declines
to a support area and then begins to rise, the traders will
jump in, believing the stock is just "coming off the pad."
Another bullish signal is flashed when a stock finally breaks
through a resistance area. In the lexicon of the chartists, the
former resistance area becomes a support area, and the stock
should have no trouble gaining further ground.

Why Might Charting Fail to Work?

It is easier for me to present the *logical* arguments against
charting. First, it should be noted that the chartist buys in
only after price trends have been established, and sells only
after they have been broken. Since sharp reversals in the
market may occur quite suddenly, the chartist will often miss
the boat. By the time an uptrend is signaled it may already
have taken place. Second, such techniques must ultimately
be self-defeating. As more and more people use it, the value
of any technique depreciates. No buy or sell signal can be
worthwhile if everyone tries to act on it simultaneously.

Moreover, traders will tend to anticipate technical signals.
If they see a price about to break through a resistance area,
they will tend to buy before, not after, it breaks through. If
it ever was profitable to use such charting techniques, it will
now be possible only for those who anticipate the signals.
This suggests that others will try to anticipate the signal still
earlier. Of course, the earlier they anticipate, the less certain
they are that the signal will occur, and in the scrambling to
anticipate signals it is doubtful that any profitable technical
trading rules can be developed.

Perhaps the most telling argument against technical
methods comes from the logical implications of profit-maxi-

mizing behavior on the part of investors. Suppose, for example, that Universal Polymers is selling at around 20 when Sam, the chief research chemist, discovers a new production technique that promises to double the company's earnings and stock price. Now Sam is convinced that the price of Universal will hit 40 when the news of his discovery comes out. Since any purchases below 40 will provide a swift profit, he may well buy up all the stock he can until the price hits 40, a process that could take no longer than a few minutes.

Even if Sam doesn't have enough money to drive up the price himself, surely his friends and the financial institutions do have the funds to move the price so rapidly that no chartist could get into the act before the whole play is gone. The point is that the market may well be a most efficient mechanism. If some people know that the price will go to 40 tomorrow, it will go to 40 today. Of course if Sam makes a public announcement of his discovery as the law requires, the argument holds with even greater force. Prices may adjust so quickly to new information as to make the whole process of technical analysis a futile exercise. In the next chapter, I'll examine whether the evidence supports such a pessimistic view of charting.

From Chartist to Technician

Though chartists are not held in high repute in Wall Street, their colorful methods, suggesting an easy way to get rich quick, have attracted a wide following. The companies that manufacture and distribute stock charts and charting paper have enjoyed a boom in their sales; and chartists themselves, at least until the bear market of 1970, found increasing employment opportunities with mutual funds and brokerage firms.

In the days before the computer, the laborious task of charting a course through the market was done by hand.

Chartists were often viewed as peculiar men, with green eyeshades and carbon on their fingers, who were tucked away in a small closet at the back of the office. Now chartists have the services of a marvelous electronic computer, replete with a large display terminal which, at the tap of a finger, can produce any conceivable chart one might want to see. The chartist (now always called a technician) can, with the glee of a little boy playing with his first electric train, produce a complete chart of a stock's past performance, including measures of volume, the 200-day moving average (an average of prices over the previous 200 days recalculated each day), the strength of the stock relative to the market and relative to its industry, and literally hundreds of other averages, ratios, oscillators, and indicators.

Once the chart has been thus displayed, another press of the button will make a xerox copy of the entire picture, which may be studied further on the train back to Larchmont and later tacked on bulletin boards around the room. The result is something akin to the Pentagon war room. One go-go fund was known to concentrate its technical information in what it called "information central." The computer also adds an aura of mystery and wonder to charting. Even if the chartist's techniques are unscientific, it is difficult to make fun of the computer, and some of the public's awe and admiration for computers has rubbed off on the technical analysts. While there is not, to my knowledge, a "Chartists' Liberation Movement," technicians have now come out of their closets and have received newfound recognition and approval.

The Technique of Fundamental Analysis

Fred Schwed, Jr., in his charming and witty 1930s exposé of the financial community, *Where Are the Customers' Yachts*, tells the story of a Texas broker who sold some stock to a customer at $760 a share at the moment when it could have been purchased anywhere else at $730. When the outraged customer found out what had happened, he complained bitterly to the broker. The Texan cut him short. "Suh," he boomed. "you-all don't appreciate the policy of this firm. This heah firm selects investments foh its clients not on the basis of Price, but of Value."

In a sense, this story illustrates the difference between the technician and the fundamentalist. The technician is interested only in the record of the stock's price, whereas the fundamentalist's primary concern is with what a stock is really worth. The fundamentalist strives to be relatively immune to the optimism and pessimism of the crowd and makes a sharp distinction between a stock's current price and its true value.

In estimating the firm-foundation value of a security, the fundamentalist's most important job is to estimate the firm's future stream of earnings and dividends. To do this, he or she must estimate the firm's sales level, operating costs, corporate tax rates, depreciation policies, and the sources and costs of its capital requirements.

Basically, the security analyst must be a prophet without the benefit of divine inspiration. As a poor substitute, the analyst turns to a study of the past record of the company, a review of the company's investment plans, and a firsthand visit to and appraisal of the company's management team. This yields a wealth of data. The analyst must then separate the important from the unimportant facts. As Benjamin Graham put it in *The Intelligent Investor,* "Sometimes he reminds us a bit of the erudite major general in 'The Pirates of Penzance,' with his 'many cheerful facts about the square of the hypotenuse.' "

Since the general prospects of a company are strongly influenced by the economic position of its industry, the obvious starting point for the security analyst is a study of industry prospects. Indeed, in almost all professional investment firms, security analysts specialize in particular industry groups. The fundamentalist hopes that a thorough study of industry conditions will produce valuable insights into factors that may be operative in the future but are not yet reflected in market prices.

A brief example will help illustrate what is involved. It involves an analysis, undertaken late in 1969 by the investment firm of Smith, Barney & Co., of the chemical industry, and of the prospects for Dow Chemical. Called "The Chemical Industry—The Image Has Changed," the Smith, Barney report first analyzed the dismal earnings performance of the industry during the 1960s.

Chemical stocks had fallen out of favor and the industry had the reputation of being very sensitive to business fluctuations and burdened with overcapacity and chaotic pricing (or what the economist calls vigorous competition). The report began by analyzing the almost uninterrupted growth of *physical* output since World War II, and the reasons investors should anticipate this trend would continue. The reasons for the poor profit performance were then discussed in detail.

Next the current and prospective supply and demand situation was investigated. The report stated that future additions to capacity would be more orderly, that pressure on prices would thus be reduced (particularly in certain product areas), and that productivity increases during the 1970s should be sufficient to prevent rising wage costs from cutting into profit margins. Consequently, the report concluded, the large growth of physical output foreseen for the 1970s was likely to be reflected in both sales and profits.

The Smith, Barney report went on to recommend a number of chemical stocks for purchase, including Dow Chemical among the larger companies. The report argued that the product mix of Dow was particularly favorable to take advantage of the propitious turn foreseen for the chemical industry. The specialty areas and consumer-product lines of Dow were ones likely to enjoy both strong growth and strong prices. Dow was expected to achieve a relatively stable 10 percent rate of growth of earnings and dividends during the 1970s and was considered to be "undervalued" by the analysts: that is, its current market price was below reasonable estimates of its firm foundation of value.

Recall that the first principle of valuation of the firm-foundation theory was that a stock is worth more—should sell at a higher price-earnings multiple—the larger is its anticipated rate of growth. In late 1969 Dow sold at a price-earnings ratio of approximately 13, while for the market as a whole the price-earnings multiple was 16. The expected growth rate of earnings and dividends for the market as a whole in 1969 was between 4 and 5 percent. But Dow was expected to grow faster; hence, by our first valuation principle, it deserved to sell at a *higher* multiple than the market as a whole. Since the stock actually sold at a lower multiple than the market (13 versus 16), it could be considered undervalued.

Of course, there were other principles of valuation mentioned in Chapter Four. By the second principle, stocks were worth more to the investors, other things being the same, if they could finance their growth and still pay out a reasonable share of their earnings in dividends. Since the dividend payout for Dow was roughly in line with the market as a whole, there was no reason to expect it to sell at a lower multiple on that score. The firm-foundation theory also suggested that stocks should sell at a lower multiple the riskier they were considered. But recall that the Smith, Barney report indicated that it was anticipated that Dow would enjoy a more stable (less risky) performance than the market. Hence, on this score the stock would deserve a premium multiple to the market.

It is also possible to use the empirical relationships discussed in Chapter Four to argue that Dow represented good value. In 1969, when the analysis was made, stocks for which a 10 percent rate of growth was expected sold, on average, at over 25 times earnings, about twice the multiple for Dow.

This further enhanced its appeal. For these reasons, Smith, Barney recommended purchase of Dow Chemical.

The Smith, Barney report represents the technique of fundamental analysis at its finest. People who followed its "buy" advice found that Dow enjoyed much better performance than the market throughout the next few years.

Why Might Fundamental Analysis Fail to Work?

Despite its plausibility and scientific appearance, there are three potential flaws in this type of analysis. First, the information and analysis may be incorrect. Second, the security analyst's estimate of "value" may be faulty. Third, the market may not correct its "mistake" and the stock price might not converge to its value estimate.

The security analyst traveling from company to company and consulting with industry specialists will receive a great deal of fundamental information. Some critics have suggested that, taken as a whole, this information will be worthless. What investors make on the valid news (assuming it is not yet recognized by the market) they lose on the bad information. Moreover, the analyst wastes considerable effort in collecting the information and investors pay heavy brokerage fees in trying to act on it. To make matters even worse, the security analyst may be unable to translate correct facts into accurate estimates of earnings for several years into the future. A faulty analysis of valid information could throw estimates of the rate of growth of earnings and dividends far wide of the mark.

The second problem is that even if the information is correct and its implications for future growth are properly assessed, the analyst might make a faulty value estimate. We have already seen how difficult it is to translate specific estimates of growth and other valuation factors into a single estimate of intrinsic value. Recall the widely different estimates of the value for IBM shown in Chapter Four. I have suggested earlier that the attempt to obtain a precise measure of intrinsic value may be an unrewarding search for a will-o'-the-wisp. Thus, even if the security analyst's estimates of growth are correct, this information may already be reflected accurately by the market, and any difference between a security's price and value may result simply from an incorrect estimate of value.

The final problem is that even with correct information and value estimates, the stock you buy might still go down. For example, suppose that Biodegradable Bottling Company is selling at 25 times earnings, and the analyst estimates that it can sustain a long-term growth rate of 10 percent. If, on average, stocks with 10 percent anticipated growth rates are selling at 30 times earnings, the fundamentalist might conclude that Biodegradable was a "cheap stock" and recommend purchase.

But suppose, a few months later, stocks with 10 percent growth rates are selling in the market at only 20 times earnings. Even if the analyst was absolutely correct in his growth rate estimate, his customers might suffer badly because the market revalued its estimates of what growth stocks in general were worth. The market might correct its "mistake" by revaluing all stocks downward, rather than raising the price for Biodegradable Bottling.

And as the chart in Chapter Four indicated, such changes in valuation are not extraordinary—these are the routine fluctuations in market sentiment that have been experienced in the past. The market can change rapidly the premium assigned to growth. Clearly, then, one should not take the success of fundamental analysis for granted.

Using Fundamental and Technical Analysis Together

Many analysts use a combination of techniques to judge whether individual stocks are attractive for purchase. One of the most sensible procedures can easily be summarized by the following three rules. The persistent, patient reader will recognize that the rules are based on principles of stock pricing I have developed in the previous chapters.

Rule 1: Confine stock purchases to companies that appear able to sustain above-average earnings growth for at least five years. An extraordinary long-run earnings growth rate is the single most important contributing element to the success of most stock investments. IBM, Xerox, American Home Products, and practically all the other really outstanding common-stock investments of the past were growth stocks. As difficult as the job may be, picking stocks whose earnings grow is the name of the game. Consistent growth not only increases the earnings and dividends of the company, but may also increase the multiple that the market is willing to pay for those earnings. Thus the purchaser of a stock whose earnings begin to grow rapidly has a chance at a *potential* double benefit—both the earnings *and* the multiple may increase.

Rule 2: Never pay more for a stock than can reasonably be justified by a firm foundation of value. While I have argued, and I hope persuasively, that you can never judge the exact intrinsic value of a stock, many analysts feel that you can roughly gauge when a stock seems to be reasonably priced. Generally, the earnings multiple for the market as a whole is a helpful benchmark. Growth stocks selling at multiples in line with or not very much above this multiple often represent good value. The Dow Chemical study just described is a good example.

There are important advantages to buying growth stocks at very reasonable earnings multiples. If your growth estimate turns out to be correct you may get the double bonus I mentioned in connection with Rule 1: The price will tend to go up simply because the earnings went up, but also the multiple is likely to expand in recognition of the growth rate that is established. Hence the double bonus. Suppose, for example, you buy a stock earning $1 per share and selling at $15. If the earnings grow to $2 per share and if the price-earnings multiple increases from 15 to 30 (in recognition that the company now can be considered a growth stock) you don't just double your money—you quadruple it. That's because your $15 stock will be worth $60 (30, the multiple, times $2, the earnings).

Now consider the other side of the coin. There are special risks involved in buying "growth stocks" where the market has already recognized the growth and has bid up the price-earnings multiple to a hefty premium over that accorded more run-of-the-mill stocks. Stocks like International Flavors and Fragrances, Avon Products, and other recognized growth companies had earnings multiples well above 50 when the first edition of *Random Walk* came out. They may still turn out to be fine investments for the years ahead, and the following comments are not directed at them. But the potential risks involved with very-high-multiple stocks are enormously high.

The problem is that the very high multiples may already fully reflect the growth that is anticipated, and if the growth does not materialize and earnings in fact go down (or even grow more slowly than expected), you will take a very unpleasant bath. The double benefits that are possible if the earnings of low-multiple stocks grow can become double damages if the earnings of high-multiple stocks decline. When earnings fall the multiple is likely to crash as well. But the crash won't be so loud if the multiple wasn't that high in the first place. Reread the grim stories of National Student Marketing and Four Seasons Nursing in Chapter

Three if you want more evidence of the enormous risks involved with very-high-multiple stocks.

What is proposed, then, is a strategy of buying unrecognized growth stocks whose earnings multiples are not at any substantial premium over the market. Of course, it is very hard to predict growth. But even if the growth does not materialize and earnings decline, the damage is likely to be only single if the multiple is low to begin with, while the benefits may double if things do turn out as you expected. This is an extra way to put the odds in your favor.

We can summarize the discussion thus far by restating the first two rules: *Look for growth situations that the market has not already recognized by bidding the stock's earnings multiple to a large premium. If the growth actually takes place you will often get a double bonus—both the earnings and the price-earnings multiple can rise, producing large gains. Beware of very-high-multiple stocks where many years of growth are already discounted in the price of the stock. If earnings decline rather than grow you will usually get double trouble—both the earnings and the multiple drop, causing heavy losses.*

Rule 3: It helps to buy stocks whose stories of anticipated growth are ones on which investors can build castles in the air. I have stressed the importance of psychological elements in stock price determination. Individual and institutional investors are not computers that calculate warranted price-earnings multiples and print out buy and sell decisions. They are emotional human beings—driven by greed, gambling instinct, hope, and fear in their stock market decisions. This is why successful investing demands both intellectual and psychological acuteness.

Stocks that produce "good vibes" in the minds of investors can sell at premium multiples for long periods even if the growth rate is only average. Those not so blessed may sell at low multiples for long periods even if their growth rate is above average. To be sure, if a growth rate appears to be established, the stock is almost certain to attract some type of following. The market is not irrational. But stocks are like people—what stimulates one may leave another cold, and the multiple improvement may be smaller and slower to be realized if the story never catches on.

So Rule 3 says to ask yourself whether the story about your stock is one that is likely to catch the fancy of the crowd. Is it a story from which contagious dreams can be generated? Is it a story on which investors can build castles in the air— but castles in the air that really rest on a firm foundation?

You don't have to be a technician to follow Rule 3. You might simply use your intuition or speculative sense to judge whether the "story" on your stock is likely to catch the fancy of the crowd—particularly the notice of institutional investors. Technical analysts, however, would look for some tangible evidence before they could be convinced that the investment idea was, in fact, catching on. This tangible evidence is, of course, the beginning of an uptrend or a technical signal that could "reliably" predict that an uptrend would develop.

While the rules I have outlined seem sensible, the important question is whether they really work. After all, lots of other people are playing the game and it is by no means obvious that anyone can win consistently.

In the next two chapters I shall look at the actual record. Chapter Six asks the question: Does technical analysis work? Chapter Seven looks at the performance record of fundamentalists. Together they should help us evaluate how well professional investment people do their job and what value we should put on their advice.

CHAPTER SIX

Technical Analysis and the Random-Walk Theory

Things are seldom what they seem, Skim milk masquerades as cream.—Gilbert and Sullivan, *H.M.S. Pinafore*

Not earnings, nor dividends, nor risk, nor gloom of high interest rates stay the chartists from their assigned task: studying the price movements of stocks. Such single-minded devotion to numbers has somehow yielded the most colorful theories and has produced much of the folk language of Wall Street:

"Hold the winners, sell the losers."

"Switch into the strong stocks."

"Sell this issue, it's acting poorly."

"Don't fight the tape."

All are popular prescriptions of technical analysts as they cheerfully collect their brokerage fees for churning your account.

Technical analysts build their strategies upon dreams of castles in the air and expect their tools to tell them which castle is being built and how to get in on the ground floor. The question is: Do they work?

Holes in Their Shoes and Ambiguity in Their Forecasts

University professors are sometimes asked by their students, "If you're so smart, why aren't you rich?" The question usually rankles professors, who think of themselves as passing up worldly riches to engage in such an obviously socially useful occupation as teaching. The same question might more appropriately be addressed to technicians. For, after all, the whole point of technical analysis is to make money, and one would reasonably expect that those who preach it should practice it successfully in their own investments.

On close examination, technicians are often seen with holes in their shoes and frayed shirt collars. I, personally, have never known a successful technician, but I have seen the wrecks of several unsuccessful ones. (This is, of course, in terms of following their own technical advice. Commissions from urging customers to act on their recommendations are very lucrative.) Curiously, however, the broken technician is never apologetic about his method. If anything, he is more enthusiastic than ever. If you commit the social error of asking him why his is broke, he will tell you quite ingenuously that he made the all-too-human error of not believing his own charts. To my great embarrassment, I once choked conspicuously at the dinner table of a chartist friend of mine when he made such a comment. I have since made it a rule never to eat with a chartist. It's bad for digestion.

While technicians might not get rich following their own advice, their store of words is precious indeed. Consider this advice offered by one technical service:

> The market's rise after a period of reaccumulation is a bullish sign. Nevertheless, fulcrum characteristics are not yet clearly present and a resistance area exists 40 points higher in the Dow, so it is clearly premature to say the next leg of the bull market is up. If, in the coming weeks, a test of the lows holds and the market breaks out of its flag, a further

rise would be indicated. Should the lows be violated, a continuation of the intermediate term downtrend is called for. In view of the current situation, it is a distinct possibility that traders will sit in the wings awaiting a clearer delineation of the trend and the market will move in a narrow trading range.

If you ask me exactly what all this means, I'm afraid I cannot tell you, but I think the technician probably had the following in mind: "If the market does not go up or go down, it will remain unchanged." Even the weather forecaster can do better than that.

Obviously, I'm biased against the chartist. This is not only a personal predilection but a professional one as well. Technical analysis is anathema to the academic world. We love to pick on it. Our bullying tactics are prompted by two considerations: (1) the method is patently false; and (2) it's easy to pick on. And while it may seen a bit unfair to pick on such a sorry target, just remember: it's your money we are trying to save.

While the advent of the large-scale electronic computer may have enhanced the standing of the technician for the time being, it will ultimately prove to be his undoing. Just as fast as the technician creates charts to show where the market is going, the academic gets busy constructing charts showing where the technician has been. Since it's so easy to test all the technical trading rules on the computer, it has become a favorite pastime for academics to see if they really work.

Is There Momentum in the Stock Market?

The technician believes that knowledge of a stock's past behavior can help predict its probable future behavior. In other words, the sequence of price changes prior to any given day is important in predicting the price change for that day. This might be called the wallpaper principle. The technical analyst tries to predict future stock prices just as we might predict that the pattern of wallpaper behind the mirror is the same as the pattern above the mirror. The basic premise is that there are repeatable patterns in space and time.

Chartists believe there is momentum in the market. Supposedly, stocks that have been rising will continue to do so, and those that begin falling will go on sinking. Investors should, therefore, buy stocks that start rising and continue to hold their strong stocks. Should the stock begin to fall or "act poorly," investors are advised to sell.

These technical rules have been tested exhaustively by using stock price data on both major exchanges going back as far as the beginning of the twentieth century. The results reveal conclusively that past movements in stock prices cannot be used to foretell future movements. The stock market has no memory. The central proposition of charting is absolutely false, and investors who follow its precepts will accomplish nothing but increasing substantially the brokerage charges they pay.*

One set of tests, perhaps the simplest of all, simply compares the price change for a stock in a given period with the price change in a subsequent period. For example, technical lore has it that if the price of a stock rose yesterday it is more likely to rise today. It turns out that the correlation of past price movements with present and future price movements is essentially zero. Last week's price change bears no relationship to the price change this week, and so forth.

Economists have also examined the technician's thesis that there are often sequences of price changes in the same direction over several days (or several weeks or months). Stocks are likened to fullbacks who, once having gained some momentum, can be expected to carry on for a long gain. It

* References to all the studies cited may be found in the bibliography.

turns out that this is simply not the case. Sometimes one gets positive price changes (rising prices) for several days in a row; but sometimes when you are flipping a fair coin you also get a long string of "heads" in a row, and you get sequences of positive (or negative) price changes no more frequently than you can expect random sequences of heads or tails in a row. What are often called "persistent patterns" in the stock market occur no more frequently than the runs of luck in the fortunes of any gambler playing a game of chance. This is what the economist means when he says that stock prices behave as a random walk.

Just What Exactly Is a Random Walk?

To many people the economist's disclaimer appears to be arrant nonsense. Even the most casual reader of the financial pages can easily spot patterns in the market. For example, look at the stock chart below.

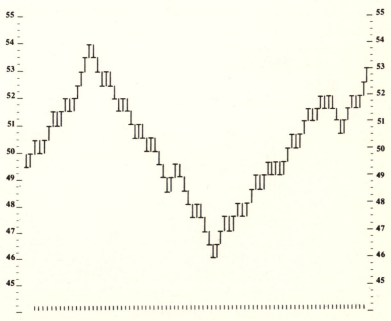

The chart seems to display some obvious patterns. After an initial rise the stock turned down, and once the decline got underway the stock headed persistently downhill. Happily for the bulls, the decline was arrested and the stock had another sustained upward move. One cannot look at a stock chart like this without realizing the self-evidence of these statements. How can the economist be so myopic that he cannot see what is so plainly visible to the naked eye?

The persistence of this belief in repetitive patterns in the stock market is due to statistical illusion. To illustrate, let me describe an experiment in which I recently asked my students to participate. The students were asked to construct a normal stock chart showing the movements of a hypothetical stock initially selling at $50 per share. For each successive trading day, the closing stock price would be determined by the flip of a fair coin. If the toss was a head, the students assumed that the stock closed $\frac{1}{2}$ point higher than the preceding close. If the flip was a tail, the price was assumed to be down by $\frac{1}{2}$. The chart displayed above was actually the hypothetical stock chart derived from one of these experiments.

The chart derived from random coin tossings looks remarkably like a normal stock price chart and even appears to display cycles. Of course, the pronounced "cycles" that we seem to observe in coin tossings do not occur at regular intervals as true cycles do, but neither do the ups and downs in the stock market.

It is this lack of regularity that is crucial. The "cycles" in the stock charts are no more true cycles than the runs of luck or misfortune of the ordinary gambler. And the fact that stocks seem to be in an uptrend, which looks just like the upward move in some earlier period, provides no useful information on the dependability or duration of the current uptrend. Yes, history does tend to repeat itself in the stock market, but in an infinitely surprising variety of ways that confound any attempts to profit from a knowledge of past price patterns.

In other simulated stock charts derived through student coin tossings, there were head-and-shoulders formations, triple tops and bottoms, and other more esoteric chart patterns. One of the charts showed a beautiful upward breakout from an inverted head and shoulders (a very bullish formation). I showed it to a chartist friend of mine who practically jumped out of his skin. "What is this company?" he exclaimed. "We've got to buy immediately. This pattern's a classic. There's no question the stock will be up 15 points next week." He did not respond kindly to me when I told him the chart had been produced by flipping a coin. Chartists have no sense of humor.

My students used a completely random process to produce their stock charts. With each toss, as long as the coins used were fair, there was a 50 percent chance of heads, implying an upward move in the price of the stock, and a 50 percent chance of tails and a downward move. Even if they flip ten heads in a row, the chance of getting a head on the next toss is still 50 percent. Mathematicians call a sequence of numbers produced by a random process (such as those on our simulated stock chart) a random walk. The next move on the chart is completely unpredictable on the basis of what has happened before.

To a mathematician, the sequence of numbers recorded on a stock chart behaves no differently from those in the simulated stock charts—with one exception. There is a long-run uptrend in most averages of stock prices in line with the long-run growth of earnings and dividends. After adjusting for this trend, there is essentially no difference. The next move in a series of stock prices is unpredictable on the basis of past price behavior. No matter what wiggle or wobble the prices have made in the past, tomorrow starts out fifty-fifty. The next price change is no more predictable than the flip of a coin.

Now, in fact, the stock market does not quite measure up to the mathematician's ideal of the complete independence of present price movements from those in the past. There have been some *very slight* dependencies found. But any systematic relationships that exist are so small that they are not useful for an investor. The brokerage charges involved in trying to take advantage of these dependencies are far greater than any advantage that might be obtained. This is the consistent finding of the academic research on stock prices. Thus, an accurate statement of the "narrow form" of the random-walk hypothesis goes as follows: *

> The history of stock-price movements contains no useful information that will enable an investor consistently to outperform a buy-and-hold strategy in managing a portfolio.

If the narrow form of the random-walk hypothesis is a valid description of the stock market, then, as my colleague Richard Quandt says, "Technical analysis is akin to astrology and every bit as scientific."

I am *not* saying that technical strategies never make money. They very often do make profits. The point is rather that a simple "buy-and-hold" strategy (that is, buying a stock or group of stocks and holding on for a long period of time) typically makes as much or more money.

When scientists want to test the efficacy of some new drug they usually run an experiment where two groups of patients are administered pills—one containing the drug in question, the other a worthless placebo (a sugar pill). The results of the administration to the two groups are compared and the drug is deemed effective only if the group receiving the drug did better than the group getting the placebo. Obviously, if both groups got better in the same period of time the drug should not be given the credit, even if the patients did recover.

---

* Academics love to split hairs. Thus we have created two forms of the random walk—both narrow and broad. The broad form of the hypothesis will be discussed in the next chapter.

In the stock-market experiments, the placebo with which the technical strategies are compared is the buy-and-hold strategy. Technical schemes often do make profits for their users, but so does a buy-and-hold strategy. Indeed, as we shall see later, a naïve buy-and-hold strategy, undertaken over a reasonably long time period, has generally provided investors with an average annual rate of return of approximately 9 percent. Only if technical schemes produce better returns than the market can they be judged effective. To date, none can pass that test.

Some More Elaborate Technical Systems

Devotees of technical analysis may argue with some justification that I have been unfair. The simple tests I have just described do not do justice to the "richness" of technical analysis. Unfortunately for the technician, even some of his more elaborate trading rules have been subjected to scientific testing. Since many of the systems tested are very popular, let's briefly examine a few in detail.

THE FILTER SYSTEM

Under the popular "filter" system a stock that has reached a low point and has moved up, say 5 percent (or any other percent you wish to name here and throughout this discussion) is said to be in an uptrend. A stock that has reached a peak and has moved down 5 percent is said to be in a downtrend. You're supposed to buy any stock that has moved up 5 percent from its low and hold it until the price moves down 5 percent from a subsequent high, at which time you sell the stock and, perhaps, even sell short. The short position is maintained until the price rises at least 5 percent from a subsequent low.

This scheme is very popular with brokers, and forms of

it have been recommended by such popular investment books as Ira Cobleigh's *Happiness Is a Stock That Doubles in a Year,* and Nicholas Darvas' *How I Made Two Million Dollars in the Stock Market.* Indeed, the filter method is what lies behind the popular "stop loss" order favored by brokers, where the client is advised to sell his stock if it falls 5 percent below his purchase price to "limit his potential losses." The argument is that presumably a stock that falls by 5 percent will be going into a downtrend anyway.

Exhaustive testing of various filter rules has been undertaken. The percentage drop or rise that filters out buy and sell candidates has been allowed to vary from 1 percent to 50 percent. The tests covered different time periods from 1897 to the present, and involved individual stocks as well as assorted stock averages. Again, the results are remarkably consistent. When the higher brokerage commissions incurred under the filter rules are taken into consideration, these techniques cannot consistently beat a policy of simply buying the individual stock (or the stock average in question) and holding it over the period during which the test is performed. The individual investor would do well to avoid employing any filter rule and, I might add, any broker who recommends it.

THE DOW THEORY

The Dow theory is a great tug-of-war between resistance and support. When the market tops out and moves down, that previous peak defines a resistance area, since people who missed selling at the top will be anxious to do so if given another opportunity. If the market then rises again and nears the previous peak, it is said to be "testing" the resistance area. Now comes the moment of truth. If the market breaks through the resistance area, it is likely to keep going up for a while and the previous resistance area becomes a support area. If, on the other hand, the market "fails to penetrate the resistance area" and instead falls through the preceding low where there was previous support, a bear-market signal is given and the investor is advised to sell.

The basic Dow principle implies a strategy of buying when the market goes higher than the last peak and selling when it sinks through the preceding valley. There are various wrinkles to the theory, such as penetration of a double or triple top being especially bullish, but the basic idea is followed by many chartists and is part of the gospel of charting.

Unhappily, the signals generated by the Dow mechanism have no significance for predicting future price movements. The market's performance after *sell* signals is no different from its performance after *buy* signals. Relative to simply buying and holding the representative list of stocks in the market averages, the Dow follower actually comes out a little behind, since the strategy entails a number of extra brokerage costs as the investor buys and sells when the strategy decrees.

THE RELATIVE-STRENGTH SYSTEM

Here an investor buys and holds those stocks that are acting well, that is, outperforming the general market indices in the recent past. Conversely, the stocks that are acting poorly relative to the market should be avoided or, perhaps, even sold short. While there do seem to be some time periods when a relative-strength strategy would have outperformed a buy-and-hold strategy, there is no evidence that it can do so consistently. A computer test of relative-strength rules over a twenty-five-year period suggests that such rules do not, after accounting for brokerage charges, outperform the placebo of a buy-and-hold investment strategy.

PRICE-VOLUME SYSTEMS

These strategies suggest that when a stock (or the general market) rises on large or increasing volume, there is an unsatisfied excess of buying interest and the stock can be expected to continue its rise. Conversely, when a stock drops on large volume, selling pressure is indicated and a sell signal is given.

Again, the investor following such a system is likely to be disappointed in the results. The buy and sell signals generated by the strategy contain no information useful for predicting future price movements. As with all technical strategies, however, the investor is obliged to do a great deal of in-and-out trading, and thus his brokerage costs are far in excess of those necessitated in a buy-and-hold strategy. After accounting for these brokerage charges, the investor does worse than he would by simply buying and holding a diversified group of stocks.

READING CHART PATTERNS

Perhaps some of the more complicated chart patterns, such as were described in the preceding chapter, are able to reveal the future course of stock prices. For example, is the downward penetration of a head-and-shoulders formation a reliable bearish omen? As one of the gospels of charting, *Technical Analysis,* puts it, "One does not bring instantly to a stop a heavy car moving at seventy miles per hour and, all within the same split second, turn it around and get it moving back down the road in the opposite direction." Before the stock turns around, its price movements are supposed to form one of a number of extensive reversal patterns as the smart-money traders slowly "distribute" their shares to the "public." Of course, we know some stocks do reverse directions in quite a hurry (this is called an unfortunate V formation), but perhaps these reversal patterns and other chart configurations can, like the Roman soothslayers, accurately foretell the future. Alas, the computer has even tested these more arcane charting techniques, and the technician's tool (magician's wand) has again betrayed him.

In an elaborate recent study, the computer was pro-
grammed to draw charts for 548 stocks traded on the New
York Stock exchange over a five-year period. It was instructed
to scan all the charts and identify any one of thirty-two of
the most popularly followed chart patterns. The computer
was told to be on the lookout for heads and shoulders, triple
tops and bottoms, channels, wedges, diamonds, and so forth.
Since the machine is a very thorough (though rather dull)
worker, we can be sure it did not miss any significant chart
patterns.

Whenever the machine found that one of the bearish
chart patterns such as a head and shoulders was followed by
a downward move through the neckline toward décolletage
(a most bearish omen), it recorded a sell signal. If, on the
other hand, a triple bottom was followed by an upside breakout (a most favorable augury) a buy signal was recorded. The
computer then followed the performance of the stocks for
which buy and sell signals were given and compared them
with the performance record of the general market.

Again, there seemed to be no relationship between the
technical signal and subsequent performance. If you had
bought only those stocks with buy signals, and sold on a sell
signal, your performance after brokerage costs would have
been no better than that achieved with a buy-and-hold
strategy. Indeed, the strategy that came closest to producing
above-average returns (not accounting for brokerage costs)
was to buy right after one of the bear signals.

A Gaggle of Other Technical Theories
to Help You Lose Money

Once the academic world polished off most of the standard
technical trading rules, it turned its august attention toward
some of the more fanciful schemes. The world of financial
analysis would be much quieter and duller without the chartists, as the following techniques amply demonstrate.

"BULL MARKETS AND BARE KNEES"

Not content with price movements, some technical analysts have broadened their investigations to include other movements as well. One of the most charming of these schemes has been called by Ira Cobleigh the "bull markets and bare knees" theory. Check the hemline of women's dresses in any given year and you'll have an idea of the level of stock prices. There does seem to be a loose tendency for bull markets in stocks to be associated with bare knees, and bear markets in stocks to be associated with bear markets for girl watchers, as the following chart reveals.

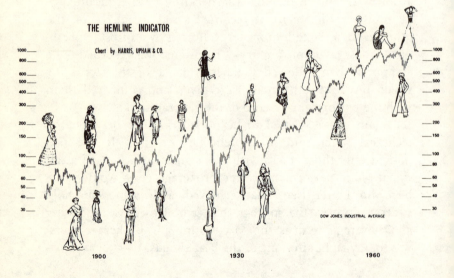

THE HEMLINE INDICATOR

Chart by HARRIS, UPHAM & CO.

DOW JONES INDUSTRIAL AVERAGE

1900   1930   1960

Source: *The AIC Journal,* Bureau of Business Research, American International College, Winter 1972.

For example, in the late nineteenth and early part of the twentieth centuries, the stock market was rather dull, and so were hemlines. But then came rising hemlines and the great bull market of the twenties, to be followed by long skirts and the crash of the thirties. (Actually, the chart cheats a bit:

Hemlines fell in 1927, prior to the most dynamic phase of the bull market.)

Unfortunately, things do not work out as well in the post-World War II period. The market declined sharply during the summer of 1946, well in advance of the introduction of the "New Look" featuring longer skirt lengths in 1947. Similarly, the sharp stock-market decline that began at the end of 1968 preceded the introduction of the midi skirt, which was high fashion in 1969 and especially in 1970.

There is also a problem for those who seriously would try to project these relationships into the future. While there is no theoretical ceiling on the level of stock prices, there obviously is a ceiling on dress heights. The advent of fanny-high micro-mini skirts and hot pants would seem to suggest that stock prices have gone about as far as they can, and everyone should sell out. After all, hemlines cannot possibly go any higher. Or can they?

THE ODD-LOT THEORY

This theory holds that except for the man who is always right, no person can contribute more to successful investment strategy than a man who is known to be invariably wrong. The "odd-lotter," according to popular superstition, is precisely that kind of person. Thus success is assured by buying when the odd-lotter sells and selling when the odd-lotter buys.

Odd-lotters are the people who trade stocks in less than 100-share lots (called round lots). Most amateurs in the stock market cannot afford the $5,000 investment to buy a round lot (100 shares) of stock selling at $50 a share. They are more likely to buy, say, ten shares for a more modest investment of $500.

By examining the ratio of odd-lot purchases (the number of shares these amateurs bought during a particular day) to odd-lot sales (the number of shares they sold) and by looking at what particular stocks odd-lotters buy and sell, one can supposedly make money. These uninformed amateurs, presumably acting solely out of emotion and not with professional insight, are lambs in the street being led to slaughter. They are, according to legend, invariably wrong.

It turns out that the odd-lotter isn't such a stupendous dodo after all. A little stupid? Maybe. There is some indication that the performance of odd-lotters might be slightly worse than the stock averages. However, the available evidence (which admittedly does not match what has been accumulated in testing many of the other technical strategies) indicates that knowledge of his actions is not useful for the formulation of investment strategies.

One of the available studies examines the theory that an investor can make use of data on odd-lot sales and odd-lot purchases in selecting stocks. Supposedly, a switch from net odd-lot buying (where odd-lot shares purchased exceed odd-lot shares sold) to net odd-lot selling (odd-lot sales greater than odd-lot purchases) should be taken as a "buy" signal, since the boobs who sell odd lots obviously don't know what they're doing. The data did not support this contention. Indeed, the rule failed to indicate the major turning points for individual stocks or for the market as a whole. Moreover, the odd-lot index was a very volatile one, switching back and forth from net sales to net purchases quite frequently. This suggests that an investor who followed the strategy would incur very heavy brokerage charges, which would eat substantially into his capital.

With the exception of a few technicians who sell their services to the public, few professional investment people believe in the odd-lot theory anymore. Indeed, some professional investors have seriously suggested that a new odd-lot theory is applicable to today's institutionally dominated market. Instead of looking at the behavior of the little guy in the market, it is suggested that the yo-yos who run the big mutual funds are the odd-lotters of today, and that investors should look at what they are doing and then do the opposite.

A FEW MORE SYSTEMS

To continue this review of technical schemes would soon generate rapidly diminishing returns. Probably few people seriously believe that the sunspot theory of stock-market movements can make money for them. But do you believe that by following the ratio of advancing to declining stocks on the New York Stock Exchange you can find a reliable leading indicator of general stock-market peaks? A careful computer study says no. Do you think that a rise in short interest (the number of shares of a stock sold short) is a bullish signal (since eventually the stock will be repurchased by the short seller to cover his position)? Exhaustive testing indicates no relationship either for the stock market as a whole or for individual issues. Do you think a moving-average system (for example, buy a stock if its price goes higher than its average price over the past 200 days and sell it if it goes below the average) can lead you to extraordinary stock-market profits? Not if you have to pay commissions to buy and sell! And so we could go on through the whole list.

Why Are Technicians Still Hired?

It seems very clear that under scientific scrutiny chart-reading must share a pedestal with alchemy. There has been a remarkable uniformity in the conclusions of all studies done on all forms of technical analysis. Not one has outperformed the placebo of a buy-and-hold strategy. Technical methods cannot be used to make useful investment strategies. This is the fundamental conclusion of the random-walk theory.

A former colleague of mine who believed that the capitalist system would be sure to weed out all useless growths such as the flourishing technicians, was convinced that the technical cult was just a passing fad. "The days of these modern-day soothsayers on Wall Street are numbered," he would say. "Brokers will soon learn they can easily do without the technicians' services."

The chartist's durability, and the fact that over the year he has been hired in increasing numbers, suggests that the capitalist system may garden like most of the rest of us. We like to see our best plants grow, but as summer wears on somehow the weeds often manage to get the best of us. And as I often tell my wife when she remarks about the abundance of weeds in our lawn, "At least they're green."

The point is, the technicians often play an important role in the greening of the brokers. Chartists recommend trades—almost every technical system involves some degree of in-and-out trading. Trading generates commissions, and commissions are the lifeblood of the brokerage business. The technicians do not help produce yachts for the customers, but they do help generate the trading that provides yachts for the brokers. Until the public catches on to this bit of trickery, technicians will continue to flourish.

Appraising the Counterattack

As you might imagine, the random-walk theory's dismissal of charting is not altogether popular among technicians. Academic proponents of the theory are greeted in some Wall Street quarters with as much enthusiasm as Golda Meier addressing a meeting of the Fedayeen. Technical analysts consider the theory and its implications to be "just plain academic drivel" in the words of one veteran professional. Let us pause then and appraise the counterattack from the beleaguered technicians.

Perhaps the most common complaint about the random-walk theory is based on a distrust of mathematics and a misconception of what the theory means. "The market isn't random" the complaint goes, "and no mathematician is going to convince me it is." Even so astute a commentator on the Wall Street scene as "Adam Smith" displays this misconception when he writes:

> I suspect that even if the random walkers announced a perfect mathematic proof of randomness I would go on believing that in the long run future earnings influence present value, and that in the short run the dominant factor is the elusive *Australopithecus,* the temper of the crowd.

Of course earnings and dividends influence market prices, and so does the temper of the crowd. We saw ample evidence of this in earlier chapters of the book. The random-walk theory does not deny that a news event indicating unexpectedly higher earnings for a company will tend to raise the price of its stock. Indeed, the theory suggests that the market is an extremely efficient mechanism: so efficient, in fact, that it adjusts to such new information right away, not gradually over time. Surely, if new information is published that indicates a much higher value for Standard Squinch, investors and traders will use this information to buy the stock today. As a result, the stock will rise in price *today* and not *tomorrow* or gradually over time forming a long uptrend.

But new information about a company (a big mineral strike, the death of the president, etc.) is unpredictable. It will occur randomly over time. Indeed, successive appearances of news items must be random. If an item of news were not random, that is, if it were *dependent* on an earlier item of news, then it wouldn't be news at all. The narrow form of the random-walk theory says only that stock prices cannot be predicted on the basis of past stock prices. Thus criticisms of the type quoted above are not valid.

The technical analyst will also cite chapter and verse that the academic world has certainly not tested every technical scheme that has been devised. That is quite correct. No economist or mathematician, however skillful, can prove conclusively that technical methods can never work. All that can be said is that the small amount of information contained in stock-market pricing patterns has not been shown to be sufficient to overcome the brokerage costs involved in acting on that information. Consequently, I expect this particular chapter to elicit a flood of letters condemning me for not mentioning a pet technical scheme the author will be convinced actually works.

Being somewhat incautious, I will climb out on a limb and argue that no technical scheme whatever could work for any length of time. I suggest first that methods which people are convinced "really work" have not been adequately tested; and second, that even if they did work the schemes would be bound to destroy themselves.

Each year a large number of pathetic people visit the gambling parlors of Las Vegas and examine the last hundreds of numbers of the roulette wheel in search of some repeating pattern. Usually they find one. And so they stay until they lose everything because they do not retest the pattern.* The same thing is true for technicians.

If you examine past stock prices in any given period, you can almost always find some kind of system that would have worked in a given period. If enough different criteria for selecting stocks are tried, one will eventually be found that selects the best ones of that period.

Let me illustrate. Suppose we examine the record of stock prices and volume over the five-year period 1968 through 1972 in search of technical trading rules that would have worked during that period. After the fact it is always possible to find a technical rule that works. For example, it might be that you should have bought all stocks whose names began with the letters X or I, whose volume was at least 3,000 shares a day, and whose earnings grew at a rate of 10 percent or more during the 1960–68 period. The point is that it is

---

* Edward O. Thorp actually did find a method to win at blackjack. Thorp wrote it all up in *Beat the Dealer,* but only after the casinos changed the rules of the game so it didn't work anymore.

obviously possible to describe, after the fact, which categories of stocks had the best performance. The real problem is, of course, whether the scheme works in a different time period. What most advocates of technical analysis usually fail to do is to test their schemes with market data derived from other periods than those during which the scheme was developed.

Even if the technician follows my advice, tests his scheme in many different time periods, and finds it a reliable predictor of stock prices, I still believe that technical analysis must ultimately be worthless. For the sake of argument, suppose the technician had found that there was a reliable year-end rally, that is, every year stock prices rose between Christmas and New Year's Day. The problem is that once such a regularity is known to market participants, people will act in a way that prevents it from happening in the future.*

Any successful technical scheme must ultimately be self-defeating. The moment I realize that prices will be higher after New Year's Day than they are before Christmas I will start buying before Christmas ever comes around. If people know a stock will go up *tomorrow,* you can be sure it will go up *today.* Any regularity in the stock market that can be discovered and acted upon profitably is bound to destroy itself. This is the fundamental reason why I am convinced that no one will be successful in employing technical methods to make money in the stock market.

Implications for Investors

The past history of stock prices cannot be used to predict the future in any meaningful way. Technical strategies are usually amusing, often comforting, but of no real value. This

---

* If such a regularity was known to only one individual, he would simply practice the technique until he had collected a large share of the marbles. He surely would have no incentive to share a truly useful scheme by making it available to others.

is the narrow form of the random-walk theory and it is the consistent conclusion of research done at universities such as Chicago, M.I.T., Pennsylvania, Princeton, and Stanford. It has been published mainly in investment journals, but also in more esoteric ones such as *Kyklos* and *Econometrica*. Technical theories enrich only the people preparing and marketing the technical service or the brokerage firms who hire technicians in the hope that their analyses may help encourage investors to do more in-and-out trading and thus generate commission business for the brokerage firm.

The implications of this analysis are simple. If past prices contain no useful information for the prediction of future prices, there is no point in following any technical trading rule for timing the purchases and sales of securities. A simple policy of buying and holding will be at least as good as any technical procedure. Discontinue your subscriptions to worthless technical services, and eschew brokers who read charts and are continually recommending the purchase or sale of securities.

There is another major advantage to a buy-and-hold strategy that I have not yet mentioned. Short-term trading (buying and selling within six months), to the extent it is profitable at all, tends to generate short-term capital gains, which are taxed at regular income-tax rates. Buying and holding enables you to postpone or avoid gains taxes. By following any technical strategy, you are likely to realize most of your capital gains and pay larger taxes (as well as paying them sooner) than you would under a buy-and-hold strategy. Thus simply buying and holding a diversified portfolio suited to your objectives will enable you to save on investment expense, brokerage charges, and taxes; and, at the same time, to achieve an overall performance record at least as good as that obtainable using technical methods.

CHAPTER SEVEN

The Clay Pedestal of SuperAnalyst, or How Good Is Fundamental Analysis?

> How could I have been so mistaken as to have trusted the experts?—John F. Kennedy (after the Bay of Pigs fiasco)

In the beginning he was a statistician. He wore a white, starched shirt and threadbare blue suit. He quietly put on his green eyeshade, sat down at his desk, and recorded meticulously the historical financial information about the companies he followed. The result: writer's cramp.

But then a metamorphosis began to set in. He rose from his desk, bought blue button-down shirts and gray flannel suits, threw away his eyeshade, and began to make field trips to visit the companies that previously he had known only as a collection of financial statistics. His title now became security analyst.

As time went on, his stature continued to grow. Portfolio managers increasingly relied on his reports and recommendations in deciding which stocks should be bought and sold. In recent years his shirts acquired stripes and, yes, he even sprouted sideburns! He became . . . SuperAnalyst!

As a SuperAnalyst, he is a special person. His job is to divine the future. He is trained to evaluate all that he hears and reads. He studies his industries exhaustively, inspects the firms' plants and operations, asks penetrating questions of the companies' officers, and talks with their customers and suppliers. He plays golf on weekends with company presidents and flies down to Washington to check the political weather. But the supreme accolade is that SuperAnalyst, once the humble statistician, is now a bona fide *chartered financial analyst!*

The Mystique of SuperAnalyst

Some of Wall Street's portfolio managers actually invest on the basis of charts and various technical schemes described in the last chapter. But even on Wall Street, technicians are considered a rather strange cult, and little faith is put in their recommendations. Thus the preceding studies casting doubt on the efficacy of technical analysis would not be considered surprising by most professionals. The really important question is whether fundamental analysis is any good. For most professional investment managers rely on an army of highly paid security analysts for their basic information—and SuperAnalyst is a fundamentalist.

Two extreme views have been taken in appraising the effectiveness of SuperAnalyst. One popularly held view regards him as almost omnipotent. Together with other Super-Analysts he is known as They.

> They are the people who move stocks. They get the information first, maybe They even create the information; and They are about to put the stock up or down. They are mysterious, anonymous, powerful, and They know everything.

Nothing fazes Them. They are the powers of the market-place.

"Adam Smith," who wrote that in *The Money Game,* goes on to suggest that professional portfolio managers and their teams of SuperAnalysts are becoming more powerful and more skilled all the time. The individual has scarcely a chance against them.

An opposite-extreme view is taken by much of the academic community. Some academicians have gone so far as to suggest that a blindfolded monkey throwing darts at the *Wall Street Journal* could select stocks with as much success as SuperAnalyst. They have argued that fund managers and their SuperAnalysts can do no better at picking stocks than a rank amateur. Many have concluded that the value of professional investment advice is nil.

My own view of the matter is somewhat less extreme than that taken by many of my academic colleagues. Nevertheless, an understanding of the large body of research on these questions is essential for any intelligent investor. This chapter will recount the major battle in an ongoing war between academics and market professionals that has shaken Wall Street to its bedrock. Current field reports have the academics claiming victory and the professionals screaming "Foul."

Can Security Analysts See into the Future?

Forecasting future earnings is the security analysts' *raison d'être.* As a top Wall Street professional put it in his fraternity magazine, *The Institutional Investor:* "Expectation of future earnings is still the most important single factor affecting stock prices." As we have seen, growth (in earnings and therefore in the ability to pay dividends) is the key element needed to estimate a stock's firm foundation of value. The analyst who can make accurate forecasts of the future will be

richly rewarded. "If he is wrong," *The Institutional Investor*
puts it, "a stock can act precipitously, as has been demonstrated time and time again. Earnings are the name of the
game and always will be."

To predict future directions, analysts generally start by
looking at past wanderings. "A proven score of past performance in earnings growth is," one analyst told me recently, "a
most reliable indicator of future earnings growth." If management is really skillful, there is no reason to think it will
lose its Midas touch in the future. If the same adroit management team remains at the helm, the course of future earnings
growth should continue as it has in the past, or so the argument goes.

Such thinking represents SuperAnalyst's first mistake,
according to the academic world. Calculations of past earnings growth are no help in predicting future growth. If you
knew the growth rates of all companies over, say, the 1950–
60 period, this would not have helped you at all in predicting
what growth they would achieve in the 1960–70 period. And
knowing the fast growers of the sixties has not helped analysts
find the fast growers of the early seventies. This startling
result was first reported by British researchers for companies
in the United Kingdom in an article charmingly titled
"Higgledy Piggledy Growth." Learned academicians at
Princeton and Harvard applied the British study to U.S.
companies—and, surprise, the same was true here!

"IBM," the cry immediately went up. "Remember IBM."
I do remember IBM: a steady high grower for decades. It is
an exception (though for how much longer is open to question). I also remember Litton Industries and dozens of other
firms that chalked up consistent large growth rates until the
roof fell in. I hope you remember *not* the exception but
rather the rule: there is no reliable pattern that can be
discerned from past records to aid the analyst in predicting
future growth.

A good SuperAnalyst will argue, however, that there's

much more to predicting than just the past record. Rather than measure every factor that goes into the actual forecasting process, those of us at Princeton's Financial Research Center decided to concentrate on the end result: the prediction itself.

Donning our cloak of academic detachment, we wrote to nineteen major Wall Street firms engaged in fundamental analysis. The nineteen firms, which asked to remain anonymous, included some of the major brokerage firms, mutual fund management companies, investment advisory firms, and banks engaged in trust management. They are among the most respected names in the investment business.

We requested—and received—past earnings predictions on how these firms felt earnings for specific companies would behave over both a one-year and a five-year period. These estimates, made at several different times, were then compared with actual results to see how well the analysts forecast short-run and long-run earnings changes. Rude as it may seem, we wound up defrocking SuperAnalyst.

Bluntly stated, the careful estimates of security analysts (based on industry studies, plant visits, etc.) do little, if any, better than those that would be obtained by simple extrapolation of past trends, which we have already seen are no help at all. Indeed, when compared with actual earnings growth rates, the five-year estimates of security analysts were actually worse than the predictions from several naïve forecasting models.

For example, one placebo with which the analysts' estimates were compared was the assumption that every company in the economy would enjoy a growth in earnings of about 4 percent over the next year (approximately the long-run rate of growth of the national income). It turned out that if you used this naïve forecasting model you would make smaller errors in forecasting long-run earnings growth than by using the professional forecasts of the analysts.

Our method of determining the efficacy of the security

analyst's diagnoses of his companies is exactly the same as was used before in evaluating the technicians' medicine. We compared the results obtained by following the experts with the results from some naïve mechanism involving no expertise at all. Sometimes these naïve predictors work very well. For example, if you want to forecast the weather tomorrow you will do a pretty good job by predicting that it will be exactly the same as today. It turns out that while this system misses every one of the turning points in the weather, for most days it is quite reliable. How many weather forecasters do you suppose do any better?

When confronted with the poor record of their five-year growth estimates, the security analysts honestly, if sheepishly, admitted that five years ahead is really too far in advance to make reliable projections. They protested that while long-term projections are admittedly important, they really ought to be judged on their ability to project earnings changes one year ahead.

Believe it or not, it turned out that their one-year forecasts were even worse than their five-year projections. It was actually harder for them to forecast one year ahead than to estimate long-run changes.

The analysts gamely fought back. They complained it was unfair to judge their performance on a wide cross section of industries, since earnings for electronics firms and various "cyclical" companies are notoriously hard to forecast. "Try us on utilities," one analyst confidently asserted. So we tried it, and They didn't like it. Even the forecasts for the stable utilities were far off the mark. Those the analysts confidently touted as high growers turned out to perform much the same as the utilities for which only low or moderate growth was predicted. This led to the second major finding of our study: There is not one industry that is easy to predict.

Moreover, no analysts proved consistently superior to the others. Of course, in each year some analysts did much better than average, but there was no consistency in their pattern of performance. Analysts who did better than average one year were no more likely than the others to make superior forecasts in the next year.

Amidst all these accusations and counterassertions, there is a deadly serious message. It is this: Security analysts have enormous difficulty in performing their basic function of forecasting earnings prospects for the companies they follow. Investors who put blind faith in such forecasts in making their investment selections are in for some rude disappointments.

Why the Crystal Ball Is Clouded

It is always somewhat disturbing to learn that a group of highly trained and well-paid professionals may not be terribly skillful at their calling. Unfortunately, this is hardly unusual. Similar types of findings could be made for most groups of professionals. There is, for example, a classic example in medicine. At a time when tonsillectomies were very fashionable, the American Child Health Association surveyed a group of 1,000 children, eleven years of age, from the public schools of New York City, and found that 611 of these had had their tonsils removed. The remaining 389 were then examined by a group of physicians, who selected 174 of these for tonsillectomy and declared the rest had no tonsil problem. The remaining 215 were reexamined by another group of doctors, who recommended 99 of these for tonsillectomy. When the 116 "healthy" children were examined a third time, a similar percentage were told their tonsils had to be removed. After three examinations, only 65 children remained who had not been recommended for tonsillectomy. These remaining children were not examined further because the supply of examining physicians ran out.

Numerous other studies have shown similar results. Radiologists have failed to recognize the presence of lung disease in about 30 percent of the X-ray plates they read, despite the clear presence of the disease on the X-ray film. A recent experiment proved that professional staffs in psychiatric hospitals could not tell the sane from the insane. The point is that we should not take for granted the reliability and accuracy of any judge, no matter how expert. When one considers the low reliability of so many kinds of judgments, it does not seem too surprising that security analysts, with their particularly difficult forecasting job, should be no exception.

There are, I believe, four factors that help explain why security analysts have such difficulty in perceiving the future. These are: (1) the influence of random events; (2) the creation of dubious reported earnings through "creative" accounting procedures; (3) the basic incompetence of many of the analysts themselves; and (4) the loss of the best analysts to the sales desk or to portfolio management. Each factor deserves some discussion.

1. THE INFLUENCE OF RANDOM EVENTS

A company is not an entity unto itself. Many of the most important changes that affect the basic prospects for corporate earnings are essentially random, that is, unpredictable.

Take the utility industry, to which I referred earlier. Presumably it is one of the most stable and dependable groups of companies. During the early 1960s almost every utility analyst expected Florida Power and Light to be the fastest-growing utility. The analysts saw a continued high population growth, increased demands for electric power among existing customers, and a favorable regulatory climate.

Everything turned out exactly as forecast except for one small detail. The favorable Florida regulatory climate turned distinctly unfavorable as the sixties progressed. The Florida Public Utilities Commission ordered Florida Power and Light to make several substantial rate cuts and the utility was not able to translate the rapid growth in demand for electric power into higher profits. As a result, the company closed the decade with a mediocre growth record, far below the ebullient forecasts.

U.S. government budgetary and contract decisions can have enormous implications for the fortunes of individual companies. So can the incapacitation of key members of management, the discovery of a major new product, the finding of defects in a current product, the shut-off of mideast oil, natural disasters such as floods and hurricanes, etc. The stories of unpredictable events affecting earnings are endless.

2. THE CREATION OF DUBIOUS REPORTED EARNINGS THROUGH "CREATIVE" ACCOUNTING PROCEDURES

A firm's income statement may be likened to a bikini bathing suit—what it reveals is interesting but what it conceals is vital. National Student Marketing, one of the concept stocks I mentioned in Chapter Three, led the beauty parade in this regard. Andrew Tobias describes it all in *The Funny Money Game*.

In its fiscal 1969 report, National Student Marketing made generous use of terms such as "deferred new product development and start-up costs." These were moneys actually spent during 1969 but not charged against earnings in that year. "Unamortized costs of prepared sales programs" carried the ploy even further. These were advertising expenses that were not charged against earnings on the flimsy excuse that they would produce sales in the future. Subsidiary losses were easily handled: the companies were simply sold, removing their unfavorable results from the consolidated accounting statement. Actually it wasn't quite that simple, because the sales were consummated after the close of the fiscal year— but the accountants had no difficulty in arranging for the sale retroactively.

Since expenses were uncounted, why not count unearnings? No sooner said than done. These were duly noted in the sales column as unbilled receivables, on the justification that the actual billing of the sales could be expected to materialize in the future. Finally, came "the $3,754,103 footnote." Almost $4 million was added to net income in the form of earnings from companies whose acquisitions were "agreed to in principal and closed subsequent" to the end of fiscal 1969.

It turned out that even accepting the rest of the creative accounting, if you didn't count the earnings of companies that were not legally part of National Student Marketing in 1969, the company barely broke even. Of course, the imprimatur of a prestigious accounting firm was affixed to the bottom of a statement assuring the public that the accounts were prepared in accordance with "generally accepted accounting principles." *

The above is admittedly an extreme example, but the general problem is not uncommon. Seeming miracles can be accomplished with depreciation; the peculiarities of conglomerate accounting; the franchise accounting game; and the special features of the reports of land-sales companies, computer leasing companies, and insurance companies. It is small wonder that security analysts have trouble estimating reported future earnings.

3. THE BASIC INCOMPETENCE OF MANY
OF THE ANALYSTS THEMSELVES

The overall performance of analysts in many respects reflects the limit of their abilities. Their record with regard to STP Corporation is certainly a good example.

In early 1971, Andy Granatelli's STP was the darling of

* In 1972 the Securities and Exchange Commission charged National Student Marketing Corp., its auditors, two law firms, and fifteen individuals with violations of federal securities laws. Included in the SEC suit was a charge that the company had issued "materially false and misleading" financial statements.

the Wall Street fraternity. Report after report indicated why it was likely to enjoy a large, long-term growth rate. Analysts pointed to its consistent pattern of growth over ten years. On the argument that the future would be more of the same, and that STP could continue to create its destiny through its marvelously successful advertising campaign, the Wall Street fraternity gave STP an estimated 20 percent growth rate for earnings in future years. As STP's stock price rose, analysts recommended the shares with greater and greater enthusiasm. Needless to say, but said nevertheless, STP management actively encouraged this enthusiasm.

Few analysts bothered to ask about the company's major product, STP oil treatment, which apparently accounted for three-quarters of the firm's revenues and earnings. What did the product really do? Could one really believe that STP helped cars start faster in winter and made engines run longer, quieter, and cooler in summer?

Admittedly, some analysts had a queasy feeling, but this was carefully reasoned away. For example, in the May 17 issue of the *Wall Street Transcript*, one analyst was quoted as saying: "The risk is that it is difficult to prove what exactly the product accomplishes, and people fear that the FTC might attack the company on an efficacy basis. We feel there is a very low probability of that happening and in the meantime consumers think the product works and that's the important thing. It is sort of a 'cosmetic company' for the car." If ever there was a castle in the air, STP certainly qualified.

While the above analyst was being quoted, *Consumer Reports* was completing its report on STP. This was published in July 1971 and stated that STP was a worthless oil thickener, not a panacea that would make ailing engines healthy again. Indeed, the consumer magazine reported that "STP can change the viscosity of a new car's oil to a considerably thicker grade than certain auto manufacturers recommend." The magazine went on to say that the major auto manufacturers positively discouraged the practice of using such additives, and suggested that STP might modify the properties of a car's engine oil so much that the new-car warranty terms might be affected.

The stock fell abruptly and the company's consistent record of past earnings growth came to an untimely end. As one analyst confided after the debacle, "I guess we just didn't ask the right questions."

To be perfectly blunt, many security analysts are not particularly perceptive, critical, or competent. I learned this early in the game as a young Wall Street trainee. In attempting to learn the techniques of the pros, I tried to duplicate some analytic work done by a metals specialist named Louie. Louie had figured that for each 1¢ increase in the price of copper, the earnings for a particular copper producer would increase by $1 per share. Since he expected a 3¢ increase in the price of copper, he reasoned that this particular stock was "an unusually attractive purchase candidate."

In redoing the calculation, I found that Louie had misplaced a decimal point. A penny increase in the price of copper would increase earnings by 10¢, not by $1. When I pointed this out to Louie (feeling sure he would want to put out a correction immediately) he simply shrugged his shoulders and declared, "Well, the recommendation sounds more convincing if we leave the report as is." Attention to detail was clearly not the forte of this particular analyst. From then on I referred to him as Sloppy Louie (not to denigrate the excellent fish restaurant of the same name near the New York financial district).

To balance this inattention to detail and careful work, we have those who glory in it. Take Railroad Roger, for example. Roger will accurately recount every conceivable statistic on track miles and freight carloadings for hours on end. But Roger does not have the faintest clue what the rails will earn next year, or which should be favored for purchase. Oil Analyst Doyle performs in a similar manner. His knowledge concerning refinery capacity and allowables in

Texas is encyclopedic, but he lacks the critical acumen to translate this into judgments useful for investment decision-making.

Many analysts, however, emulate Louie. Generally too lazy to make their own earnings projections, they prefer to copy the forecasts of other analysts or to swallow the ones released by corporate managements without even chewing. Then it's very easy to know whom to blame if something goes wrong. "That ***!!! treasurer gave me the wrong dope." And it's much easier to be wrong when your professional colleagues had all agreed with you. As Keynes put it, "Worldly wisdom teaches that it is better for reputation to fail conventionally than to succeed unconventionally."

Corporate management goes out of its way to ease the forecasting task of the analyst. Let me give you a personal example: A two-day field trip was arranged by a major corporation to brief a whole set of Wall Street security analysts on its operations and future programs.

We were picked up in the morning by the company's private plane for visits and briefings at three of the company's plants. In the evening we were given first-class accommodations and royally wined and dined. After two more plant visits the next day, we had a briefing, replete with slide show, indicating a "most conservative five-year forecast" of robustly growing earnings.

At each stop we were showered with gifts—and not only the usual souvenir mock-ups of the company's major products. We also received a variety of desk accessories for the office, a pen and pencil set, cigarette lighter, tie bar, cuff links, and a tasteful piece of jewelry to "take home to the wife or mistress, as the case may be." Throughout each day liquor and wine flowed in abundance. As one bleary-eyed analyst confided at the end of the trip, "It's very hard not to have a warm feeling for this company."

I do not mean to imply that most Wall Street analysts typically receive payola for touting particular stocks. Indeed, from my own experience, I would judge that the standards of ethics in Wall Street are very high. Sure, there are crooks; but I would guess far fewer than in other professions.

I do imply that the *average* analyst is just that—a well-paid and usually highly intelligent person who has an extraordinarily difficult job and does it in a rather mediocre fashion. Analysts are often misguided, sometimes sloppy, perhaps self-important, and at times susceptible to the same pressures as other people. In short, they are really very human beings.

4. THE LOSS OF THE BEST ANALYSTS TO THE SALES DESK OR TO PORTFOLIO MANAGEMENT

My fourth argument against the profession is a paradoxical one: many of the best security analysts are not paid to analyze securities. They are either very high-powered institutional salesmen; efficient new-business getters, successful in bringing new underwriting business to their firms; or get promoted to be prestigious portfolio managers.

Brokerage houses that pride themselves on their research prowess project an aura of respectability by sending a security analyst to chaperone the regular salesman on a call to a financial institution. Institutional investors like to hear about a new investment idea right from the horse's mouth, and so the regular salesman usually sits back and lets the analyst do the talking. Thus most of the articulate analysts find their time is spent with institutional clients, not with financial reports and corporate treasurers. They also find that their monetary rewards are heavily dependent upon their ability to bring commission business to the firm.

Another magnet away from the study of stocks is the ability of some analysts to attract to their firm profitable underwriting clients, that is, companies who need to borrow money or sell new common stock to raise funds for expansion. The analyst on a field trip who is looking for new, small, expanding companies as potential investment recommendations may put a great deal of effort into selling his firm's investment banking services. I have seen many a security analyst make his reputation by his ability to attract such clients to the firm. He may not come up with good earnings forecasts or select the right stocks for investment, but he brings the bacon home to his firm and that is the name of the game.

Finally, both the compensation and prestige structures within the securities industry induce many analysts away from research work into portfolio management. It's far more exciting and remunerative to "run money" in the line position of portfolio manager than only to advise in the staff position of security analyst. Small wonder that many of the best-respected security analysts do not remain long in their jobs.

Do Security Analysts Pick Winners? The Performance of the Mutual Funds

I can almost hear the chorus in the background as I write these words. It goes something like this: The real test of the analyst lies in the performance of the stocks he recommends. Maybe Sloppy Louie, the copper analyst, did mess up his earnings forecast with a misplaced decimal point; but if the stocks he recommended made money for his clients, his lack of attention to detail can surely be forgiven. "Analyze investment performance," the chorus is saying, "not earnings forecasts."

Fortunately, the records of one group of professionals—the mutual funds—are publicly available. Better still for my argument, many of the men at the funds are the embodiment of the SuperAnalyst concept—they are the best and highest-paid analysts and portfolio managers in the business. They stand at the pinnacle of the investment profession.

"They" allegedly are the first to learn and act on any new fundamental information that becomes available. By their own admission "they" can clearly make above-average returns. As one investment manager recently put it: "It will take many years before the general level of competence rises enough to overshadow the startling advantage of today's aggressive investment manager." "Adam Smith" echoes a similar statement:

> All the players in the Game are getting rapidly more professional. . . . The true professionals in the Game—the professional portfolio managers—grow more skilled all the time. They are human and they make mistakes, but if you have your money managed by a truly alert mutual fund or even by one of the better banks, you will have a better job done for you than probably at any time in the past.

Statements like these are just too tempting to the lofty-minded men in the academic world. Given the wealth of available data, the time available to conduct such research, and the overwhelming desire to prove academic superiority in such matters, it was only natural that academia would zero in on the performance of SuperAnalyst.

MUTUAL FUNDS VERSUS RANDOMLY SELECTED PORTFOLIOS

Again the evidence from several studies, including a series conducted at the Wharton School of Finance, is remarkably uniform. Investors have done no better with the average mutual fund than they could have done by purchasing and holding an unmanaged broad stock index. In other words, over long periods of time mutual fund portfolios have not outperformed randomly selected groups of stocks.

When Nobel Prize-winning economist and M.I.T. professor Paul Samuelson testified to this effect before the powerful Senate Banking and Currency Committee, he aroused the curiosity of Senator Thomas McIntyre of New Hampshire, who decided to conduct a test. The senator tacked a listing of all stocks traded on the New York Stock Exchange to a dart board and proceeded to select his random portfolio by casually lofting darts in the direction of the board.

The result: his random portfolio had a better overall performance over a ten-year period than even the average of funds whose objective was maximum long-term capital growth.

The cost: 29½¢ per year. This included the dart board, dart, thumbtacks, newspaper, and brokerage fees, which were zero after the first year. The senator did admit to one problem, however. Being a fairly poor shot, he often missed the board completely and it took some time to select his portfolio.

THE INCONSISTENCY OF PERFORMANCE

Many readers will say, politely and otherwise, that the senator's record was a fluke. It certainly doesn't jibe with the yearly performance rankings of mutual funds that one sees listed in financial magazines. These *always* show a substantial number of funds beating the averages each year—and some by significant amounts. What these rankings do not always make clear, however, is that occasionally superior performance is commonplace. Only consistency of performance can be accepted as evidence that SuperAnalyst clearly possesses superior powers. And the evidence points to the reverse— there seems to be no relationship between good performance in one period and superior returns in the next.

It turns out that the mutual fund portfolio managers as a group have as many bad years—that is, worse than average —as good years. And a mutual fund that has had one better-than-average year has only a 50 percent chance of repeating that record the next year. This is just what you would expect if mutual fund investing were a random process.

In compiling yearly rankings for thirty-nine funds over a ten-year period, Eugene Fama of the University of Chicago has nicely illustrated how inconsistent fund performance can actually be. The table below shows the yearly rankings for three funds over a period of ten years. These funds have gone back and forth from the top of the ranking (1) right to the bottom (39).

Funds and their Rankings

Year	Keystone S-4	Chemical Fund	International Resources
1	29	1	10
2	1	39	37
3	38	14	39
4	5	27	22
5	3 (tied)	3 (tied)	35
6	8	33	1
7	35	1	37
8	1	27	39
9	1 (tied)	4	1 (tied)
10	36	23	11

Just as past earnings growth cannot predict future earnings, neither can past fund performance predict future results. Fund managements are also subject to random events—they may grow fat, become lazy, or break up. An investment approach that works very well for one period can easily turn sour the next. One is tempted to conclude that a very important factor in determining poll ranking is our old friend Lady Luck.

PERFORMANCE AND PORTFOLIO TURNOVER, LOADING FEES, AND SIZE

Another way to study the performance of SuperAnalyst is to examine the value of the buy and sell decisions made by portfolio managers directly. This is done by comparing the performance of each manager's actual portfolio with what he would have achieved if he had simply held his beginning-of-period portfolio throughout the time studied. Evidence indicates that portfolio managers succeeded in outperforming this buy-and-hold strategy only about 50 percent of the time. Thus their trades seem not to have improved their portfolio performance.

Other studies have asked whether fund managers have been able to predict market trends—buying at the bottom and selling off at the peak of speculative enthusiasm, thus both benefiting their shareholders and stabilizing the market. Again the mutual funds show no special abilities. They are just as likely to be buying at the top and selling on the way down. Bradbury K. Thurlow, a well-known professional, summed it up by noting, "The funds behaved like the worst of small investors, showing speculative exuberance at the top, dire forebodings at the bottom, and steadfast timidity during the recovery."

And how about that old maxim that you pay for what you get? Don't look for it in this area of Wall Street. There seems to be no relationship between performance and the fees paid to portfolio managers or the sales charge collected by many popular mutual funds. Load and no-load funds (I'll explain the differences in Chapter Eleven) do just about the same. Nor is there a consistent relationship between size or portfolio turnover and average performance. The only dependable relationship that exists in explaining mutual fund performance is the tendency for funds assuming greater risks to earn, on average, a larger long-run rate of return.

Risk Has Its Reward

One of the best-documented propositions in the field of investment is that on average investors receive higher rates of return for bearing greater risk. Risk, as discussed in Chapter Four, is considered to be the relative volatility of returns. An investment promising a stable and dependable 9 percent each year is less risky than (and preferable to) one that may return 36 percent in a year when the market is strong and lose 18 percent in a year when the market falls. At least this seems to be the view of the majority of investors. Return in this context is composed of both dividends and any appreciation (or depreciation) in the market value of the shares held.

I know that there are some mutual fund salesmen who will tell you not to worry about what happens in down markets because the major trend is up. The trouble is that every now and then stock markets have a habit of suffering fairly sharp setbacks and may not recover their former highs for a considerable period of time. And often investors are forced to sell during such a bear market because they need money and can't get it from the bank. It may be true that eventually their stocks will recover again, but that will be small consolation to them because other investors will be holding them.

Thus few, if any, investors can fail to be concerned with the downside risk of their investments. And because downside risk is so universally distasteful, investors who hold portfolios of riskier shares whose price swings are wider must be and actually are compensated with a somewhat higher long-run return.

The differences that exist in mutual fund returns can be explained almost entirely by differences in the risk they have taken. The chart on the following page illustrates this relationship over the 1957–72 period for a representative group of mutual funds.

Risk is measured by the relative sensitivity of the fund's performance to swings in the general market. A volatility number of 1.2 suggests that the fund was 1.2 times as volatile as the market index—it tended to fluctuate about 20 percent more than the market. This relative volatility index also goes by the name "beta" and is explained more fully in the fol-

Rate of Return (%)

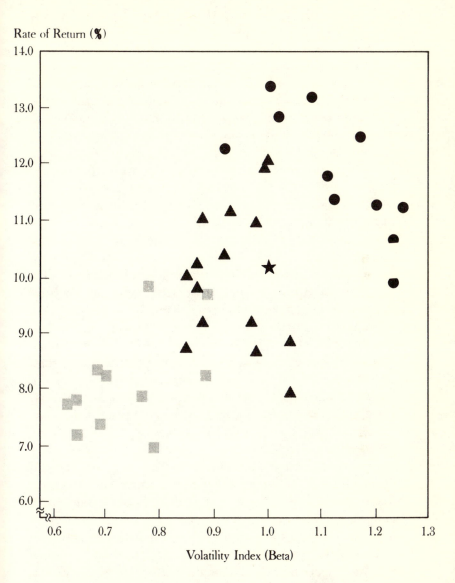

Volatility Index (Beta)

■ BALANCED INCOME FUND ▲ GROWTH AND INCOME FUND ● GROWTH FUND
★ STANDARD AND POOR'S 500-STOCK INDEX

Performance of Selected Mutual Funds: 1957–1972

lowing chapter. A fund that tends to do very well when the market goes up but falls out of bed when the market falters gets a high risk rating. A fund with more stable returns from year to year gets a low risk rating. The chart also shows the rate of return for the market as measured by the Standard & Poor's (S&P) 500 Stock Index, which by definition gets a volatility rating of one.

The chart shows that by and large the riskiest funds—the growth-oriented ones—have had the largest average return. But these are also the funds whose annual returns were most volatile and that fell most sharply when the market turned sour. The safest funds—those balanced with high-quality bonds—tended to have the lowest but most stable returns. To be sure, over the whole period (including up and down markets) the growth funds outdistanced their safer counterparts and even tended to do better than a broad stock-market average. But this was not a matter of skill—added risk was the price of that performance. Randomly selected portfolios of riskier stocks also tended to outdistance the market. Indeed, you could have bought the stocks making up the market average (say the Dow-Jones thirty industrials) on margin (that is, borrowing some of the funds needed to pay for the purchase) and increased both your return and your risk.

This last point is sufficiently important and so little understood—even by some market professionals—that I would like to provide an example of how this can be accomplished. Suppose that, on *average,* the return in the market—counting both dividends and capital gains—is somewhere around 10 percent per year. (A massive computer study financed by the Merrill Foundation and done at the University of Chicago suggests this is not far from the mark over reasonably long time periods.) Now suppose you have $1,000 to invest. This means that in a *typical* year you would make about 10 percent and would end up with $1,100.

But what if you wanted a bit more action for your $1,000?

Just talk to your friendly broker and borrow an extra $1,000 at, say, 8 percent. (This is called buying on margin.) Now for your $1,000 investment (this is all you put up) you can buy $2,000 worth of stock; and in a typical year a 10 percent return will make your total portfolio grow to $2,200. At the end of this year you repay your broker the $1,080 you owe him (the borrowed $1,000 plus $80 interest) and you will have $1,120 ($2,200 minus $1,080). Through the magic of leverage you were able to increase the return on your $1,000 investment from 10 percent to 12 percent.

In general, leverage will tend to give you a larger average return. You will always increase your return if your borrowing rate is lower than what you earn on your investment. But if you get out your pencil and paper, you'll quickly see that in a year when the market doesn't do well you really can take a bath with your leveraged (and highly risky) investment stance. Leverage is a two-edged sword, which is exactly the point of the story. You were able to get a larger average return only by taking on more risk. There ain't no such thing as a free lunch. And don't let the mutual funds fool you. As the chart shows very clearly, the funds with the largest average returns also took on the most risk. If you held one of the supposedly better-performing but riskier funds, don't ascribe this to any genius on the fund manager's part. Your extra return was simply a just reward due you for bearing extra risk.

Can't Even Some of the Analysts Pick Some of the Winners?

The preceding paragraphs constitute rank heresy as far as Wall Street is concerned. My allegation that mutual funds generally do about the same as the market averages—with perhaps a bit of extra return for the particularly risky ones— flies in the face of its conventional (and convenient) wisdom.

Is there not a group of "performance-oriented" funds whose whole *raison d'être* is the achievement of above-average returns and which, by their own admission, have clearly achieved their goals? All right, let's now see if these are exceptions to the generally mediocre performance I reported for the industry at large.

PERFORMANCE INVESTING

I mentioned in Chapter Three that performance investing was a product of the 1960s and became especially prominent during the 1967–68 strong bull market. This was the period when money managers changed their image. The old Scrooge-type image of the fiduciary counting his golden sovereigns with meticulous care and probity was out. Capital preservation gave way to capital productivity. The key word was "performance" and the financial press reported at frequent intervals the latest rank-ordered performance results for the funds, just like the daily horse-race results.

The fund managers who turned in the best results for the period were written up like sports celebrities in both the popular and professional organs. New public money no longer flowed to the old-line names in the fund game—only the new breed of money managers really did well in attracting new investments.

The star system had come to Wall Street. Everyone wanted to hitch his wagon to a SuperAnalyst—and Wall Street listened and brought forth well over a hundred new funds. Their names were reminiscent of the days of the South Sea Bubble: Explorer, Vanguard, Viking, Magellan, Polaris, and even New Era. But as one fund manager put it to a new salesman, "We aren't selling mutual funds, we're selling dreams," and those are the names on which dreams are dreamed. For a while it all worked. When the performance polls were published in 1967 and 1968, the go-gos

with their youthful gunslingers as managers were right at
the top of the pack, outgunning all the competition by a
wide margin.

SOME TRICKS OF THE TRADE

How did the performance funds do it? By doing what comes
naturally, of course. When the market is going up and you
hold a portfolio of very risky (defined as very volatile) stocks,
it follows that your portfolio can be expected to go up substantially more than the market. When the bulls are in command, risk can easily be forgotten. Thus it was that the performance-fund manager was honored and even believed in
his own glory. After all, it was far easier to persuade himself
that the big gains were the result of financial acumen than
to admit they were the normal concomitant of holding volatile stocks in a rising market.

Self-delusion is a very human failing, but some fund managers indulged in practices that could not be so easily par-
doned. These were the use of so-called "letter stock" and the
buying up of large positions in very small and thinly capitalized companies. Such devices were among the unhealthiest
developments of the performance era.

"Letter" or "restricted" stock is stock whose sale is subject to several restrictions, generally because it has not been
registered with the Securities and Exchange Commission.
This means that there is no prospectus to tell about the
company's business, past record, etc. While unregistered stock
may not be sold publicly, it may be sold privately. The buyer
is required to sign an "investment letter" pledging that he
bought the stock for investment purposes and indicating that
he anticipates hanging onto the shares for a considerable
period of time. Hence the name letter stock.

Companies often sold letter stock to large funds because
it was a way of raising money quickly and of avoiding certain

disclosures required by the SEC. The funds bought such stock at discounts of 20 percent to 50 percent. Now watch carefully for the trick. Suppose that a fund buys some letter stock at $50 per share, while the market price is $100. When the fund makes its next report, it might write the value of the stock to $75. Result: instant performance. On the next report, performance can be maintained simply by writing up the value even higher. Who cares if the stock is not readily marketable, as long as it boosts performance? Very few cared in the late 1960s.

Another performance trick involved the purchase of substantial blocks in companies with relatively few shares outstanding. The market for many of these issues was so thin (so few shares were available for trading) that a fund willing to take a big position could make the price almost anything it wished. It may be that in the long run these companies do, in fact, produce a higher return than the blue chips. (They should, because they are riskier.) But the funds interested in immediate performance were more concerned with what happened to the price in the short run when the next performance poll would be published. The better the record, the easier it was to sell new shares in the fund, and the more money would be available to buy up other small companies. Small wonder that many funds playing this game opened themselves to charges of market manipulation.

No one seemed to worry that these blocks of stock were not easily salable. But what would happen if the fund had to sell some of these shares—perhaps to meet redemptions during less favorable times? I am reminded of the classic story of the broker who suggested that his client, Sam, invest in some shares of a thinly capitalized company selling at fifty cents a share. Sam bought up several hundred shares, after which his friendly broker informed him that the price was now $1.00. "Excellent," Sam exclaimed, "buy more." Dutifully the broker executed his order and reported back that the price was now $1.50. "Fine," exclaimed our performance in-

vestor, "sell all my holdings." "Sure, Sam," the broker replied quizzically, "but to whom?"

RISK HAS ITS PENALTY

The game ended unceremoniously with the bear market that
commenced in 1969 and continued until 1971. The go-go
funds suddenly went into reverse. It was fly now and pay
later, for the performance funds with their portfolios of volatile stocks were no exception to the financial law of gravity.
They went down just as sharply as they had gone up. The
new breed of SuperAnalysts got clobbered in the 1969–71
period, as the fall of the performance funds was substantially
sharper than for the averages as a whole. Perhaps the most
dramatic way of describing the debacle is with the aid of the
following table showing the rankings of the top funds in
1968 and their disastrous performance in the ensuing years.

The Mates Fund led the pack in 1968, with a gain of
153.48 percent. (What performance!) Its net value, however,
had to be calculated as of the close of business on December 19. On December 20, Mates temporarily stopped redeem-
ing its shares and calculating their value. Twenty percent
of Mates Fund was invested in thinly capitalized Omega Securities when the SEC announced the untimely suspension of
trading in Omega (while it investigated for hanky-panky).

At the end of 1973, the Mates Fund sold at about one-tenth
of its 1968 value. Beware the mutual fund salesman who tries
to build up your dreams by selling you the fund with the
best recent performance! So many dreams have turned into
nightmares that performance investing is now a dirty word
on Wall Street.

There is an interesting footnote to the Mates story. In
1974, Mates threw in the towel and left the investment community to enter a business catering to a new fad. In New York
City he started a singles' bar appropriately named "Mates."
At Mates' place women were encouraged to approach men

Some Results of the Performance Derby

1968 Rank	Fund	1969 Rank **	1970 Rank **	1971 Rank **	1972 Rank **	1973 Rank **	1968 Net Asset Value * Per Share	1973 Net Asset Value Per Share
1	Mates Investment Fund	312	424	512	465	531	15.51	1.61
2	Neuwirth Fund	263	360	104	477	397	15.29	8.01
3	Gibraltar Growth Fund (4)	172	456	481			17.27	
4	Insurance Investors Fund (1)	77	106	317	417	224	7.45	10.50
5	Pennsylvania Mutual	333	459	480	486	519	11.92	2.02
6	Puerto Rican Investors Fund	30	308	387	435		19.34	
7	Crown Western-Dallas	283	438	207	244	380	13.86	5.70
8	Franklin Dynatech Series	342	363	112	120	453	14.47	6.95
9	First Participating Fund (2)	49	283	106	27	220	19.25	19.51
10	Connecticut Western Mutual Fund (3)	5	202				127.27	
11	Enterprise Fund	334	397	133	364	250	11.88	5.70
12	Ivy Fund	357	293	233	161	312	12.37	6.93
13	Century Shares Trust	120	55	62	62	127	13.09	13.39
14	Mutual Shares Corporation	284	272	152	452	62	22.18	14.81
15	Putnam Equities Fund	376	384	45	54	354	17.05	8.39
16	Financial Industrial Income Fund	244	222	277	231	35	8.40	5.83
17	Consumers Investment (4)	354						
18	Columbia Growth Fund	33	322	27	370	332	14.23	11.88
19	Templeton Growth Fund	1	241	163	1	81	4.00	7.33
20	Schuster Fund	129	231	253	425	445	12.29	7.40

(1) Insurance Investors Fund is now First Sierra Fund.
(2) First Participating Fund is now American General Growth Fund.
(3) Connecticut Western is now Channing Bond Fund, which is no longer surveyed by Lipper.
(4) No longer surveyed by Lipper.
* The net asset values for 1968 have been adjusted for all subsequent splits.
** Out of 381 funds surveyed in 1969; 463 in 1970; 526 in 1971; 537 in 1972; 536 in 1973.

Source: Arthur Lipper Corporation

rather than the other way around, and "liberated aggressive females" could feel free to "do their own thing." According to preliminary reports, Mates' success in the barroom business was little better than his more recent record in the market. When a reporter visited the bar on a Friday night soon after it opened he could find only Mates, a bartender, and a single customer.

Is There Anything Good to Be Said about Professional Investment Management?

Professionally managed mutual fund portfolios do not, on average, appear to perform any better than broad unmanaged indices of securities. While larger returns have been realized by investment funds specializing in riskier portfolios, the same is true of the returns from randomly selected portfolios of riskier stocks. It's true that a few funds have outperformed random portfolios with equivalent risk, but the number of funds with above-average records is no larger than might be attributed to chance.

In any activity in which large numbers of people are engaged, while the average is likely to predominate, the unexpected is bound to happen. The very small number of really good performers we find in the investment management business is not at all inconsistent with the laws of chance. Indeed, as I mentioned earlier, the fact that good past performance of a mutual fund is no help whatever in predicting future performance only serves to emphasize this point. The preceding table shows just how inconsistent fund performance can be.

Perhaps the laws of chance should be illustrated. Let's engage in a coin-tossing contest. Those who can consistently flip heads will be declared winners. The contest begins and 1,000 contestants flip coins. Just as would be expected by chance, 500 of them flip heads and these winners are allowed to advance to the second stage of the contest and flip again.

As might be expected, 250 flip heads. Operating under the laws of chance, there will be 125 winners in the third round, 63 on the fourth, 31 on the fifth, 16 on the sixth, and 8 on the seventh.

By this time, crowds start to gather to witness the surprising ability of these expert coin-tossers. The winners are overwhelmed with adulation. They are celebrated as geniuses in the art of coin-tossing—their biographies are written and people urgently seek their advice. After all, there were 1,000 contestants and only 8 could consistently flip heads. The game continues and there are even those who eventually flip heads nine and ten times in a row.* The point of this analogy is not to indicate that investment fund managers can or should make their decisions by flipping coins, but that the laws of chance do operate and they can explain some amazing success stories.

Some readers will complain that I am being unfair in using the performance of mutual funds to generalize about the quality of investment management. After all, mutual funds labor under some very severe handicaps. Many are so large that when they try to buy a position in a security the very activity of their purchase tends to move the price against them.

For example, I sit on the finance committee of a fund with assets of approximately $2½ billion. Whenever this fund tries to accumulate a position in a security it must anticipate that it may sometimes move the price of that security several points before its transaction is completed.

Some funds are also often forced to sell during market panics when redemptions are high. At such times the market is likely to be disorganized and large blocks of securities can be sold only at substantial discounts. Other readers may point out that mutual funds account for only about 20 percent of

---

* If we had let the losers continue to play (as mutual fund managers do, even after a bad year) we would have found several more contestants who flipped eight or nine heads out of ten and were therefore regarded as expert tossers.

the stock holdings of institutional investors, and that it may not be fair to say their performance is typical of all professionals.

Academic researchers, curious souls that they are, have also examined the performance of many other professional investors. The records of life insurance companies, property and casualty insurance companies, foundations, college endowments, state and local trust funds, personal trusts administered by banks, and individual discretionary accounts handled by investment advisors have all been studied, though not in nearly the same detail as mutual funds. This research suggests that there are no sizable differences in the investment performance of any of these professional investors or between the investment performance of these groups and that of the market as a whole. *No scientific evidence has yet been assembled to indicate that the investment performance of professionally managed portfolios as a group has been any better than that of randomly selected portfolios.*

Are there exceptions to this general rule? Of course there are. As I noted earlier, a few mutual funds have enjoyed outstanding long-run records. But many more had outstanding records through 1968.

The record of one major investment advisory service has, over a recent seven-year period, proved superior to random selection. But this service's longer-run record is only mediocre and it remains to be seen if it can beat the averages consistently in the future.

Another well-publicized success story concerns one of the major New York banks, which began a contest in early 1970, asking thirty-four brokerage firms to manage a fictitious $100 million common-stock portfolio. At the end of 1972 the average performance of the thirty-four contestants was considerably better than the Standard & Poor's index. Again, the time period is very short and the performance on paper should not be taken as a yardstick in the real world, where the attempt to purchase or sell substantial blocks of stock can have a large impact on the market price.

Isolated instances of success should not a SuperAnalyst make. As we examine more and more types of professional investors, we should expect more and more exceptions. So long as there are averages, some people will beat them. With large numbers of players in the money game, chance will—and does—explain some super performance records.

The very great publicity given occasional success in stock selection reminds me of the famous story of the doctor who claimed he had developed a cure for cancer in chickens. He proudly announced that in 33 percent of the cases tested remarkable improvement was noted. In another third of the cases, he admitted, there seemed to be no change in condition. He then rather sheepishly added, "And I'm afraid the third chicken ran away."

The Broad Form of the Random-Walk Theory

The academic world has rendered its judgment: Fundamental analysis is no more effective than technical analysis in beating the market. Security analysts may have difficulty perceiving the future, but we must readily concede that they are very good at interpreting whatever new information does become available and acting on it quickly. This is the fundamental problem preventing SuperAnalyst from beating the market. Information is disseminated too rapidly today, and it gets reflected almost immediately in market prices. By reacting so quickly, the analysts make it extremely difficult to realize a significant profit in the stock market on the basis of fundamental analysis.*

---

* It might actually be very inconvenient for SuperAnalyst if it could be shown that he did make above-average returns. This would imply that some other group (presumably the public) was earning below-average returns. Think of the reformers who would press to restrict SuperAnalyst's activities so as to protect the public.

Professor Samuelson sums up the situation as follows:

> If intelligent people are constantly shopping around for good value, selling those stocks they think will turn out to be overvalued and buying those they expect are now undervalued, the result of this action by intelligent investors will be to have existing stock prices already have discounted in them an allowance for their future prospects. Hence, to the passive investor, who does not himself search out for under- and overvalued situations, there will be presented a pattern of stock prices that makes one stock about as good or bad a buy as another. To that passive investor, chance alone would be as good a method of selection as anything else.

This is the broad form of the random-walk theory. The narrow form of the theory said that technical analysis—looking at past stock prices—could not help investors. The broad form states that fundamental analysis is not helpful either. It says that all that is known concerning the expected growth of the company's earnings and dividends, all of the possible favorable and unfavorable developments affecting the company that might be studied by the fundamental analyst, are already reflected in the price of the company's stock. Thus throwing darts at the financial page will produce a portfolio that can be expected to do as well as any managed by professional security analysts. In a nutshell, the broad form of the random-walk theory states:

> Fundamental analysis of publicly available information cannot produce investment recommendations that will enable an investor consistently to outperform a buy-and-hold strategy in managing a portfolio.

The random-walk theory does not, as some critics have proclaimed, state that stock prices move aimlessly and erratically and are insensitive to changes in fundamental information. On the contrary, the point of the random-walk theory is just the opposite: The market is so efficient—prices move so quickly when new information does arise—that no one can consistently buy or sell quickly enough to benefit. Indeed, the growing power and quickness of SuperAnalyst will help fulfill the random-walk theory by insuring that current prices reflect all known information. This theory believes that a random guess will enable you to predict the next market move with the same (or higher) degree of accuracy as the estimate provided through either technical or fundamental analysis. Needless to say, it is not popular in the brokerage houses.

The random-walk theory does recognize, however, that it is possible for insiders acting on the basis of information about an important mineral strike to make profits at the expense of public investors not privy to that information. Such things happened in the past with too much frequency. But Texas Gulf Sulphur situations, where insiders allegedly profited from news of mineral discoveries at the expense of the public, are now less likely to occur than in the past.

In recent years, the Securities Exchange Commission has taken an increasingly tough stand against anyone profiting from information not generally available to the public. The SEC has put the investment community on notice that corporate officials and anyone else acting on material nonpublic information do so at their own peril. More recently it has extended this warning to *any* investor acting on this information, even if he hears about it thirdhand—such as through his broker. It is small wonder that many a company president who thinks he has told a visiting security analyst some relevant piece of information he has not made available to others will immediately issue a public press release to rectify the situation.

Thus tightened rules on disclosure make time lags in the dissemination of new information much shorter than they may have been in previous years. Of course, the more quickly information is disseminated to the public at large, the more closely the market may be expected to conform to the random-walk model.

While the random-walk theory does recognize the potential disruptiveness of inside information, it does not consider this to be of crucial importance. Corporate insiders are so often wrong that it hardly seems worth the legal risk involved to try to act on inside information. Many professional investors would agree. Wall Street's legendary Armand Erpf was fond of citing a statement by Talleyrand that he had managed to lose a fortune by never speculating except on inside information. Bernard Baruch echoed this thought: "Given time, I believe that inside information can break the Bank of England or the U.S. Treasury."

A Personal Viewpoint

Just to show how truly contrary a former analyst turned academic can be, I am now going to present my personal thoughts. But first, let's briefly recap the diametrically opposed viewpoints. The view of many of the managers themselves is that professionals have almost supernatural powers—they are all-knowing, all-powerful, and can certainly outperform all amateur and casual investors in managing money. Much of the academic community believes that professionally managed investment portfolios cannot outperform randomly selected portfolios of stocks with equivalent risk characteristics. Random walkers claim that the stock market adjusts so quickly and perfectly to new information that amateurs buying at current prices can do just as well as the pros. Thus the value of professional investment advice is nil—at least insofar as it concerns choosing a stock portfolio.

I walk a middle road. While I believe that investors must reconsider their faith in SuperAnalyst, I am not as ready as many of my academic colleagues to damn the entire field. I mentioned earlier that most of the evidence we have now

concerns large funds, which operate under a variety of constraints. While it is true that there seems to be no difference
in the performance of large and small funds, I still think it
is necessary to round out the statistical picture with more evidence on many different kinds of investors.

I am also cautious because the random-walk theory rests
on several fragile assumptions. The first is that there is perfect pricing in the market. As the quote from Paul Samuelson
indicates, the random-walk theory holds that at any time
stocks sell at the best estimates of their intrinsic values. Thus
uninformed investors buying at today's structure of prices are
really getting full value for their money, whatever securities
they purchase.

The problem is that this line of reasoning is uncomfortably close to that used by proponents of the greater-fool
theory. We have seen ample evidence in earlier chapters that
stocks sometimes do not sell on the basis of anyone's estimate
of value (as hard as this is to measure) but are often swept up
in waves of frenzy. To be sure, the market pros as a group
do not seem to have the ability to recognize such periods of
speculative excess or the independence and courage to take a
contrary course. Professional managers were largely responsible for three major speculative waves of the 1960s and for
more recent instances such as the Levitz furniture roller-
coaster of 1972–73. But the existence of these broader influences on market prices at least raises the possibility that
investors might not want to accept the current tableau of
market prices as being the best reflection of intrinsic values.

There are other assumptions behind the random-walk
theory that can also be questioned. News does not travel
instantaneously, as the random walkers suggest, and I doubt
that there will ever be a time in the future when all useful
inside information is immediately disclosed to all. Moreover,
the random-walk theory implies that no one possesses monop-
olistic power over the market and that stock recommendations
based on unfounded beliefs do not lead to large buying.

Neither assumption is more than approximated in today's markets. Brokerage firms specializing in research services to institutions wield enormous power in the market and can direct tremendous money flows in and out of stocks. Many speculators (and indeed even fund managers) will rush to buy and sell a stock simply because they believe a large firm is about to recommend some action on it. In this environment it is quite possible that erroneous beliefs about a stock by some professionals can for a considerable time be self-fulfilling.

Finally, there is the enormous difficulty of translating known information about a stock into estimates of true value. We have seen that the major determinants of a stock's value concern the extent and duration of its growth path far into the future. Both the estimation of the growth path from known information and the translation of the growth path into a value estimate require art as much as science. In such an environment there is considerable scope for an individual to exercise superior intellect and judgment to turn in superior performance.

But while I believe in the possibility of superior professional investment performance, I must emphasize that the evidence we have thus far does not support the view that such competence in fact exists; and while I may be excommunicated from some academic sects because of my only lukewarm endorsement of the random walk, I make no effort to disguise my heresy in the financial church. It is clear that if there are exceptional financial managers they are very rare. This is a fact of life with which both individual and institutional investors will have to deal. Precisely how investors should adjust to these realities is the subject of Part Three.

CHAPTER EIGHT

What Every Intelligent Investor Ought to Know about Beta

. . . Practical men, who believe themselves to be quite exempt from any intellectual influence, are usually the slaves of some defunct economist. Madmen in authority, who hear voices in the air, are distilling their frenzy from some academic scribbler of a few years back.—J. M. Keynes, *General Theory of Employment, Interest, and Money*

Throughout this book, I have attempted to explain the theories used by professionals—simplified as the Firm Foundation and Castle in the Air Theories—to predict the valuation of stocks. As we have seen, many academics have earned their reputations by attacking these theories. While not denying that these theories tell us a good deal about how stocks are valued, the academics maintain that they cannot be relied upon to yield extraordinary profits.

As graduate schools continued to grind out bright young economists and statisticians, the attacking academics became so numerous that it seemed obvious—even to them—that a new strategy was needed. Ergo, the academic community busily went about erecting its own theories of stock market valuation.

This chapter deals with these theories. Being an academic, my biased viewpoint is that they are important and that every intelligent investor should be acquainted with them. So, sit down in a straightbacked chair, prop your eyelids open, and read on. The kinds of questions I want to consider are why investors need to diversify their holdings among several securities, and how a model of portfolio selection can aid them. Following that, I will explain the implications this work has for security pricing. Specifically, I will describe the "theory of capital-asset pricing" and elaborate on the thesis of this book that extra returns can be obtained only by assuming more risks.

There is a lot to do in this chapter, and necessarily the discussion must be a bit more formal than in previous pages. The patient reader will be rewarded, however, with an understanding of a good deal of modern financial theory and of what lies behind the specific prescriptions for investment strategy contained in Part Three.

Getting Down to Basics

We academics were faced with a very basic question: if technical (Castle in the Air) and fundamental (Firm Foundation) analysis are not the keys to higher investment returns, what is? I have already touched upon our answer: risk. As the Scottish poet Alexander Smith so aptly put it, "Everything is sweetened by risk." From the academic point of view, stocks (and bonds as well) are no exception.

Risk is a most slippery and elusive concept. It's hard for investors—let alone economists—to agree on a precise definition. The American Heritage Dictionary defines risk as the possibility of suffering harm or loss. If I buy one-year Treasury bills to yield 7.5 percent and hold them until they mature, I am virtually certain of earning a 7.5 percent return. The possibility of loss is so small as to be considered nonexistent. But if I hold common stock in my local power and light company for one year on the basis of an anticipated 10 percent dividend return, the possibility of loss increases. The dividend of the company might be cut and, more important, the market price at the end of the year could be much lower, so that I might suffer a serious net loss. Risk is the chance that expected security returns will not materialize and, in particular, that the stocks you hold will fall in price.

Once academics accepted the idea that risk for investors is related to the chance of disappointment in achieving expected security returns, a natural measure suggested itself—the probable variability or dispersion of future returns. Thus, financial risk has generally been defined as the variance or standard deviation of returns. Being long-winded, we use the accompanying exhibit to illustrate what we mean. A security whose returns are not likely to depart much, if at all, from its average (or expected) return is said to carry little or no risk. A security whose returns from year to year are likely to be quite volatile (and for which sharp losses are typical in some years) is said to be risky.

Exhibit

EXPECTED RETURN AND VARIANCE:
MEASURES OF REWARD AND RISK

This simple example will illustrate the concept of expected return and variance and how they are measured. Suppose you buy a stock from which you expect the following overall returns (including both dividends and price changes) under different economic conditions:

Business Conditions	Probability of Occurrence	Expected Return
Normal economic conditions	1 chance in 3	10 percent
Rapid real growth	1 chance in 3	30 percent
Recession with inflation (Stagflation)	1 chance in 3	−10 percent

If, on average, a third of past years have been "normal," another third characterized by rapid growth, and the remaining third characterized by "stagflation," it might be reasonable to take these relative frequencies of past events and treat them as our best guesses (probabilities) of the likelihood of future business conditions. We could then say that an investor's *expected return* is 10 percent. A third of the time the investor gets 30 percent, another third 10 percent, and the rest of the time he suffers a 10 percent loss. This means that, *on average,* his yearly return will turn out to be 10 percent.

$$\text{Expected Return} = \tfrac{1}{3}(.30) + \tfrac{1}{3}(.10) + \tfrac{1}{3}(-.10) = .10$$

The yearly returns will be quite variable, however, ranging from a 30 percent gain to a 10 percent loss. The "variance" is a measure of the dispersion of returns. It is defined as the average squared deviation of each possible return from its average (or expected) value, which we just saw was 10 percent.

$$\begin{aligned} \text{Variance} &= \tfrac{1}{3}(.30-.10)^2 + \tfrac{1}{3}(.10-.10)^2 + \tfrac{1}{3}(-.10-.10)^2 \\ &= \tfrac{1}{3}(.20)^2 + \tfrac{1}{3}(.00)^2 + \tfrac{1}{3}(-.20)^2 = .0267 \end{aligned}$$

The square root of the variance is called the *standard deviation*. In this example, the standard deviation equals .0517.

———————

Dispersion measures of risk such as variance and standard deviation have failed to satisfy everyone. "Surely riskiness is not related to variance itself" the critics say. "If the dispersion results from happy surprises—that is, from outcomes turning out better than expected, no investors in their right minds would call that risk."

It is, of course, quite true that only the possibility of downward disappointments constitutes risk. Nevertheless, as a practical matter, as long as the distribution of returns is symmetric—that is, as long as the chances of extraordinary gain are roughly the same as the probabilities for disappointing returns and losses—a dispersion or variance measure will suffice as a risk measure. The greater the dispersion or variance, the greater the possibilities for disappointment.

While the pattern of historical returns from individual securities has not usually been symmetric, the returns from well-diversified portfolios of stocks do seem to be distributed approximately symmetrically. The following chart shows the twenty-five year distribution of monthly security returns for a portfolio consisting of equal dollar amounts invested in 100 stocks. It was constructed by dividing the range of returns into equal intervals (of approximately $1\frac{1}{4}$ percent) and then noting the frequency (the number of months) with which the returns fell within each interval. On average the portfolio returned about 0.9 percent per month or 10.7 percent per year. In periods when the market declined sharply, however, the portfolio also plunged losing as much as 13 percent in a single month.

For symmetric distributions such as this one, a helpful rule of thumb is that two-thirds of the monthly returns tend to fall within one standard deviation of the average return and 95 percent of the returns fall within two standard deviations. Recall that the average return for this distribution was just under 1 percent per month. The standard deviation (our measure of portfolio risk) turns out to be about $4\frac{1}{2}$ percent per month. Thus, in two-thirds of the months the returns from this portfolio were between $5\frac{1}{2}$ percent and minus $3\frac{1}{2}$ percent, and 95 percent of the returns were between 10 and —8 percent. Obviously, the higher the standard deviation (the more spread out are the returns), the more prob-

Distribution of Monthly Returns for a 100-Security
Portfolio January 1945–June 1970

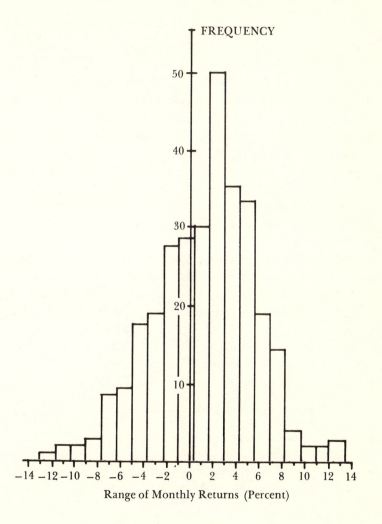

Range of Monthly Returns (Percent)

Source: Modigliani and Pogue, "An Introduction to Risk and Return," *Financial Analysts Journal*, March–April, 1974.

able it is (the greater the risk) that at least in some periods
you will take a real bath in the market. That's why a measure
of variability such as standard deviation * is so often used
and justified as an indication of risk.

Portfolio Theory

Portfolio theory begins with the premise that all investors
are like my wife—they are risk-averse. They want high returns
and guaranteed outcomes. The theory tells investors how to
combine stocks in their portfolios to give them the least risk
possible, consistent with the return they seek. It also gives a
rigorous mathematical justification for the time-honored investment maxim that diversification is a sensible strategy for
individuals who like to reduce their risks.

The theory was invented in the 1950s by Harry Markowitz.
His book, *Portfolio Selection,* was an outgrowth of his Ph.D.
dissertation at the University of Chicago. Markowitz is a
scholarly academic "computenick" type with a most varied
background. His experience has ranged from teaching at
UCLA to designing a computer language at RAND Corporation and helping General Electric solve manufacturing problems by computer simulations. He has even practiced money
management, serving as president of Arbitrage Management
Company, which ran a "hedge fund."** What Markowitz

* Standard deviation or its square, the variance, are used interchange-
ably as risk measures. They both do the same thing and it's purely a
matter of convenience which one we use.

** Basically what Markowitz did was to search with the computer for
situations where a convertible bond sold at a price that was "out of
line" with the underlying common stock. He admitted, however, that
it was "no great trick" and that competitors would be joining him in
increasing numbers. "Then when we start tripping over each other,
buying the same bonds almost simultaneously, the game will be over.
Two, three years at most." I spoke to Harry in the summer of 1974 and
he admitted that convertible hedges were no longer attractive in the

discovered was that portfolios of risky (volatile) stocks might be put together in such a way that the portfolio as a whole would actually be less risky than any one of the individual stocks in it.

The mathematics of portfolio theory is recondite and forbidding; it fills the journals and, incidentally, keeps a lot of academics busy. That in itself is no small accomplishment. Fortunately, there is no need to lead you through the labyrinth of quadratic programming to understand the core of the theory. A single illustration will make the whole game clear.

Let's suppose we have an island economy with only two businesses. The first is a large resort with beaches, tennis courts, a golf course, and the like. The second is a manufacturer of umbrellas. Weather affects the fortunes of both. During sunny seasons the resort does a booming business and umbrella sales plummet. During rainy seasons the resort owner does very poorly, while the umbrella manufacturer enjoys high sales and large profits. The following table shows some hypothetical returns for the two businesses during the different seasons:

	Umbrella Manufacturer	*Resort Owner*
Rainy Season	50%	−25%
Sunny Season	−25%	50%

Suppose that, on average, one-half the seasons are sunny and one-half are rainy, (i.e., the probability of a sunny or rainy season is ½). An investor who bought stock in the umbrella manufacturer would find that half the time he earned a 50 percent return and half the time he lost 25 percent of his investment. On average, he would earn a return of 12½ percent. This is what we have called the investor's

_____

market. Consequently, he had moved on to do hedging operations on the newly formed Chicago Board Options Exchange.

expected return. Similarly, investment in the resort would produce the same results. Investing in either one of these businesses would be fairly risky, however, because the results are quite variable and there could be several sunny or rainy seasons in a row.

Suppose, however, that instead of buying only one security an investor with two dollars diversified and put half his money in the umbrella manufacturer's and half in the resort owner's business. In sunny seasons, a one-dollar investment in the resort would produce a fifty-cent return, while a one-dollar investment in the umbrella manufacturer would lose 25 cents. The investor's total return would be 25 cents (50 cents minus 25 cents), which is 12½ percent of his total investment of two dollars.

Note that during rainy seasons exactly the same thing happens—only the names are changed. Investment in the umbrella manufacturer produces a good 50 percent return while the investment in the resort loses 25 percent. Again, however, the diversized investor makes a 12½ percent return on his total investment.

This simple illustration points out the basic advantage of diversification. Whatever happens to the weather, and thus to the island economy, by diversifying investments over both of the firms an investor is sure of making a 12½ percent return each year. The trick that made the game work was that while both companies were risky (returns were variable from year to year), the companies were affected differently by weather conditions. (In statistical terms, the two companies had a negative covariance).* As long as there is some lack of

---

* Statisticians use the term *covariance* to measure what I have called the degree of parallelism between the returns of the two securities. If we let R stand for the actual return from the resort and R̄ be the expected or average return, while U stands for the actual return from the umbrella manufacturer and Ū is the average return, we define the covariance between U and R (or COV_{UR}) as follows:

parallelism in the fortunes of the individual companies in the economy, diversification will always reduce risk. In the present case, where there is a perfect negative relationship between the companies' fortunes (one always does well when the other does poorly), diversification can totally eliminate risk.

Of course, there is always a rub, and the rub in this case is that the fortunes of most companies move pretty much in tandem. When there is a recession and people are unemployed, they may buy neither summer vacations nor umbrellas. Therefore, one should not expect in practice to get the neat kind of total risk elimination just shown. Nevertheless, since company fortunes don't always move completely in parallel, investment in a diversified portfolio of stocks is likely to be less risky than investment in one or two single securities.

It is easy to carry the lessons of this illustration to actual portfolio construction. Suppose you were considering combining General Motors and its major supplier of new tires in a stock portfolio. Would diversification be likely to give you much risk reduction? Probably not. It may not be true that "as General Motors goes, so goes the nation" but it surely

---

$$\text{COV}_{UR} = \text{Prob. rain } (U, \text{ if rain} -\bar{U}) (R, \text{ if rain} -\bar{R}) + \text{prob. sun } (U, \text{ if sun} -\bar{U}) (R, \text{ if sun} -\bar{R}).$$

From the preceding table of returns and assumed probabilities we can fill in the relevant numbers:

$$\text{COV}_{UR} = \tfrac{1}{2}(.50-.125) (-.25-.125) + \tfrac{1}{2}(-.25-.125) (.50-.125) = -.141.$$

Whenever the returns from two securities move in tandem (when one goes up the other always goes up) the covariance number will be a large positive number. If the returns are completely out of phase, as in the present example, the two securities are said to have negative covariance.

does follow that if General Motors' sales slump, G.M. will be buying fewer new tires from the tire manufacturer. In general, diversification will not help much if there is a high covariance between the returns of the two companies.

On the other hand, if General Motors were combined with a government contractor in a depressed area, diversification might reduce risk substantially. It usually has been true that as the nation goes, so goes General Motors. If consumer spending is down (or if an oil crisis comes close to paralyzing the nation) General Motors' sales and earnings are likely to be down and the nation's level of unemployment up. Now, if the government makes a habit during times of high unemployment of giving out contracts to the depressed area (to alleviate some of the unemployment miseries there) it could well be that the returns of General Motors and those of the contractor do not move in phase. The two stocks might have very little or, better still, negative covariance.

The example may seem a bit strained, and most investors will realize that when the market gets clobbered just about all stocks go down. Still, at least at certain times, some stocks do move against the market. Gold stocks are often given as one example, and foreign stock markets may not always move in the same direction as our own. The point to realize in setting up a portfolio is that while the variability (variance) of the returns from individual stocks is important, even more important in judging the risk of a portfolio is covariance, the extent to which the securities move in parallel. It is this covariance that plays the critical role in Markowitz's portfolio theory.

True diversification depends on having stocks in your portfolio that are not all dependent on the same economic variables (consumer spending, business investment, housing construction, etc.). Wise investors will diversify their portfolios not by names or industries but by the determinants that influence the fluctuations of various securities.

Asset-Pricing Theory

Portfolio theory has important implications for how stocks are actually valued. If investors seek to reduce risk in anything like the manner Harry Markowitz described, the stock market will tend to reflect these risk-reducing activities. This brings us to what is called "capital-asset pricing theory," worked out by Stanford professor William Sharpe and others.

I've mentioned that the reason diversification cannot usually produce the miracle of risk elimination, as it did in my mythical island economy, is that usually stocks tend to move up and down together. Still, diversification is worthwhile—it can eliminate some risks. What Sharpe did was to focus directly on what part of a security's risk could be eliminated by diversification and what part couldn't.

Can you imagine any stockholder saying, "We can reasonably describe the total risk in any security (or portfolio) as the total variability (variance or standard deviation) of the returns from the security"? He'd probably scare away the few individual customers who are left. But we who teach are under no such constraints, and we say such things often. We go on to say that part of total risk or variability may be called the security's *systematic risk* and that this arises from the basic variability of stock prices in general and the tendency for all stocks to go along with the general market, at least to some extent. The remaining variability in a stock's returns is called *unsystematic risk* and results from factors peculiar to that particular company; for example, a strike, the discovery of a new product, and so on.

Systematic risk, also called market risk, captures the reaction of individual stocks (or portfolios) to general market swings. Some stocks and portfolios tend to be very sensitive to market movements. Others are more stable. This relative volatility or sensitivity to market moves can be estimated on the basis of the past record, and is popularly known by the Greek letter beta.

You are now about to learn all you ever wanted to know about beta but were afraid to ask. Despite the mathematical manipulations involved, the basic idea behind the beta measurement is one of putting some precise numbers on subjective feelings money managers have had for years. The beta calculation is essentially a comparison between the movements of an individual stock (or portfolio) and the movements of the market as a whole.

The calculation begins by assigning a beta of 1 to a broad market index, such as the NYSE index or the S&P 500. If a stock has a beta of 2, then on average it swings twice as far as the market. If the market goes up 10 percent, the stock rises 20 percent. If a stock has a beta of 0.5, it tends to be more stable than the market (it will go up or down 5 percent when the market rises or declines 10 percent.) Professionals often call high-beta stocks aggressive investments and label low beta stocks as defensive.

Now the important thing to realize is that *systematic risk cannot be eliminated by diversification*. It is precisely because all stocks move more or less in tandem (a large share of their variability is systematic) that even diversified stock portfolios are risky. Indeed, if you diversified perfectly by buying a share in the S&P index (which by definition has a beta of 1) you would still have quite variable (risky) returns because the market as a whole fluctuates widely.

Unsystematic risk is the variability in stock prices (and, therefore, in returns from stocks) that results from factors peculiar to an individual company. Receipt of a large new contract, the finding of mineral resources on the company's property, labor difficulties, the discovery that the corporation's treasurer has had his hand in the company till—all can make a stock's price move independently of the market. The risk associated with such variability is precisely the kind that diversification can reduce. The whole point of portfolio theory was that, to the extent stocks don't move in tandem all the time, variations in the returns from any one security will tend to be washed away or smoothed out by complementary variation in the returns from other securities.

The following diagram illustrates the important relationship between diversification and total risk. Suppose we randomly selected securities for our portfolio that tended on average to be just as volatile as the market. (The average betas for the securities in our portfolio will always be equal to 1.) The chart shows that as we add more and more securities the total risk of our portfolio declines, especially at the start.

How Diversification Reduces Risk

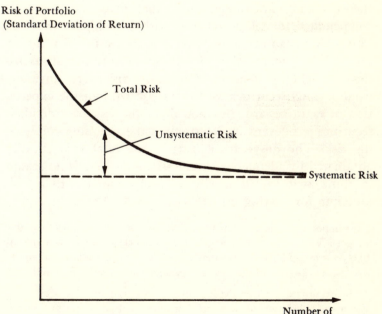

Source: Modigliani and Pogue, *op. cit.*

When ten securities are selected for our portfolio, a good deal of the unsystematic risk is eliminated and additional diversification yields little further risk reduction. By the time twenty securities are in the portfolio, the unsystematic part of risk is substantially eliminated and our portfolio (with a beta of 1) will tend to move up and down essentially in tandem with the market.* Of course, we could perform the same experiment with stocks whose average beta is $1\frac{1}{2}$. Again we would find that diversification quickly reduces unsystematic risk but that the remaining systematic risk would be larger. A portfolio of 20 or more stocks with an average beta of $1\frac{1}{2}$ would tend to be 50 percent more volatile than the market.

Now comes the key step in the argument. Both financial theorists and practitioners agree that investors should be compensated for taking on more risk by a higher expected return. Stock prices must therefore adjust to offer higher returns where more risk is perceived, to insure that all securities are held by someone. Obviously, risk-averse investors wouldn't buy securities with extra risk without the expectation of extra reward. But not all of the risk of individual securities is relevant in determining the premium for bearing risk. The unsystematic part of the total risk is easily eliminated by adequate diversification. So there is no reason to think that investors will be compensated with a risk premium for bearing unsystematic risk.** The only part of

* It's important that we draw the stocks for our portfolio to insure that we get a well-diversified selection. Twenty stocks drawn at random are likely to provide a portfolio that comes close to eliminating unsystematic risk, but twenty oil stocks will provide for less effective diversification.

** If investors did get an extra return (a risk premium) for bearing unsystematic risk, it would turn out that diversified portfolios made up of stocks with large amounts of unsystematic risk would give larger returns than equally risky portfolios of stocks with less unsystematic risk. In such a situation, investors looking for superior performances would bid up the prices of stocks with large unsystematic risk and sell stocks with equivalent betas but lower unsystematic risk. This would continue until total risk that investors will get paid for bearing is systematic risk, the risk that diversification cannot help. And since it's our old friend beta that measures systematic risk, capital-asset pricing theory says that returns (and, therefore, risk premiums) for any stock (or portfolio) will be related to beta, the measure of systematic risk.

The key relationship of the theory is shown in the following chart. As the systematic risk (beta) of an individual stock (or portfolio) increases, so does the return an investor can expect. If an investor's portfolio has a beta of zero, as might be the case if all his funds were invested in a bank savings cerificate (beta would be zero since the returns from the certificate would not vary at all with swings in the stock market), the investor would receive some modest rate of return, which is generally called the risk-free rate of interest. As the individual takes on more risk, however, the return should increase. If the investor holds a portfolio with a beta of 1 (as, for example, holding a share in one of the broad stock market averages) his return will equal the general return from common stocks. This return has over long periods of time exceeded the risk-free rate of interest, but the investment is a risky one. In certain periods the return is much less than the risk-free rate and involves taking substantial losses. This, as we have said, is precisely what is meant by risk.

The diagram shows that a number of different expected returns are possible simply by adjusting the beta of the portfolio. For example, suppose the investor put half of his money in a savings certificate and half in a share of the market averages. In this case he would receive a return midway between the risk-free return and the return from the market, and his portfolio would have an average beta of

the prospective returns of stocks with the same betas were equalized and no risk premium could be obtained for bearing unsystematic risk. Any other result would be inconsistent with the existence of efficient markets.

Risk and Return According to the Capital-Asset Pricing Theory *

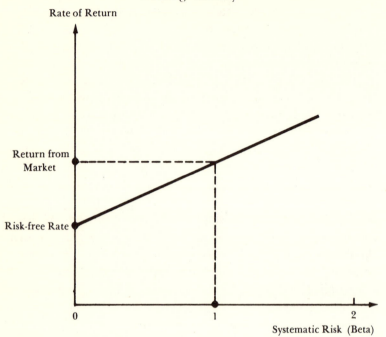

* Those who remember their high school algebra will recall that any straight line can be written as an equation. The equation for the straight line in the diagram is

Rate of Return = Risk-free Rate + Beta (Return from Market − Risk-free Rate)

Alternately, the equation can be written as an expression for the risk premium, that is, the rate of return on the portfolio or stock over and above the risk-free rate of interest.

Rate of Return − Risk-free Rate = Beta (Return from Market − Risk-free Rate)

The equation says that the risk premium you get on any stock or portfolio increases directly with the beta value you assume. Some readers may wonder what relationship beta has to the covariance concept that was so critical in our discussion of portfolio theory. The beta for any security is essentially the same thing as the covariance between that security and the market index as measured on the basis of past experience.

0.5.* The theory then asserts very simply that to get a higher average long-run rate of return you should just increase the beta of your portfolio. An investor can get a portfolio with a beta larger than 1 either by buying high-beta stocks or by purchasing a portfolio with average volatility on margin. (See the following illustration.) There was an actual fund proposed by a West Coast bank that would have allowed an investor to buy the S&P average on margin, thus increasing both his risk and potential reward. Of course, in times of rapidly declining stock prices, such a fund would have enabled an investor to lose his shirt in a hurry. This may explain why the fund found few customers.

Illustration of Portfolio Building *

Desired Beta	Composition of Portfolio	Expected Return From Portfolio
0	$1 in risk-free asset	8%
½	$.50 in risk-free asset, $.50 in market portfolio	$\frac{1}{2}(.08) + \frac{1}{2}(.11) = 9\frac{1}{2}\%$
1	$1 in market portfolio	11%
1½	$1.50 in market portfolio borrowing $.50 at an assumed rate of 8 percent	$1\frac{1}{2}(.11) - \frac{1}{2}(.08) = 12\frac{1}{2}\%$

* Assuming expected market return is 11 percent and risk-free rate is 8 percent.

Just as stocks had their fads, so beta came into high fashion by the early 1970s. The *Institutional Investor,* the glossy prestige magazine that spent most of its pages chronicling the accomplishments of professional money managers,

* In general, the beta of a portfolio is simply the weighted average of the betas of its component parts.

put its imprimatur on the movement in 1971 by featuring on its cover the letters BETA on top of a temple and including as its lead story "The Beta Cult! The New Way to Measure Risk." The magazine noted that money men whose mathematics hardly went beyond long division were now "tossing betas around with the abandon of Ph.D.s in statistical theory." Even the Securities and Exchange Commission gave beta its approval as a risk measure in its *Institutional Investor Study*.

In Wall Street the early beta fans boasted that they could earn higher long-run rates of return simply by buying a few high-beta stocks. Those who thought they were able to time the market thought they had an even better idea. They would buy high-beta stocks when they thought the market was going up, switching to low-beta ones when they feared the market might decline. To accommodate the enthusiasm for this new investment idea, beta measurement services proliferated among brokers, and it was a symbol of progressiveness for an investment house to provide its own beta estimates.* The beta boosters in "the street" oversold their product with an abandon that would have shocked even the most enthusiastic academic scribblers intent on spreading the beta gospel.

Is Beta All It's Cracked Up to Be?

In Shakespeare's *Henry IV*, Glendower boasted to Hotspur, "I can call spirits from the vasty deep." "Why, so can I, or so can any man," said Hotspur, unimpressed, "but will they

---

* Beta numbers are available from many brokers, including Merrill Lynch, Pierce, Fenner and Smith and the Value Line Investment Survey. The beta estimates are actually obtained by finding the slope of the linear relationship over many periods between the returns (including dividends and price changes) from each security and the returns from a market index.

come when you do call for them?" Anyone can theorize
about how security markets work, and the capital-asset pricing model is just another theory. The really important question is, "Does it work?"

Is beta a useful measure of risk? Do high-beta portfolios
always fall farther in bear markets than low-beta ones? Is it
always true that high-beta portfolios will, over the long pull,
provide larger overall returns than lower-beta-risk ones, as
the capital-asset pricing theory suggests? And does a beta
value calculated on the basis of past history really give you
any useful information about future betas? These are subjects of intense current debate among practitioners and academics, and all the evidence is not yet in. Nevertheless, the
tentative conclusion based on what we now know is encouraging.

One might well be skeptical about the wisdom of relying
on beta estimates based on historical data. Beta really looks
suspiciously like a tool of technical analysis in academic dress
—a bastard cousin of the chartists. Small wonder that many
Wall Streeters adopted a "show me" attitude toward the beta
gurus.

To illustrate the hazards in measuring an individual
stock's beta, consider the following example: During some
periods in the 1960s, Mead Johnson and Company (now part
of Bristol-Myers Company) had a measured beta that was
negative; it tended to move against the market, and thus appeared to be precisely the kind of stock investors would seek
to reduce the risks of their portfolio. But looking behind the
reasons for this measured beta's being less than zero did not
give one very much comfort that the beta for the future—
which is after all what is really relevant—would turn out to
be anything like the beta from the past.

What happened in the Mead Johnson case was that in
1962 the Company came out with a marvelous new product
that became an instant bestseller. The product, called "Metrecal," was a liquid dietary supplement. Consumers were urged

to have a can of Metrecal rather than their normal lunch. Metrecal would provide all the vitamins and nutrients needed for health with few of the calories that usually went along with lunch. And so, in 1962, as Americans became more diet-conscious, drinking Metrecal became quite a fad, and the earnings and stock price of Mead Johnson climbed sharply at precisely the time the stock market was taking one of its worst baths since the Great Depression.

Like most fads, the Metrecal boom did not last very long; by 1963 and 1964, just when the general stock market was recovering, Americans got pretty sick and tired of drinking Metrecal for lunch, and the big boost in earnings and stock prices that Mead Johnson had earlier enjoyed began to fade away.

Later in the 1960s, just about the time the market took another slump, Mead Johnson came out with another new product. This one was called "Nutrament." Nutrament was a dietary supplement that was supposed to put on weight, and skinny teenagers bought it by the case to improve their appearance. Yes, you guessed it! Nutrament was the same product as Metrecal except that if you drank Nutrament *in addition* to lunch you could put on weight, rather than lose it. Again, Mead Johnson prospered while the market slumped, and it is this unusual combination of circumstances that produced the negative betas of the period.

The problem is, of course, whether such a fortuitous string of events could reasonably be anticipated to occur in the future. On a priori grounds we would expect not. Indeed, what was in fact measured was anything but a systematic relationship with the market. Of course, this is precisely the problem in predicting betas on the basis of past experience.

The Mead Johnson example is not just an isolated case —the exception that proves the rule. Beta estimates for individual stocks are not very accurate, and that is one reason many professionals say nasty things about beta. The people who oversold beta as a useful tool in predicting the behavior of individual stocks did the beta cause a great disservice.

Thanks to the law of large numbers, however, a number of inaccurate beta estimates on individual stocks can be combined to form surprisingly accurate estimates of the risk of a portfolio. While the beta estimates for some securities will be much too high, the estimates for many others will be too low. The result is that the average beta in a well-defined portfolio is a good predictor of performance.

The proposition that betas for portfolios are stable over time has been subjected to considerable testing. The tests have usually constructed portfolios with certain beta values on the basis of past experience and then ascertained whether the subsequent volatility of the portfolio could have been predicted on the basis of the historical evidence. It turned out that future beta coefficients were remarkably well predicted on the basis of past experience for large portfolios (25 to 50 stocks) and less well predicted for very small portfolios and for individual securities.

Mutual-fund betas are not quite as easy to predict from period to period as betas for unmanaged portfolios because fund managers will often deliberately change the risk composition of the portfolio. Still, the general investment objective of the fund (e.g., growth, stability, etc.) does put a limit on the degree of change possible, and mutual-fund betas also tend to be reasonably stable from period to period.

Tests of the capital-asset pricing theory itself have tried to ascertain if security returns are in fact directly related to beta, as the theory asserts. I have already presented some data on this question in the previous chapter. Here I would like to present some additional evidence.

The following chart shows the relationship between the performance of a large number of professionally managed funds and the beta measure of relative volatility. It is because the numbers are for the most part averages of many funds that the relationship between risk and reward is so startlingly tight. Still, the results show a remarkable consistency with the theory. Returns are related to beta in a straight-line manner, just as the theory predicts. Over the long pull, high-beta portfolios have provided larger total returns than low-risk ones.

Volatility versus Average Annual Return
Ten Years, 1964–1973

CHART I

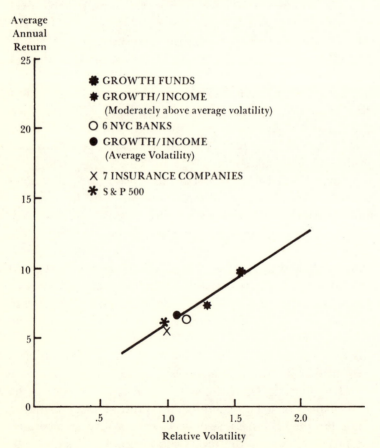

Chart prepared by D. A. Love Associates for Prudential Insurance Company.

The next two charts break down the ten-year performance into two subperiods; the six years when the market went up, and the four years when it went down. Again, the relationship is exactly as predicted by the theory. In "up" years, high-beta portfolios well outdistanced the low-beta ones. (Since

Volatility versus Average Annual Return

CHART II

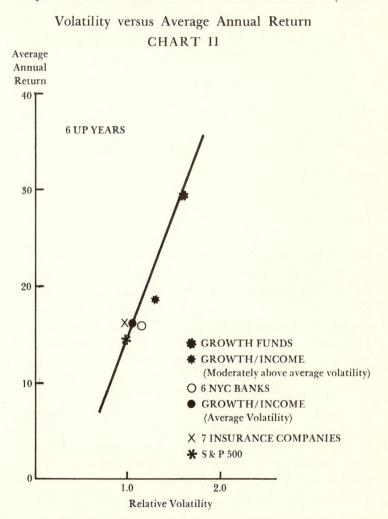

Chart prepared by D. A. Love Associates for Prudential Insurance Company.

Volatility versus Average Annual Return
CHART III

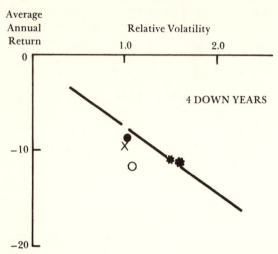

Chart prepared by D. A. Love Associates for Prudential Insurance Company.

the market was up from 1964 through 1973, this same relationship held over the whole period.) In "down" years, however the high-beta portfolio did considerably worse than the
low-volatility ones. It was the high-beta portfolios that took
the real drubbings in the bear market periods of the 1970s.
Of course, this is precisely what we mean by the concept of
risk, and this is why betas for diversified portfolios seem to be
very useful risk measures.

The possibility of obtaining higher returns over the long
pull from higher-beta portfolios is perfectly consistent with
the random-walk and efficient-market notions I have discussed
earlier. The former theories assert that there is no way to
gain superior performance (that is, extra returns) *for a given
level of risk.* The beta advocates say that the only way to gain
extra returns is to take on more risk. But this is hardly an
inefficiency in the market. It is the natural expectation in a

market where most participants dislike risk and therefore must be compensated (rewarded) to bear it.

But Beta Is Far from Perfect

Yet, beta does seem to be a useful risk measure, but it's far from perfect. While there is little doubt that security and portfolio returns are related to risk as measured by beta, not all the empirical evidence is as uniformly favorable as the studies I have reported so far.

For one thing, beta does not always perform well in the short run. In 1972, for example, which was an up market year, it turned out that safer (lower beta) stocks went up *more* than more volatile securities, contradicting the theory. *Fortune* magazine commented dryly on this well-publicized failure, "The results defied the textbooks." What happened was that in 1972 styles changed in Wall Street as institutional investors eschewed younger, more speculative companies, the "faded ladies" of the late 1960s, and became much more enamored of the highest-quality, most stable leading corporations in the so-called "first tier" of stocks. It became clear that while beta could do a good job in predicting a long-run relationship, it could not be used to guarantee investors a predictable performance over periods of a few months or even a year.

In addition, there seems to be some evidence that, over the long pull, the incremental returns on high-beta stocks and portfolios are not as large as the risk premiums predicted by the theory. There seems to be a phenomenon operating in the stock market much like that at the race track, where people tend to overbet long shots. Long shots seem to go off at somewhat shorter odds than their prospects seem to warrant. The original Adam Smith, writing in 1667, made a similar observation: "The ordinary rate of profit always rises more or less with the risk. It does not, however, seem to rise . . . so as to compensate it completely." Already economists have come up with refinements to the simple asset-pricing theory that seem better to accord with the evidence.*

Finally, some empirical tests done on individual stocks have shown that both systematic risk (beta) *and* unsystematic risk are related to security returns. This finding directly contradicts the theory, which says that only systematic risk will command a risk premium. There are severe statistical problems in testing the theory, and this phenomenon probably results from statistical biases. More recent studies on portfolios reveal that non-systematic risk has no effect on average security returns. To the great relief of assistant professors, there is still much debate within the academic community on risk measurement, and much more empirical testing needs to be done. It is clear, however, that beta is not perfect and caution is required to insure that the tool is not oversold as the final answer to the problems of building portfolios and projecting their risks and rewards. In judging risk, beta cannot be a full substitute for brains.

A Summing Up

Part Two has presented a broad overview of the random-walk theory and of the modern theory of capital markets. The stock market appears to be a most efficient mechanism which adjusts to new information very rapidly. Neither technical

---

* One implicit assumption in the simple asset-pricing theory is that the investor can borrow at the risk-free rate. (Note the Illustration of Portfolio Building shown earlier.) It's clear that in practice, borrowing rates for margin buying are considerably higher than, say, Treasury bill rates. Changing assumptions such as these alter the structure of the theory somewhat, but not its broad implications.

analysis, which analyzes the past price movements of stocks, nor fundamental analysis, which analyzes more basic information about the prospects for individual companies and the economy, seem to yield consistent benefits. It appears that the only way to obtain higher long-run investment returns is to accept greater risks—and those risks can be horrendous, as any investor who has lived through the great bear markets of the late 1960s and early 1970s can tell you.

Unfortunately, a perfect risk measure does not exist. Nevertheless, beta numbers have proved to be serviceable and useful risk estimates when applied to well-diversified portfolios rather than to individual stocks. Indeed, it's amazing how well the differences in long-run portfolio returns can be explained by that single factor. Undoubtedly, there will be future improvements in risk measurements, but for the present, beta is all we have that is easily available, and it can be of enormous help to investors. Precisely how should investors adjust to the reality that markets are highly efficient and that risk-reward tradeoffs are central to the investment decisions? These are the subjects of Part Three.

PART THREE

A Practical Guide for Random Walkers and Other Investors

CHAPTER NINE

A Fitness Manual for Random Walkers

In investing money, the amount of interest you want should depend on whether you want to eat well or sleep well.—J. Kenfield Morley, *Some Things I Believe*

Fred Schwed, Jr. was a man of keen intuition. More than thirty years ago he came to many of the same conclusions I have expressed about the efficacy of professional investment management. His conclusions were based only on casual observation and perhaps some personal pique about the incongruity of seeing in the harbor many yachts belonging to brokers—but none belonging to their customers. Little did he know that years later academicians armed with computers would also join battle with the investment pros in an attempt to finish the job he had begun. I would like to borrow and update one of his analogies in drawing the lesson of this analysis for individual investors.

Suppose you had a chance to win the coveted golf championship cup at your local club and the rules of the contest permitted you to let anyone you chose take the shots for you. Only an egotistical fool would want to play the match himself rather than let Jack Nicklaus, Lee Trevino, Arnold Palmer, or Kermit Zarley play for him. Professional golfers are consistently and demonstrably better at minimizing the strokes it takes to get the ball in the hole.

Unfortunately, the same cannot be said of professional investment managers. The pros in the investment business may give you useful information about the suitability of alternative portfolios for your objectives, offer helpful tax suggestions, execute trades efficiently, and assist investors in a number of ways; but what they apparently cannot do (whatever methods they use) is choose portfolios of common stocks that consistently outperform randomly selected diversified portfolios with equivalent risk. This is the lesson of the random-walk theory.

Now I have admitted that I am far from being a complete believer in the random-walk theory. I admit that there may be real geniuses in investment management whose above-average performance is not due to chance. There are a few exceptions to the rule; but such superior performance is extremely rare, and even if you find someone who has performed well over some past period, there is no assurance that the good record will continue. Like corporate earnings growth, investment performance is higgledy-piggledy. Thus it seems to me that the average investor, be he an individual with little savings or a large institution with millions of dollars to invest, might be wise to proceed as if it will not be possible to find a Nicklaus or Zarley to help him.

Thus far this book may be described as a "how-not-to-do-it" guide. Part Three turns the focus around and provides an instruction manual for taking a random walk down Wall Street. In the first two chapters, I shall offer general advice that should be useful to all investors even if they don't believe that security markets are highly efficient. In the final chapter I shall develop specific strategies for investors who do believe at least partially in the random-walk theory or who are convinced that even if real expertise does exist they are unlikely to find it. Even in a random-walk market, useful techniques and unique investment opportunities often exist.

Some Warming-Up Exercises

The first thing to realize—after avoiding the pitfalls that tempt you to lose money—is that common stocks are only one form of investment and should not constitute your entire assets. The only sensible way to take a random walk is after detailed and careful planning with regard to all your investments. Even if stock prices move randomly, you shouldn't. Therefore, I will first review all the available options, as well as the financial security you should have. Think of this as a set of warm-up exercises to prepare you for the flings you will soon be taking.

Exercise 1: Maintain medical and life insurance appropriate to your family situation. Insurance needs vary with age, income, family status, and whatever group benefits may be provided by your employer. The main purpose of insurance is protection, not the accumulation of assets; you'll do that later on Wall Street. Therefore, *when you buy life insurance make sure you are buying pure insurance and not insurance plus a savings plan.* "Living benefits" are the tipoff that you are buying an insurance scheme that is combined with a type of savings plan. The benefit goes to the seller, not the buyer, because these plans pay interest rates on the savings portion that are far below the levels that could be earned if your money were invested directly in bonds and stocks.

Beware of life-insurance salesmen who tell you they can provide a "whole-life" policy with "living benefits" that is really cheaper than term insurance. Even though the annual premiums are higher, the insurance salesmen stress that the whole-life policy provides a cash surrender value, whereas the term policy does not. What the salesmen do not point out is that if you bought a low-premium term insurance policy and invested the difference in annual premiums in safe bonds yourself, you could come out far ahead.*

Buy renewable term insurance; you can keep renewing your policy without the need for a physical examination. This provides death benefits alone and no buildup of cash value. So-called "decreasing term insurance," renewable for progressively lower amounts, should suit many families best since, as time passes (and the children and family resources grow) the need for protection usually diminishes. Unless you will incur heavy penalties for discontinuing your present coverage, or unless you are able to save money only if coerced by slick-talking salesmen, look for a term insurance plan. Use the money you save for your random walk down the big street.

Exercise 2. Exercise initiative and shop around for the best deal on life insurance. You'll be surprised how much money you can often save by buying insurance directly, rather than having an agent sell it to you. Agents, like stockbrokers, make their money on sales commissions. In a sense, they earn it by doing work that you should be doing yourself. Commission rates on life insurance tend to be much larger than on common stocks. About half of your first year's premium (and smaller fractions of subsequent premiums) go to pay the agent who sells you your policy. If you'd rather

* For an excellent guide on how to buy life insurance, including a demonstration of the above assertion, you may wish to consult *The Consumers Union Report on Life Insurance,* by the editors of *Consumer Reports,* published by Grossman Publishers. If you have already purchased a life insurance policy with investment features, I suggest that you borrow against the policy up to the maximum amount permitted. Many policies allow you to borrow at interest rates as low as 4½ percent. The proceeds from the borrowing can be invested in good-quality long-term corporate bonds at considerably higher rates.

keep that money, check on a "plain-pipe-rack" insurance company, one that operates without a costly network of agents and also offers low rates. In addition, some states have savings-bank life insurance, which you can buy at your local savings institution. The table on page 212 gives you an idea of the range of different premiums charged for term insurance and indicates the kind of savings that are possible.

Exercise 3. Keep some reserves in safe and liquid investments. That surely, to many, is the antithesis of investing. Why put money in a safe place when you could be picking the next winner on the stock market? To cover unforeseen emergencies, that's why! It's the height of folly to gamble that nothing will happen to you. Every family unit should have a reserve of funds to finance an unexpected medical bill or to provide a cushion during a time of unemployment.

The old rule of thumb was that a year's living expenses should be kept in assets like savings accounts. If you are protected by medical and disability insurance, this emergency reserve can be reduced safely. Indeed, even some bank trust departments—the acme of conservative money management —now estimate that three months of living expenses are satisfactory. In no case, however, should you be without at least some assets near the safe and liquid end of the spectrum.

Exercise 4. Review your overall investment objectives. Too many investors skip over this step by glibly stating that their objective is to make money. Of course. The question is: what degree of risk are you willing to assume? Some will want to run as fast as possible down Wall Street; others might prefer a more leisurely stroll.

J. P. Morgan was once asked by a friend who was so worried about his stock holdings that he could not sleep at night, "What should I do about my stocks?" Morgan replied, "I'd sell down to the sleeping point." Morgan's somewhat facetious retort contains a gem of real wisdom. Every investor

Five-Year Renewable Term Policies

This table compares twenty-year premium costs of policies from four sources open only to certain people and four conventional insurance companies. The prices shown are based on standard rates in 1972 for a man who bought the insurance at age thirty-five, and whose policy size was $50,000 or the maximum coverage available if less than $50,000. Companies were selected to illustrate a wide price range against which to compare the price of any five-year renewable term policy you may want to consider.

	Policy Size	Twenty-Year Net Payment (Gross Premiums Less Dividends)	Average Annual Cost per $1,000
Institute of Electrical and Electronics Engineers Group Plan	$50,000	$4,391.76	$4.39
Massachusetts Mutual Savings Banks	41,000	3,923.29	4.78
New York State Mutual Savings Banks	30,000	2,875.00	4.79
Teachers Insurance and Annuity Association of America Individual Policy	50,000	5,184.50	5.18
National Life Insurance Co. (Montpelier, Vt.)	50,000	6,876.50	6.87
Berkshire Life Insurance Co. (Pittsfield, Mass.)	50,000	7,307.00	7.31
Metropolitan Life Insurance (New York, N.Y.)	50,000	7,683.50	7.68 *
Nationwide Life Insurance Co. (Columbus, Ohio)	50,000	8,188.50	8.19

* Includes waiver of premium for total disability.
Source: *The Consumers Union Report on Life Insurance,* 1972 edition,

must decide the trade-off he or she is willing to make between eating well and sleeping well. The decision is up to you. As I have emphasized repeatedly, *high investment rewards can be achieved only at the cost of substantial risk taking.* This is the overriding lesson of every bit of research that has been done on security prices. And your inclination for risk taking is largely a matter of personal temperament.

Exercise 5. Set reasonable investment goals.   Many people go astray at the start by setting unattainable investment goals. They have a lot in common with a successful surgeon who recently sought my advice. I suggested he might anticipate a rate of return of perhaps 11 percent over the long pull from a diversified portfolio of relatively volatile stocks. "But I want to double my money every two or three years," he exclaimed. I told him that no one can achieve such a long-run return from the market. (Since his funds totaled $200,000 he would have been worth well over $1 billion in twenty-five years if his stocks did double every two years.) Unfortunately, my friend found a number of brokers who assured him that his goals *were* reasonable and realizable by active trading. And so the surgeon moved from broker to broker, who churned his account and managed consistently to lose his money in that hopeless search.

This story is all too typical of the greedy investor. The higher you set your objectives the more likely you are to end up with substantially inferior returns. In seeking to make fast profits you might try to outguess the market or hop from one "hot stock" to another, hoping for quick gains. Such a strategy incurs heavy brokerage costs and inevitably leads to getting "whipsawed"—buying a hot issue just after a substantial rise and before an adverse news development knocks the price down substantially.

Even if you are prepared to take large risks, you should not reach higher than an 11 or 12 percent annual average return. As unexciting as this goal might sound, it does enable

you to double your money every six and one-half years (assuming all your dividends are reinvested, and not accounting
for taxes) and have it grow to approximately eight times its
present value in twenty years. If you have a broker who promises substantially larger returns, I would strongly suggest that
you reconsider your association.

Exercise 6. Review all the investment options. Excluding
real estate, art, and various commodities, there are several
broad categories of investments in which you can put your
money to work. The table arranges them in order of the
sleeplessness they may cause.

At the safe end of the spectrum are savings accounts at
various thrift institutions such as mutual savings banks and
savings and loan associations. Interest rates on these passbook
accounts are now at a 5¼ percent stated rate. The dollar value
of your principal is perfectly safe and you can almost always
get your money out any time you wish. Somewhat less liquid,
but promising a higher rate of return, are special savings
certificates. Four-year certificates are now available at 7½ percent. They are just as safe as savings accounts, but the catch
is that you have to leave your money on deposit for a specified period in order to earn the higher rate.

A bit more risky, but quite liquid, are the so-called liquid-
asset mutual funds. The funds pool the savings of many small
investors so that they can take advantage of the higher rates
often available from Treasury bills and various short-term
obligations (bonds) of banks and corporations. I'll tell you
more about these funds in the next chapter.

Next comes investment in long-term bonds. Good quality
corporate bonds in early 1974 yielded about 8½ percent when
held to maturity in twenty or thirty years. The bonds may be
sold prior to maturity, but then the actual return will depend
on how much you can sell the bonds for, and that in turn de-

The Menu of the Major Investment Choices Available

Type of Asset	Expected Rate of Return (Start of 1974) (Before Income Taxes)	Length of Time Investment Must Be Held to Get Expected Rate of Return	Risk Level
Savings Account	5–5¼ percent	No specific investment period required. Many thrift institutions calculate interest from day of deposit to day of withdrawal.	None. Deposits up to $20,000 guaranteed by agency of the federal government.
Special Savings Certificates	5¾–7½ percent	Money must be left on deposit for periods from three months up to four years to take advantage of higher rate.	None. (as above)
Liquid-asset Mutual Funds	8 percent	Money may be withdrawn at any time.	Little, depending on the investment policies of the funds. Funds investing in lower quality corporate obligations may carry some degree of risk.
Corporate Bonds * (Good Quality)	8½ percent	Investments must be made for the period until the maturity of the bond (twenty to thirty years) to be assured of the stated rate. The bonds may be sold at any time, however, in which case the net return will depend on fluctuations in the market price of the bonds.	Little if held to maturity. Moderate fluctuations can be expected in realized returns if bonds are sold prior to maturity.
Diversified Portfolios of Blue-chip Common Stocks (Such as Mutual Funds)	9–11 percent	No specific investment periods required, and stocks may be sold at any time. The 9 percent average expected return assumes a fairly long investment period and can only be treated as a rough guide based on past experience.	Moderate to substantial. In any one year the actual return could, in fact, be negative. Diversified portfolios have at times lost 25 percent or more of their actual value.
Diversified Portfolios of Relatively Risky Stocks (Such as Aggressive Growth-Oriented Mutual Funds)	11–13 percent	Same as above. The average expected return of 10–11 percent assumes a fairly long investment period and can only be treated as a rough guide based on past experience.	Substantial. In any one year the actual return could be negative. Diversified portfolios of very risky stocks have at times lost 50 percent or more of their value.

* Good quality long-term tax exempts are available at 7 percent. As this book goes to press in mid-summer 1974, the rates applicable to bonds and to some of the savings vehicles are somewhat higher than those indicated in the table above. In addition, banks and industrial corporations have begun to offer special floating-rate notes, which have many of the same features as liquid-asset mutual funds but have some restrictions on when funds can be withdrawn.

pends on the future course of interest rates. If interest rates rise in the future, the price of your 8½ percent bonds will fall to make them competitive with new bonds offering a higher stated interest rate. The capital loss could be enough to eat up a whole year's interest—or even more. On the other hand, if interest rates fall, the price of your bonds will rise and you will not only get the promised 8½ percent interest but also a capital gain. Thus, if you sell prior to maturity, your actual yearly return could vary considerably, and that is why such bonds are riskier than savings accounts. You should also know that, unlike savings account interest, the interest on your bonds does not compound unless you specifically reinvest the payments.

Even riskier are investments in common stocks such as those that make up a typical mutual fund. No one can say for sure what the returns on common stocks will be. Nevertheless, we can make some reasonable guesses. The stock market, as Oskar Morgenstern once observed, is like a gambling casino in which the odds are rigged in favor of the players. Although stock prices have fluctuated considerably, and have been flat on their backs for years at a time, they have on the whole gone up historically.

Long-run rates of return from stocks have generally exceeded the returns from bonds and run about 9 or 10 percent a year, including both dividends and capital gains. If you start measuring from years after the market has taken a real pounding, the rate is even higher. That's why I put the 1974 expectation (after a prolonged bear market) at something between 9 and 11 percent. Don't forget that the target figures I have been using represent a *long-run average* return for an investment that is held over a considerable period of time. The actual yearly return can deviate substantially from target, and in bad years investors might well lose 25 percent of their capital or even more. Moreover, investors in common stock must be prepared to accept the possibility of suffering several bad years in a row.*

Finally, investors might want to choose a portfolio of somewhat riskier (more volatile) stocks like those in the typical aggressive growth-oriented mutual funds. Aggressive investors might avoid the established blue chips and buy younger companies in newer technologies, which promise greater growth prospects. Such companies are likely to be more volatile performers, and portfolios of these issues could easily lose half of their value in a bad market year. *On average,* however, you might expect on the basis of past experience a rate of return in the neighborhood of 11 to 13 percent per year. The chart in the preceding chapter showed very clearly that portfolios of riskier stocks have tended to outperform the market averages by small amounts. If you will have no trouble sleeping during bear markets, an aggressive portfolio may be just the right thing for you.

Exercise 7. Match your investment choices with your objectives.   Many people go astray at the start by mismatching the types of securities they buy with their investment objectives. Therefore, this last warm-up exercise is crucial. I've already mentioned that you will want to keep at least some funds in very liquid assets like savings deposits. The key decision is how you divide the rest of your assets. Let's examine two central questions: first, whether to invest in short- or long-term fixed-income securities (liquid-asset funds or long-term bonds), and, second, whether to invest in stocks or bonds.

I've mentioned that investment in liquid-asset funds or short-term bonds tends to be a safer strategy than investment

---

* As investors know painfully well, the decade from 1964 through 1973 produced an average rate of return of only 6 percent for the S&P average. During the five years ending in 1973 the overall yield from stocks was close to zero.

in long-term bonds. On the other hand, the latter generally have the higher yield as they did at the start of 1974. In mid-1974, however, the reverse was true and short rates got up to a tantalizingly high 12 percent. During such time many investors ask, "Why bother with lower yielding long-term bonds, especially since investment in long issues is riskier and less liquid?"

There is no doubt that if you hold long-term bonds when interest rates rise you will suffer a capital loss, and if rates rise substantially the loss can be considerable. The shorter the maturity of your bond, however, the less the potential loss. Suppose, your bond matures i. three months. Since the company has to pay off the full fac. amount of the loan at maturity, the bond has to sell very cl se to 100 cents on the dollar unless there is a substantial cha ice of default. Thus, the promise of full payment at maturity limits the amount of price fluctuation for short-term bonds. If maturity is twenty or thirty years down the road, however, watch out if interest rates rise.

Why, then, should any investor accept the extra risk of price fluctuation that goes along with long-term bonds if higher rates are available on short-term offerings? The reason is that interest rates may not stay as high. While investment in short-term securities could produce a much higher yield over a period of a few months or a year, the investor might have to reinvest the proceeds later at considerably lower rates. A 10 percent yield available on a 20-year bond would be much better for the long-term investor than a 12 percent rate over one year and, say, an 8 percent rate over the following 19 years. In fact, over the long pull, investing in long-term securities has usually produced a higher rate of return than continuous reinvestment in shorter-term issues.

Whenever short-term rates are higher than long rates, the market is in effect betting that yields will come down in the future. In 1966 and 1970, when this was the case, the market was correct—rates did come down, at least for a while. Of course, the market isn't always right, and nobody knows for sure if it will be in the future. What is clear, however, is that investors should not automatically infer that higher yields on shorter securities always make them preferable to longer-term bonds.

My advice is to make your decision on short- versus long-term issues on the basis of your needs and objectives. If you are putting away $5,000 to pay for your kid's tuition next year, buy only short-term liquid instruments where you can get your money when you need it without any chance of loss. On the other hand, if you want to be sure of a steady long-term source of income, buy long-term bonds and don't be dissuaded by the apparent bonus yields, if any, on short-term securities.

Next, take the question of whether to invest in bonds or stocks. The decision depends crucially on the state of your nerves. Bonds are the more conservative investment. Stocks are likely to provide a larger but much more variable overall return. If you are the type that loses sleep if your net worth bounces up and down with the whims of the market, then you probably don't want to put all your investment money in the stock market. Most people choose some ratio, such as $2 for stocks and $1 for interest-yielding investments, in making up their portfolios. The exact proportions should depend largely on your attitude toward and tolerance of risk.

One investment advisor suggests that you consider what kind of Monopoly player you were as a child. Were you a plunger? Was your greatest pleasure having hotels on Boardwalk and Park Place? True, the other players seldom landed on your property, but when they did you could win the whole game in one fell swoop. Or did you prefer the steadier sources of moderate income such as the orange monopoly of St. James, Tennessee, and New York Avenues? The answers to these questions may give you some insight into your

psychological makeup with respect to investing and may help
you choose the right categories of securities for you. Or perhaps the analogy breaks down when it comes to the money
game, which is played for keeps. In any event, it is critical
that you understand yourself before choosing specific securities for investment.

Exercise 8. Don't forget about inflation protection. Since
World War II, prices in the United States have risen at a
rate of about 3½ to 4 percent each year. But the rates of interest paid by savings institutions and by the U.S. government
on series E bonds were often below 3½ percent in this
period. Thus, such investments not only failed to keep you
ahead of the game—they didn't even allow you to stay with
the game.

For this reason many investors bad-mouth bonds and any
other investments with fixed interest and principal payments.
It is wrong, however, to say that bonds offer no protection
against inflation. One reason that interest rates are relatively
high now is that investors have clewed up to the danger of
continued inflation, and high interest rates in part compensate for the expected loss in purchasing power of the
dollar. In early 1974, good quality long-term bonds promise
a money yield of approximately 8½ percent. Perhaps 4 percent was the real rate of return anticipated (the rate of return
in constant purchasing power), and the extra 4½ percent
represented protection against inflation. Later in the year,
when the inflation rate went into the double digit range,
rates on prime quality bonds went to 10 percent and even
higher. This provided protection for a long-run inflation of
6 percent or more.

Now, I'm not saying that bonds are a good buy for everyone. And there is always the risk that the actual long-run rate
of price inflation may be considerably greater than the expected rate of 6 percent or so reflected in 1974 bond yields. But

don't automatically write bonds off for all time just because investors have had bad experiences with them in the past, when interest rates were at unrealistically low levels.

The other side of the anti-bond argument states that common stocks will protect an investor against inflation, since stock prices tend to keep pace with or exceed increases in general price levels. Unfortunately, in the short run—and, indeed, for periods as long as decades—common stocks have failed to keep pace with changes in consumer prices. In fact, significant increases in the rate of inflation have often been accompanied by falling stock prices. And some of the largest increases in stock prices have occurred during periods when the consumer prices were reasonably stable.

One reason that rapid acceleration in the rate of inflation can, in the short-run at least, be very bad for stocks is that inflation makes bond buyers demand higher interest rates to compensate them for the loss in the purchasing power of the dollar. When the rates on prime quality bonds climb to 10 percent, as they did in the summer of 1974, investors will no longer be satisfied with rates of return of only 9 or 10 percent from stocks, which are considerably riskier than bonds. Stock buyers will want returns that are larger than those available from bonds.

If investors were confident that the inflation would be reflected in higher corporate profits, then stock prices need not fall. Investors would simply adjust earnings growth rates upward (to reflect the greater inflation rate) so that stocks would provide the higher expected returns required. But rapid inflation often makes investors fear a profit squeeze and the imposition of restrictive monetary and fiscal policy, which in turns hurts corporate earnings. In the event that expected earnings growth rates are not adjusted upwards, investors can get higher overall rates of return from stocks only if stocks sell at lower prices from which they can produce higher dividend returns and better prospects for capital appreciation. Hence, it is perfectly understandable why rapidly-rising interest rates in 1974 could lead to sharply falling stock prices.

It is easy to see why many investors have decided that stocks are a very thin shield against the attack of inflation. Remember, however, that over the long pull corporate earnings and dividends have risen more rapidly than living costs, and that while the relationship is a very loose one, stock prices too have well outdistanced the rise in consumer prices.

Where, then, does all this discussion about inflation and stocks and bonds leave us? Some people say that if you expect very little inflation, bonds are a good deal. But, as I've just noted, stocks also may do extremely well with stable prices. If you expect fairly rapid inflation at rates much greater than we have been experiencing, you probably want to buy some common stocks, even if you don't sleep well knowing that the dollar value of your net worth is likely to fluctuate. While common stocks offer no guarantee that they will protect you against inflation, bond holders are certain to lose out from any rapid rise in prices. So my advice is that *at least some of your funds should be placed in common stocks or other assets that offer a degree of protection against unexpectedly rapid inflation.*

Rest Period: Hey, You Forgot about Gold, Real Estate, and Other Investments

My list does not include several investment alternatives. I have excluded convertible bonds, options and warrants, real estate, art objects, stamps, coins, oil wells, vineyards, and many more investment possibilities. Many of these have done very well, and often have provided tax shelters as well as generous returns. However, most specialized investment vehicles are very difficult for the average investor to evaluate and buy, are usually not readily salable, and are best left to the specialists or to investors whose high tax brackets make tax shelters worthwhile. It will be useful, however, to say a few things about the most popular of these alternatives.

GOLD

The price of gold has reached castle-in-the air proportions. It more than tripled from 1968 to 1973, and in 1974 gold traded at close to $200 per ounce. As might be expected, many writers now promise sure future gains from the purchase of gold. Indeed, a best-selling book on investing in 1974 suggested that everybody should sell their stocks, bonds, and real estate; purchase gold and a gun; and retire to the hills to await financial Armageddon. One can easily decry the fall-out shelter ethics of the author, and his investment advice may hardly be more respectable or profitable.

It is well to remember that gold bears no interest, and that people who bought gold on similar suggestions in the 1930s didn't make a nickel on their purchases until the late 1960s. It is true that in 1968 one could validly argue that all commodities have risen in price over the preceding three decades except gold, and that gold was due for its turn. But from 1968 to early 1974 gold more than made up for the previous rise in living costs. Overhanging the market were huge hoards of gold held by the central bankers of the world. Even a tiny trickling of these gold stocks onto the market could sharply reduce the market price. What was clearly correct advice five years before was no longer as self-evident.

The speculative boom in gold prices reminds me of the story of the wiley Chinese merchant who made an excellent living trading in sardines. His business was so successful that he hired a bright young college graduate to assist him in his endeavors. One day when the young man was entertaining his in-laws for dinner he decided to bring home a couple of cans of sardines to have as an appetizer. Upon opening the first can he found, to his great chagrin, that the can was filled with sand. He then opened the second can and found that it, too, was filled with sand. Upon informing the Chinese merchant of his experience the next day the wiley trader simply smiled and said, "Oh, those cans are for trading, not for eating."

In a sense, this story is very similar to the situation that occurs in gold trading. Practically all gold trading is for the purpose of hoarding or speculating that the bullion can be sold later at a higher price. Almost none of the gold is actually used. While there is some small demand for such uses as dental work, jewelry, and a few other specialized industrial needs, the current inventory of gold is some fifty times its annual industrial requirement—not to mention the large amounts of yet-to-be-mined metal stored below ground. Gold trading has an uncomfortably close similarity to the classic speculation in tulip bulbs.

As with any speculative movement, it is impossible to say where the boom will end. But we also know that all speculative booms ineluctably do end, and the losses suffered by players of the greater-fool game can be enormous. I would not bet on the gold-bugs' claim that the price of the metal will continue to skyrocket. My advice is to stay away from gold (and silver too).

REAL ESTATE

Real estate in good locations has proved to be an excellent investment for many people, and has also provided tax shelters. Nevertheless, I think real estate is much too specialized for the ordinary investor and is best left to the experts. Moreover, rental incomes, which usually provide the major part of the returns from real estate, have not always kept up with inflation, since periods of overbuilding and the imposition of rent controls have often restrained the rise in rents. Indeed, many real estate projects, such as hotels and apartment houses, have been squeezed by operating costs rising considerably faster than rental income. In short, it is a very specialized game with dangers at least as great as in the stock market. The unsophisticated should be extremely wary.*

While I am less than enthusiastic about real estate as a general type of investment for the ordinary investor, I make an important exception when it comes to purchasing your own house. Equity in one's own home is a basic step in inflation protection as well as an excellent source of tax benefits.

With inflation, residential property has generally risen in value over time, and the payments you make to service your mortgage give a gradual build-up of equity. Moreover, property taxes and interest on your mortgage are tax-deductible expenses, while ordinary rental payments are out. There's another advantage to owning a house on which part of the original mortgage has been paid off or which has risen in value. It can often be remortgaged if you need additional funds—for example, to get the kids through college. Don't wait for prices to come down on good homes. There may be dips from time to time, but I doubt that you can predict them any better than dips in the stock market.

OTHER INVESTMENTS

Other books on investing favor different alternatives. Readers are promised instant wealth from paintings, rare stamps

* There is one instrument—the real estate investment trust—by which individual investors can own equity interests in real estate without the hassle of evaluating and purchasing individual properties. These trusts are much like regular investment funds—they can buy a diversified portfolio of different properties and offer shares in the trust to the public. In fact, most of these trusts have been more involved in making long-term mortgage loans at fixed rates than in purchasing properties. Moreover, the trusts have usually financed their loans with short-term borrowings. As the rates on short-term borrowings rose in 1974, many of the trusts encountered severe financial difficulties and a number were on the verge of bankruptcy. In short, while the idea is a good one, these instruments have clearly been quite risky investments for the individual investor.

and coins, wines, and other assets. The authors exploit the greed in all investors—the urge to play the money game as a kind of horse-racing perfecta where small stakes can be parlayed into enormous returns. These books are terribly harmful. They suggest that such goals are reasonable and capable of fulfillment.

Of course, many of these assets have provided acceptable investment returns which in some periods have exceeded the yield from stocks and bonds. Paintings, for example, can be good buys—if you purchase future favorites before they become popular. But investing in any of these assets actually takes more skill and patience than investing in the stock and bond markets, and is best left to those who are experts in their respective fields. By the process of elimination, common stocks and fixed-income securities are (with the exception of equity in your home) usually the major practical portfolio investment media for most individuals, and my discussion will stick to these instruments.

A Final Check-Up

Now that you have completed your warm-up exercises, let's take a moment for a final check-up. The theories of valuation worked out by economists and the performance recorded by the professionals all lead to a single conclusion: there is no sure and easy road to riches. Higher returns can be achieved only through higher risk-taking (and perhaps by accepting lesser degrees of liquidity). The menu of actual investment choices shown earlier in the chapter makes painfully clear that each investor must make the difficult decision as to whether he or she wants to eat or sleep well. This is perhaps the most important investment decision you have to make.

Once you've done your warm-up exercises and decided where your "sleeping point" is, it's time to begin your walk.

You should have a clear notion of how you want to allocate your funds among the different types of securities (liquid savings instruments, bonds, stocks, etc.) marketed by the financial community. The rest of the book is a guide through the difficult decisions you will have to make along the way.

CHAPTER TEN

A Guided Tour of the Opportunities in Fixed-Income Securities and Common Stocks

> Annual income twenty pounds, annual expenditure nineteen nineteen six, result happiness. Annual income twenty pounds, annual expenditure twenty pounds ought and six, result misery.—Charles Dickens, *David Copperfield*

Now that you've reviewed your objectives, it's time for a quick prayer at Trinity Church and then a bold step forward, taking great care to avoid the graveyard on either side of you. In this chapter I'll develop some sensible rules for buying stocks and bonds. These rules can help you to avoid costly mistakes and unnecessary sales charges and to increase your yield a mite without undo risk. I can't offer anything spectacular but I do know that often a percent or two increase in the yield on your assets can mean the difference between happiness and misery.

A Stroll to the Bank

Let's start off with the safest and most conservative form of investment. When you have decided how much money to put away for unforeseen emergencies, you will probably want to deposit these funds in a bank or thrift institution. Even in such prosaic investments there are some steps you can take to improve your return.

Bank Step 1. Review the balance in your checking account. Don't leave more than you have to in assets that earn no interest. I'm always amazed at how much excess money many people leave in barren checking accounts rather than in interest-bearing investments. Money in a savings account is always available for emergencies and in the meantime it earns generous interest. You don't have to be a sharp-penciled corporate treasurer to know that a dollar shifted from checking to savings means about five cents earned per year. So try to get your checking-account balance down to the minimum needed to cover your monthly expenditures and to reduce or eliminate bank service charges. Many banks will give you free checking account services if you keep a minimum balance of about two hundred dollars on hand. It usually makes good sense to keep that minimum deposit, but there's no need to keep large excesses on deposit in checking accounts.

Bank Step 2. Shop around for the savings account paying the highest interest. If you've seen one bank, you haven't seen them all. You can earn a good deal of extra interest each year by shopping around for the highest interest available. The typical commercial bank (where you have your checking account) pays only 5 percent interest at this writing. You can receive 5¼ percent from savings and loan associations, and many offer continuous compounding of interest (so that your interest also keeps earning interest). This brings the effective yield up to close to 5½ percent. In California, thrift and loan guaranteed passbook accounts are available at a 6 percent stated rate. In addition, many accounts figure interest right up to the day of withdrawal, so you don't lose out if you have to withdraw some funds before the end of a quarter. And don't hesitate to bank by mail in response to advertisements by federally insured thrift institutions. It's easy to arrange, and convenient postage-paid bank-by-mail envelopes are supplied.

Bank Step 3. Where instant liquidity is not required, savings certificates can increase your interest return substantially. Today, if you can put your money away for four years, you can earn 7½ percent (plus an extra quarter of a percent because of the compounding feature). Somewhat lower rates are available if you invest your money for shorter periods. Again, shop around. Don't cheat yourself out of the possibility of substantial extra interest.

Liquid-Asset Funds Can Give You a Much Bigger Return on Short-Term Savings During Periods of High Interest Rates

Investors with substantial funds to invest need not be satisfied with yields of 5 percent or so on safe and liquid investments of short-term funds. In years of very high interest rates like 1974 such investors have earned double that rate on U.S. Treasury bills and short-term borrowings of leading banks and corporations. Until recently, however, small investors have been excluded from such opportunities. The reasons stemmed partly from government policy.

The government has purposely kept the rates very low on series E savings bonds and has sold higher-yielding short-term Treasury bills only in $10,000 denominations. More-over, the government has allowed commercial banks to pay 10 percent and above on so-called certificates of deposit offered in denominations of $10,000 or more, but prevents the same banks from paying higher than 5 percent on savings accounts. Edward Kane, a professor of banking at Ohio State, summed up the situation in an article entitled "Shafting the Small Saver." A journal editor with an overzealous sense of decorum later renamed the article "Short-Changing the Small Saver" but I think the original title better described the situation.

The reasons for such seemingly bizarre public policy, which favors wealthy individuals and institutions over citizens of moderate means, need not concern us here. (The explanation has to do with the fear that massive withdrawals of funds from savings and loan institutions might be induced if individuals were free to buy higher-yielding investments directly, and concern for the financial viability of these institutions.) What is of vital importance is that individuals with funds in savings institutions are not getting a fair shake in times of high inflation and high interest rates, and I want to make sure you know how to get a piece of the action.

Fortunately, private enterprise has come to the aid of the beleaguered small investor. A number of mutual funds have been established to pool the funds of many investors and to invest them in a portfolio of short-term obligations of the Treasury and of various banks and corporations. Most of these funds limit their investments to securities that mature in one year or less to insure that price fluctuations from interest-rate movements will be kept to a minimum. The safest (and lowest-yielding) of the funds invest exclusively in U.S. Treasury issues. Others try to earn even juicier yields (sometimes two to three percentage points more than is available on Treasury issues) by investing in bank and corporation issues. It's the old familiar story. Higher yields go along with greater risks. If you insist on absolute safety, stick to a fund investing exclusively in government securities.

Most of the funds have no initial sales (loading) fee but charge expenses of close to 1 percent per year. Thus, if the fund earned 10½ percent on its investments, it would pay out only about 9½ percent. The individual can cash in at any time at the asset value of the fund. One fund lets the investor write a check against the fund at a local affiliated bank. The check triggers an automatic redemption of shares sufficient to cover the payment. Appendix One lists a number of these funds together with information about them, including the minimum investment requirements and how to invest. For the small investor (and even the wealthy who have neither the time nor inclination to buy and roll over their bank certificates of deposits and other investments) the no-load variety of these funds represents a most useful financial innovation. The investor should be warned, however, that the yield advantages of such funds could disappear if interest rates fall sharply. Also, a policy of investing in longer-term securities or engaging in short-term trading operations is likely to make the fund's returns more volatile.

Investment in Floating-Rate Notes, or, You May Have a Friend at Chase Manhattan

In 1974 the parent companies of two large New York banks (First National City and Chase Manhattan) began issuing so-called floating-rate notes. Several other banks and industrial corporations quickly followed suit. These notes enabled investors to take advantage of interest rates considerably higher than those available on savings accounts.

Here is how the typical issue worked. The notes matured in about two years, after which the securities would be redeemable semiannually at the full purchase price. The interest rate started at 9.70 percent and shifted later to a flexible rate 1 percent above the yield available on short-term Treasury bills. The minimum purchase amount was $5,000—still a substantial amount, but far below the $100,000 minimum for bank certificates of deposit. The notes were not government guaranteed (as savings deposits are), but those issued by the top five or ten banks and the most blue-chip corporations are clearly prime credits. After the initial offering, these floating-rate notes trade on the market and can be purchased or sold through any broker by paying a small commission charge. (If a new issue is available, however, the notes can be bought without commission.)

In sum, the investor gives up some liquidity and a bit of safety in return for considerably higher yields. Anyone with substantial amounts in savings accounts should consider switching either to liquid-asset funds or to floating-rate notes of the top banks or industrial concerns.

A Promenade through Bond Country

We are now ready to continue our walk through bond country. Before moving off let's be sure we have a clear picture of the terrain. A bondholder of a corporation is simply a lender of money for which he receives an IOU (the bond itself) and a right to received *fixed* contractual interest payments that do not vary with the success of the business. Stockholders, on the other hand, as owners of the firm, have a claim on the company's earnings and assets only after the bondholders (and other creditors) have been paid what is due them. Consequently, stockholders participate directly in the good and bad fortunes of the corporation. Their dividends and the price of their stock will vary with the earnings success of the firm, and this is why they bear more risk than holders of corporate bonds. Bonds are also issued by such solid borrowers as the U.S. Treasury, state and local governments, public authorities, etc.

Bonds are by no means riskless, however. There are two major risks: (1) They can default on their interest. Fortunately, such occurrences have been very rare since the Great Depression of the 1930s, and thus bonds are properly considered fairly safe investments. (2) Bond prices fluctuate with interest rates. If interest rates rise in the future (perhaps because investors expect inflation to accelerate) and you want to sell your bonds *prior* to their maturity date, you will not be able to get as much as you paid and your net effective return will be lower than the contract interest rate. As long as we understand the potential pitfalls, we can now proceed.

Bond Step 1. Be unpatriotic. Don't buy U.S. savings bonds. Many government officials have eloquently proclaimed that self-interest and patriotism go hand in hand. Don't believe it! The yields on U.S. savings bonds today are far below what is available from other quality investments in corporate bonds. If you have at least $1,000 to invest (the minimum denomination of most corporate bonds) you'll be better off buying a high-quality bond of your local AT&T affiliate than a U.S. Treasury security.*

Series E savings bonds do have some advantages, however. For example, the tax on the interest can be deferred until you cash them in. (Also, if interest rates rise you won't suffer a capital loss. Unlike corporate bonds, series E bonds can be redeemed at face value prior to maturity, although there is

---

* There is one exception I must mention here. Some long-term U.S. Treasury securities held in the estate of a decedent are redeemable at face value ($1,000) for the payment of estate taxes. Such bonds can be bought at the present time for about 80 percent of face value and are clearly worthwhile for many older investors who wish to plan for the payment of estate taxes. These securities are called "flower bonds" since their major advantage comes when their buyers are six feet underground and pushing up the flowers.

an interest penalty for cashing in early.) But if you are in a high enough tax bracket to make the tax deferral worthwhile, you'll probably be better off buying tax-exempt bonds in the first place. We'll get to these later in the walk. (And if you're likely to cash in your savings bonds before maturity, a bank savings certificate will give you a higher yield with equivalent guarantees.)

Bond Step 2. Buy newly issued corporate bonds rather than those already outstanding and trading in the market.   Each week several major U.S. corporations float new issues of bonds. There are two main advantages in buying such issues. First, the yields available from new shares are typically higher than those available from already outstanding bonds. The market generally requires some form of yield sweetener on new issues to enable it easily to digest the big chunks of money that are raised at a single time. New issues can often yield as much as $1/4$ of 1 percent more than already outstanding bonds of comparable quality. Second, the investor can buy new issues without incurring any brokerage costs. The corporation issuing the bonds pays the broker's commission on the initial sale.

Bond Step 3. Buy only new issues with a Moody's rating of Baa or better (Standard & Poor's rating of BBB or better). Two main rating services, Moody's and Standard & Poor's, rate the credit worthiness of each issuer. The ratings, which are easily obtained from your broker, generally run from A to C. For example, Standard & Poor's bond ratings run as follows: AAA—highest grade; AA—high grade; A—upper medium grade; BBB—medium grade; BB—lower medium grade, etc. The yields available get higher the lower the bond's quality, to compensate investors for assuming the added risk. The ratings are far from perfect but they do, I believe, provide a good rough guide to investment quality.

My suggestion is to avoid the very top AAA quality bonds —leave them to conservative bank trust officers. On the other hand, if you don't know how to evaluate credit worthiness, don't ever go below BBB-rated bonds in quality (or Baa on the Moody's rating scheme). Inexperienced investors will feel more comfortable with bonds rated A. This will reduce the chance of picking up any bonds with a substantial risk of default.

Bond Step 4. There are often bargains in bonds—shop around for them. Bonds of similar quality don't always offer the same yield, and investors willing to shop around can often get themselves some easy extra interest. For example, in recent years the bonds issued by public utilities have been offering higher interest rates than bonds of industrial companies with comparable risk rating.

Utilities have had especially high capital requirements, and their bonds have literally been glutting the market. To create a demand for this glut, they have been forced to increase their yield relative to comparable industrial bonds. You can get some nice extra interest now by buying utilities. Of course, this bonus may not continue to exist, but it is worthwhile for you to check with your broker (or check yourself in the financial pages) what kinds of yields are being offered on different bonds of similar quality.

Bond Step 5. Tax-exempt bonds might be just right for you, particularly if you are in a high bracket. Interest income from banks and from U.S. Treasury and corporate bonds is fully taxed at regular income-tax rates. The interest on bonds issued by state and local governments and by various governmental authorities (such as port authorities or toll roads) is tax exempt. You don't even have to report it on your tax form, and bonds from the state in which you live are typically exempt from any state income taxes.

This tax exemption gives a subsidy to state and local governments since they can issue bonds at lower interest rates than if the bonds were fully taxable. Economists have argued that it's an inefficient subsidy (it would be cheaper for the U.S. Treasury just to pay the state and local governments to issue taxable bonds), but since that's the present law there is no reason why you shouldn't take advantage of it.

The attractiveness of municipal bonds depends on your tax bracket and the yields available from other types of bonds. At the start of 1974, good quality long-term corporate bonds were yielding about 8½ percent. Tax-exempt issues of comparable quality offered yields around 6½ percent. Suppose you are in the 40 percent tax bracket. By this I mean the rate at which your last dollar of income was taxed—not your average rate. The table on the following page shows the savings involved for a $10,000 bond purchase.

After-tax income is $100 higher on the tax-exempt security, and is clearly the better investment in your tax bracket. Even

	Interest Paid	Applicable Taxes (40 Percent Rate)	After-Tax Income
Buy 6½ percent tax-exempt bond	$650	$ 0	$650
Buy 8½ percent taxable bond	850	340	510

in the 30 percent tax bracket tax exempts might pay depending on the exact yields available in the market when you make your purchase.

Bond Step 6. Look carefully at new long-term revenue bond issues of various public authorities. They often provide very attractive tax-exempt investment vehicles. Large issues of "term" (meaning long-term) bonds (often called dollar

bonds) offered by various port authorities, established turn-
pikes, power authorities, etc. usually give particularly attractive yields. Again, I would suggest that you buy new issues
rather than already outstanding securities, and also that you
stick with issues rated at least Baa by Moody's rating service.
These term bond issues usually mature in thirty years or
more but they often enjoy a good trading market after they
have been issued. Thus, if you want to sell the bonds later
you can do so with reasonable ease, particularly if you own
at least $5,000 worth of a single issue.

Avoid serial bonds. These are tax-exempt bonds that
mature serially over perhaps thirty different years or more.
These issues are usually tougher to sell than term bonds if
you have to raise funds prior to maturity. Also, yields on
serial issues (especially the shorter-term ones) tend to be
lower than on term bonds, in part because they are particularly attractive to institutions like banks that pay taxes at
high corporate rates. Unless you have funds to invest for
some specific period of time and want to match the maturity
of the bond you buy with the timing of your fund requirements, these bonds are best left to institutional buyers.

So ask your broker how the "new-issue calendar" looks.
By waiting a week or so until a high-yielding revenue term
bond comes out, you may be able to improve your interest
return substantially.

*Bond Step 7. Make sure the bonds you buy have a call-
protection feature.*   There is one nasty "heads I win, tails
you lose" feature of bonds that you should know about. If
interest rates go up, the price of your bonds will go down, as
I noted earlier. But if interest rates go down, in many cases
the issuer can "call" the bonds away from you (repay the debt
early) and then issue new bonds at lower rates.

To protect yourself, make sure your bonds have a call-protection provision that prevents the issuer from calling your bonds to refund them at lower rates. New corporate issues now usually have a five-year protection against call for refunding—some have even longer protection. Many tax-exempt revenue issues offer about ten years of call protection. After that the bonds are callable, but typically at a premium over what you paid for them. Make sure to ask about call protection, especially during periods when interest rates are high compared with historical precedent, as they are as this is written in 1974.

Bond Step 8. Keep fit; don't buy load-type bond mutual funds. In recent years a number of bond mutual funds, both corporate and tax-exempt, have been started and now are being sold to the public. These funds enable you to purchase a share in a whole bond portfolio rather than in a single issue or two. In return, you pay a sales commission to buy into the fund, plus a management fee to those running it. That's a waste of money. If you have followed the previous rules and confined your purchases to high quality bonds, there's no need for you to diversify among many different securities. You'll get more interest return if you do it yourself. You may not want to avoid all funds, however, as the next step indicates.

Bond Step 9. Investigate the discounts offered by closed-end bond funds.   There is a certain class of bond funds that has afforded investors an opportunity to buy bonds at discounts of 15 percent or more from their market values. These are the so-called closed-end bond funds, and such discounts can make these funds excellent investments. In the next chapter I will discuss the whole concept of closed-end funds and offer specific rules for their purchase. For the present, keep in mind that these funds can be quite useful for individual investors.

How to Avoid Stumbling at the Corner of Broad and Wall Streets: Some General Guide-lines for Buying Common Stocks

We've now arrived at the critical stage of the walk where the rewards are larger but the footing becomes more treach-erous. Common stocks represent the very heart of Wall Street. It is here at the site of the New York Stock Exchange that you must pit all the expertise you have acquired against the randomness of the market. To help gird you for that I offer the following general guidelines—all of which build on the discussion in the first two parts of the book.

Stock Step 1. You can expect an average yearly return of 9–11 percent over the long pull, but be prepared for substantial losses from stocks in any year, or even over several years. The first rule is just to remind you of the extra risks involved in stocks and to advise you to stay away if you can't stand the risk. As Harry Truman used to say, "If you can't stand the heat, get out of the kitchen." I know I've said it before, but I can't emphasize it enough. Also, the 9–11 percent expectation is based on past experience. No one can guarantee how stocks will do in the future.

Stock Step 2. Maintain a diversified portfolio suited to the risk level you are prepared to assume. It's an old but true saw: don't put all your eggs in one basket. We saw in Chapter Eight how diversification reduces risk and makes it far more likely that you will achieve the kind of good average long-run return that meets your investment objective. Of course, by diversifying you do miss the chance of perhaps being lucky enough to put all your eggs in a Xerox or IBM basket. But just think how few and far between the IBMs and Xeroxes are. By trying to put all your money in the IBM of the future, you may in fact buy stock in one of the many promising companies that eventually fizzle out.

If you find, after establishing a liquid reserve, that you have less than $20,000 to invest, it will be very difficult and costly for you to obtain the diversification you need by buying stocks directly. Commissions on small purchases are relatively high, and you have little alternative but to buy shares in a mutual fund. How you should go about doing this I discuss in the next chapter.

The decision concerning what kinds of stocks (or what kind of mutual fund) you want to buy should depend on the risk level you want to assume. Safer (that is, more stable) stocks should go into the portfolios of those who seek a somewhat greater return than can be obtained from bonds but who wish to limit extreme fluctuations in the market values of their portfolios. Those seeking larger returns and willing and able to bear sharp fluctuations should choose a portfolio (or fund) made up of riskier (more volatile) stocks, often small firms or companies associated with newer technologies and products.

Stock Step 3. Your tax status and income needs should also influence the type of portfolio chosen.   Other things being equal, investors in high tax brackets (who often don't need high current dividends for living expenses) will usually find stocks paying relatively low dividends and promising most of their returns in less highly taxed capital gains better suited to their needs. Of course, low-dividend payers, which promise most of their return through growth of capital values, are often riskier than more mature companies paying high dividends. So if you are in a high tax bracket and want to end up with a less volatile portfolio you will probably have to balance your low-dividend-paying "growth" stocks with tax-exempt bonds to keep your overall risk level low.

Investors with a need for high dividend returns for living expenses (who typically are in relatively low tax brackets) will find stocks or mutual funds paying generous dividends more suitable and also less volatile. It is, of course, possible for such investors to buy low-dividend payers and sell off a few shares each quarter for living expenses, but such a process can be quite costly.* Remember that brokerage commissions are particularly high on small sales.

While we are on the subject of taxes, there are a few stocks available at the present time that pay dividends that are partially tax exempt. Ask your broker about these if you are in a high tax bracket and want relatively stable stocks paying high dividends. Also, I want to point out once again that there are other investments available in such things as low-income housing, oil drilling, etc. that currently have tax advantages for investors in relatively high brackets. Tax laws can change quickly, however, and these types of investment may not always be available.

Stock Step 4. Dollar-cost averaging can help you minimize the risks of putting all your money in the market at an inopportune time. Don't be alarmed by the fancy-sounding name. Dollar-cost averaging simply means investing the same fixed amount of money in, for example, the shares of some mutual fund, at regular intervals—say every month or quarter—over a long period of time. Periodic investments of equal dollar amounts in common stocks can substantially reduce (but not avoid) the risks of equity investment by insuring that the entire portfolio of stocks will not be purchased at temporarily inflated prices. The investor who makes equal dollar investments will buy fewer shares when prices are high and more shares when prices are low. As illustrated in the following table, the average cost per share

---

* It is possible, however, to invest in mutual funds that regularly distribute capital gains and that have automatic withdrawal privileges.

is actually lower than the average of the share prices during the period when the investments are made.

Period	Investment	Price of Fund Shares	Shares Purchased
1	$150	$75	2
2	150	25	6
3	150	50	3

Total Cost   .   . $450

Average Price $50

Total Shares Owned 11

Average Cost: Approximately $41

By the process of dollar-cost averaging, you have purchased 11 shares, now worth $50 apiece, for a total market value of $550. You have invested only $450 over the period. In other words, your average share cost ($\frac{\$450}{11} = \$40.91$) is lower than the average ($50) of the market price of the fund's shares during the periods in which they are accumulated. So you've actually made money despite the fact that the average price at which you bought is the same as the current price. It works because you bought more shares when they were cheap and fewer when they were dear.

Don't think that dollar-cost averaging will solve all of your investment problems. No plan can protect you against a loss in market value during declining stock markets. And a critical feature of the plan is that you have both the cash and the courage to continue to invest during bear markets as regularly as you do in better periods. No matter how pessimistic you are (and everybody else is), and no matter how bad the financial and world news is, you must not interrupt the plan or you will lose the important benefit of insuring that you buy at least some of your shares after a sharp market decline. Indeed, if whenever the market declines by 25 percent or more you buy a few extra shares, your dollar-cost averaging will work even better.

There is one drawback to dollar-cost averaging. Remember, brokerage commissions are relatively high on small purchases. For that reason, it is often cheaper to buy larger blocks of securities over longer time intervals. For example, it is cheaper to buy $150 worth of stock each quarter, or $300 worth semiannually, than to invest $50 each month. Of course, if you pick a no-load mutual fund (see next chapter) for your dollar-cost averaging, this problem disappears. You can invest as little $50 per month in most no-load funds, with no brokerage charges at all. Also, some of the closed-end investment companies (which I'll also discuss in the next chapter) pool small monthly contributions from their shareholders to enable their customers to get the advantage of lower commission rates on volume purchases.

To further illustrate the benefits of dollar-cost averaging, let's move from a hypothetical to a real example. The table on the following page shows the results (ignoring taxes) of a $500 initial investment made on January 1, 1959, and thereafter $100 per month, in the shares of the T. Rowe Price Growth Stock Fund, a no-load mutual fund.

While no one can be sure that the next fifteen years will prove to be as good as the past fifteen, the table does illustrate the tremendous *potential* gains possible from consistently following a dollar-cost averaging program, even when we do the final accounting after a disastrous year in the market like 1973.

Stock Step 5. If possible, keep a small reserve to take advantage of market declines and buy a few extra shares if the market is down sharply. I'm not suggesting for a minute that you try to forecast the market. However, it's usually a good time to buy after the market has fallen out of bed and no one can think of any reason why it should rise. Just as hope and greed feed on themselves to produce speculative bubbles, so do pessimism and despair react to produce market panics. The greatest market panics are just as unfounded as the most pathological speculative explosions. No matter how bleak the outlook has been in the past, things usually get better.

Illustration of Dollar-Cost Averaging with T. Rowe Price Growth Stock Fund

($500 Initial Investment on 1/1/59, and $100 Monthly Investment Thereafter—All Dividends and Capital Gains Distributions Reinvested)

Year Ended 12/31	Total Cost of Cumulative Investments	Total Value of Shares Acquired
1959	$ 1,600	$ 1,799
1960	2,800	3,248
1961	4,000	5,369
1962	5,200	5,914
1963	6,400	8,319
1964	7,600	10,577
1965	8,800	14,673
1966	10,000	15,755
1967	11,200	21,312
1968	12,400	24,393
1969	13,600	26,507
1970	14,800	25,735
1971	16,000	35,293
1972	17,200	42,053
1973	18,400	32,497

The last two general guidelines follow directly from the careful studies of investment performance I discussed in Part Two. The gist of both is to do as little stock trading as possible.

Stock Step 6. Adopt a buy-and-hold strategy. Trade as little as possible. Above all, do not let your broker churn your account. Even if you do not believe fully in the broad form the random-walk theory, one fact stands out very clearly. A great deal of investment advice is more or less worthless. Brokers often recommend that you switch into and out of particular stocks (or in and out of the market as a whole) on tips, hunches, or research reports that represent a rehashing of information or "news" items that are already reflected in the market prices of the shares. The surest way I know of to turn the favorable odds of stock-market investing against you is to let a broker churn your account. Never forget that the trader is playing a game against all other investors, and we have seen that their collective judgment is, in general, quite good. Stock prices quickly reflect all fundamental information that is known. Brokers make money when you trade—not when you hold on. What is good for general brokers is not necessarily good for the American public.

Look at the odds against you if you ignore my advice and jump from security to security. First we have seen that the chances of finding one of those rare individuals who can consistently give you good advice are overwhelmingly against you. Very often your trades simply won't work out. Remember—you have to be right twice, first on the purchase and then on the sale. A mistake on either side blows the whole transaction. Even the pros don't beat a buy-and-hold strategy. Second, brokerage costs are expensive. Commissions alone amount to almost 3 percent for an in-and-out trip in a $20.00 stock—even if you do buy in 100-share (so-called round) lots. In addition, you may have to pay up to 5 percent extra in middleman's markup to the specialist or dealer who "makes a market" in your stock.

The scenario often runs this way: The specialist may quote your stock 19½ bid—20½ asked. This means that when you sell, the specialist buys your stock at his bid price of 19½ (or he may fill an order in his book at that price). When you buy you get your stock at 20½, the specialist's offering price. This point difference is equal to 5 percent of the stock's average price. Maybe now you will understand why so often it seems you have bought at the high for the day and sold at the low.

If the brokerage costs and middleman's markup aren't enough to convince you, let me add a third reason—taxes. Whenever you sell a stock that has gone up, Uncle Sam collects his due in capital-gains taxes. No taxes are due if you don't sell.* To come out ahead in a trade, the stock you buy has to outperform the one you sell by an amount sufficient to offset the taxes and all the commissions. Sometimes I think the capital-gains tax is a blessing in disguise for investors. It has actually saved them a lot more money than it has cost them. I know your broker will hate me, but do yourself a favor—think one more time before making that trade your broker has been suggesting.

I would make only one exception to my buy-and-hold rule. It is good strategy to sell out stocks on which you have losses. With few exceptions, I sell out any of my own stocks on which I have a loss before the end of each calendar year (and usually within six months). The reason is that losses are deductible (up to certain amounts) for tax purposes, or can offset gains you may already have taken. Thus, taking losses can actually save you money. For example, if you are in the 50 percent tax bracket and have $1,000 of short-term capital losses (the sale to give you a loss was made within six months of the purchase) and no other gains or losses, you can deduct the loss from your income and pay $500 less in taxes.

---

* Thus you can defer paying taxes and have the use of the tax money for investment. In fact, if you hold the stock until you die, neither you nor your heirs have to pay the capital-gains tax on your capital gains. The tax base to your heirs will be the value of the stock on the date of death.

Stock Step 7. Avoid short-term switch-hitting to outguess the market.   There's a great temptation to use the latest market predictions as a basis for switching from stocks to bonds to take advantage of general market movements. "Bulls can make money in the stock market—bears can make money in the stock market, but hogs never can," goes a very popular Wall Street maxim. It was propagated by resourceful brokers trying to encourage their customers to step in and out of the market more frequently so that they could earn more commissions. I don't believe there is anyone who can consistently foresee short-term fluctuations in stock prices. And to gain from such a strategy the investor has to make two correct decisions in every market decline and recovery.

Don't try to outguess turns in the market. Don't try to switch from stock to stock in the hope of improving performance. Buy a diversified portfolio (or mutual fund) suited to your risk preferences, need for income, and tax status. Sell only to establish tax losses (where Uncle Sam will subsidize a part of the loss), when your requirements change, or when you need the money. If your need for funds is a temporary one, borrow against your portfolio rather than sell stock at a gain, to avoid incurring capital-gains taxes. By this procedure you will minimize brokerage costs and taxes and give yourself a much better chance of being a winner in the market

Another Rest Period. The Author Intrudes Again.

I hope I haven't appeared to damn all brokers. First, I am convinced that many are sincerely misguided, not brazenly mendacious. Just examine what a mess they often make of their own accounts and you'll see what I mean. Also, brokerage houses do consciously try to monitor the activities of their salesmen to insure that they are not churning their accounts.

As I've said before, I do not think the brokerage community is peculiarly dishonest—I believe its standards of ethics are usually extremely high. But investors must recognize the terrible conflict of interest inherent in the broker's situation. He makes money by recommending trades. He makes particularly generous commissions by selling you offerings of stocks the firm is underwriting, or by selling you load-type mutual funds, which I'll discuss in the next chapter. None of these activities is necessarily in your interest.

It is best to treat your broker as if he were a friendly adversary like any other salesman—not a trusted guardian. I don't mean to do a hatchet job on brokers; I only want to prevent them from doing a hatchet job on you.

Appendix One

Information on Liquid-Asset Mutual Funds

Name and Address of Fund	Telephone Number	Sales Charge on Minimum Investment	Minimum Initial Investment (Dollars)	Year Organized	Net Assets (Millions of Dollars) 7/1/74	Offering Price (Dollars) 7/1/74	Yield, Standard & Poors Estimate (Percent)	Investment Policy
Anchor Reserve Westminster at Parker Elizabeth, N.J. 07207	(201) 354-1770	8¾%	100	Dec., 1971	15.3	11.36	8.5	Primarily debt securities with up to 1 year maturity, some corporate bonds up to 5 year maturity; short-term trading.
Capital Preservation 459 Hamilton Avenue Palo Alto, Calif. 94301	(415) 328-1550	none	1,000	Oct., 1971	4.2	95.84	9.0	Primarily debt securities with up to 1 year maturity, some longer maturity issues, limited short-term trading.
Dreyfus Liquid Assets 600 Madison Avenue New York, N.Y. 10022	(800) 223-5525 (212) 935-8700	none	5,000	Sept., 1973	145.1	9.98	10.19	Debt securities all with up to 1 year maturity; short-term trading.

Fund / Address	Telephone	Load	Minimum	Date	Assets ($ mil.)	Price	Yield	Portfolio
Fidelity Daily Income Trust 35 Congress Street Boston, Mass. 02109	(800) 225-6190 (617) 726-0200	none	5,000 [1]	May, 1974	5.8	1.00	10.97	Debt securities all with up to 1 year maturity; short-term trading.
Money Market Management 421 Seventh Avenue Pittsburgh, Pa. 15219	(412) 288-1900	none	1,000	Oct., 1973	52.9	1.00	10.62	Debt securities all with up to 1 year maturity; limited short-term trading.
Oppenheimer Monetary Bridge 1 New York Plaza New York, N.Y. 10004	(212) 825-4000	4¼	1,000	Apr., 1974	4.6	10.02	9.60	Debt securities all with up to 1 year maturity; limited short-term trading.
Reserve Fund 1301 Avenue of the Americas New York, N.Y. 10019	(212) 977-9880	none	5,000 [1]	Feb., 1970	238.4	1.00	11.59	Primarily debt securities with up to 1 year maturity, some longer maturity issues; no short-term trading.
Temporary Investment Fund 1730 Pennsylvania Avenue Washington, D.C. 20006	(202) 785-6690	none	50,000	Oct., 1973	76.0	1,000	10.60	Debt securities up to 6 months maturity; no short-term trading; open only to institutional investors.

1 Through brokers, $1,000.
Source: Standard & Poor's *Outlook*, July 8, 1974, p. 677, and fund prospectuses.

CHAPTER ELEVEN

A Measured Step through the Mutual Fund Mire

> Beware of false prophets, which come to you in sheep's clothing, but inwardly they are ravening wolves. Ye shall know them by their fruits.—Matthew 7:15–16

Mutual fund salesmen will tell you that their product helps investors avoid the risk of putting all their eggs in a single basket. Perhaps a more appropriate analogy would be that a mutual fund permits the small investor to purchase not just one fragile and highly perishable egg, but fractional shares in a very large basket of eggs. A fund takes the money of thousands of investors and places it in a multimillion-dollar marketbasket of stocks and sometimes other securities. Each investor shares proportionately in the net income and in the capital gains and losses of the fund's portfolio. Thus, if some of the eggs in the basket turn out to be rotten, each investor bears part of the loss. On the other hand, if some of the eggs turn out to be quite valuable, all share in this good fortune. But there ain't no such thing as a free lunch, and mutual funds are no exception. Investors pay for the services of the fund manager in the form of a management fee and in some cases in large acquisition (loading) fees when the funds are bought.

We have already seen how the academic world feels about mutual funds. On average, the funds do not outperform either the stock averages or randomly selected portfolios. Does this mean that the random walker should discretely sheathe his dart as he tiptoes through mutual fund land?

Despite their average records, there are good reasons for many investors to buy funds. Investors with limited amounts of cash and unfamiliar with the intricacies of buying securities will find that mutual funds provide convenient diversification, freedom from having to select stocks, and relief from paperwork and record keeping for tax purposes. Most funds also offer a variety of special services such as automatic reinvestment of dividends and regular cash-withdrawal plans. Mutual funds are particularly attractive as an investment vehicle for retirement savings for the self-employed and their employees.* Moreover, as this book is written, there are some excellent buys in funds.

I believe, therefore, it is worth our while to take a measured tread through the mutual fund mire. So strap on your boots and read further.

Open-End and Closed-End Funds

There are two broad categories of funds: open-end and closed-end. Open-end mutual funds issue and redeem shares

---

* The Self-Employed Individual's Tax Retirement Act of 1962 (also known as the Keogh Act) provided that up to $1,250 a year (amended in 1966 to $2,500 a year) could be invested in a mutual fund with the total amount deductible for income tax purposes. Until you retire, no income tax on any dividends or capital gains distributions need be paid.

at the net asset value of the share at the time of the transaction. They are "open" because the number of shares in the fund can increase indefinitely. Closed-end funds (officially called closed-end investment companies), on the other hand, neither issue nor redeem shares after the original offering. Thereafter, if an investor wants to sell or buy closed-end fund shares, he must do so on the market—generally on the New York Stock Exchange. The price of the shares depends on what other investors are willing to pay for them and is not necessarily related to net asset value, as is true of the open-end funds. Thus, closed-end funds can sell at a premium above or at a discount below their net asset values.

Load versus No-Load Funds

Since most funds are of the open-end variety, let's examine that kind first. Within this broad category there are two varieties: load and no-load. A load is the commission that is tacked on to pay the salesmen who sell most fund shares to the public. The typical loading fee is advertised at 8½ percent, but the real charge comes out to 9.3 percent of your stake in the fund. For example, if you buy a load mutual fund with a net asset value of $10.00 per share, you pay $10.93 per share, not $10.85. The extra 93¢ turns out to be 8½ percent of the $10.93 you are charged.

No-load funds employ few salesmen, and most do not advertise heavily. With no initial commission charge, these funds sell at their net asset value. So, if the fund in the example above went no-load, you would pay only $10.00 per share rather than $10.93. It's easy to tell the difference between the two. Just look at the price quotations in the newspapers. The following pages shows some taken from the January 2, 1974 edition of *The Wall Street Journal*.

Note that for some funds the asked price at which you can buy the shares is larger than the bid price; the difference is

Price Quotations for Some Representative Mutual Funds
(Net Asset Values as of Start of 1973)

	Bid Price (Net Asset Value)	Asked Price
Fidelity Capital Fund	10.71	11.70
Hartwell Growth Fund	9.34	9.34
One William Street Fund	16.10	16.10
Oppenheimer Fund	6.68	7.30
Smith, Barney Equity Fund	9.64	9.64
T. Rowe Price Growth Stock Fund	11.91	11.91
Wellington Fund	10.26	11.21
Value Line Fund	4.91	5.38

Source: *Wall Street Journal,* January 2, 1974

the commission you pay. That is the sign that these are load
funds. No-load funds have identical bid and asked prices.

How to Buy Mutual Funds

The following steps should help you avoid the pitfalls involved in buying mutual funds and alert you to some real
bargains that are currently available.

*Fund Step 1: Never buy a load fund. No-loads perform as
well and are particularly advantageous for dollar-cost averaging.*   From the facts presented so far, it seems foolish to buy
a load fund. Why spend some of your investment money on
sales commissions, unless you believe in capital punishment?
Yet, most fund investors (about 90 percent) put their money
into the load funds. Why? The answer in this case is that
while silence may be golden, it doesn't sell. The load funds
have hotshot salesmen touting their product throughout the
country. They back up their efforts by million-dollar ad-

vertising campaigns, by lions walking out of subways and herds stomping through the prairies. Who will counter such a dynamic approach? No one. No-load funds typically do not have teams of salesmen out in the field. You must beat the path to their door; they will not come to yours.

For example, a friend of mine, Oliver, recently wrote to a load fund for information (the address was in an ad) and then tried to find the address of a no-load fund. Since Oliver did not know where to find the latter, he called the brokerage firm whose name was associated with the load fund. The person answering referred him to another number; that number in turn gave him another number to call. Being a persistent soul, Oliver did. The last number hung up on him.

Oliver never did find out any information about the no-load fund. The load fund, on the other hand, has sent him three packages containing well-illustrated material describing its growth and performance. A salesman called at the office three times, and at home (during the dinner hour) four times. When the salesman finally became convinced that my friend was not interested in buying a load fund (Oliver had, after all, only asked for information), he did admit that his firm had a no-load fund and promised to send material on it. This has not yet been received.

In such a situation, the average investor—who wanted to put his money into a mutual fund—would probably have fallen prey to the blandishments of the salesman and bought the load fund. The mutual fund is perhaps the best example of a product of which even more might be sold if they raised the price—that is, if they increased the loading charge. Such an increase would only accentuate the already powerful incentive for hard-selling salesmen to push their customers into load-type funds. Unfortunately, most prospective investors don't know the facts and cannot dispute the many claims of the fund salesman. That is one of the reasons why I have written this book.

Most brokers will candidly admit that Oliver's search for information on a no-load versus a load fund is typical, but then they will quickly state that the load funds perform better. This is not true, and it is hard to believe that such widespread ignorance can exist honestly on Wall Street. A number of careful studies of mutual fund performance have failed to document any evidence of significant differences in performance between the load and no-load funds.* Indeed, some of the best performing funds in the past have been of the no-load variety.

Most no-load funds allow you to buy in for as little as $50, and to make further investments at that figure. A program of investing $50 per month (and having all dividends and distributions automatically reinvested) can, over a period of years, produce a substantial nest egg, as I indicated earlier. If you are not able to invest that much, you could make your investments bimonthly or even quarterly.

Remember, however, that while you are not legally obligated to continue the periodic payments, you must stick to whatever plan you choose in order to obtain the advantages of dollar-cost averaging. And once you have chosen a mutual fund that meets your objectives, there's no need to switch from fund to fund; the long-run records of all funds are generally pretty much the same when adjusted for the degree of risk they assume. Incidentally, if you already own a load fund, there is little point in switching to a no-load type. Just make sure that all new investments go into no-load funds.**

---

* These studies are listed in the bibliography for Chapter Seven.
** A possible exception to this rule may be applicable to those individuals who have signed up for contractual plans and agreed to invest a certain amount per year. Such plans could involve heavy penalties for discontinuance. In general, contractual plans should be especially avoided by all investors. If you are already in one, however, it can sometimes be better to continue with it than discontinue.

It's easier than you think to buy a no-load fund. In Appendix One to this chapter there is a listing of the major no-load funds at the present time, together with their mailing addresses, an indication of any minimum amounts required for investment, and also a tabulation of their expense ratios. Once you have selected the fund or funds you want, simply send them a postcard asking for information on the fund and its investments, fill out the subscription form they send (indicating whether you want your cash dividends and distributions reinvested), write out a check or money order, and mail them in to the fund. True, you have to take the initiative, but it's really as easy to do as banking by mail.

Fund Step 2. Pick a mutual fund on the basis of your willingness to take risks.   How *much* volatility are you willing to accept from your fund? This should be the major consideration in your choice. Don't forget that capital-gain or growth-oriented funds tend to specialize in more volatile types of stocks. Income-oriented funds generally hold more stable issues.

Look back at the charts in Chapters Seven and Eight. The more volatile funds have tended to produce a somewhat larger long-run return than more stable funds. But they often show sharp fluctuations in value. That can cause heartburn and loss of sleep for nervous individuals not temperamentally suited to risk taking. Unfortunately, the marketing labels such as "growth" used by the funds can only be taken very loosely to indicate the approximate risk or volatility zone. Fortunately, an annual book known as the "bible" of the mutual-fund industry, and a monthly pamphlet, provide the necessary information to help make a sensible choice.

The book, *Investment Companies,* and the pamphlet, *Wiesenberger Performance Monthly,* published by Wiesenberger Services, Inc., contain risk (volatility) ratings for most mutual funds. You can find these publications in most libraries.

The risk ratings provided by Wiesenberger are the same relative volatility measures used in the charts in Chapters Seven and Eight. These volatility ratings, also known as betas, were described more fully in Chapter Eight. The following table shows you a sample.

Volatility Ratings (Betas) of Mutual Fund Shares

Name of Fund	Beta over Ten-Year Period * to 12/31/73
NYSE Common Stock Index (Composite)	1.00
Afuture Fund	1.90
One William Street	1.03
Smith, Barney Equity	1.23
T. Rowe Price Growth	1.04

* Or shorter period if fund has not been in existence for ten years.
Source: Wiesenberger Services, Inc. *Mutual Fund Performance Monthly,* Year-end Edition, January 1974.

The volatility ratings show the characteristic fluctuations of the fund's asset values relative to the market. A beta of 1 means the fund tended to be exactly as volatile as the market, as measured by the New York Stock Exchange Composite Index—if the market went up 10 percent, so did the fund. The market itself gets a volatility rating of 1. Thus Afuture Fund, which had a beta close to 2, is for investors willing to accept above-average risk for a chance to achieve above-average gains. The fund has been almost twice as volatile as the general market (when the market fluctuated by 20 percent, the fund fluctuated by close to 40 percent, on average).

Often smaller funds, like Afuture, are able to "swing" by concentrating their investments in small companies and, therefore, have relatively high volatility ratings. On the other hand, larger funds, like the T. Rowe Price Growth Stock Fund, with hundreds of millions of dollars under management, are usually forced to spread their investments out more widely. Consequently, their net asset values are unlikely to go soaring or plummeting on the basis of the fortunes of a few companies.

In Appendix Two, volatility ratings for the no-load funds are shown up through the end of 1973. More up-to-date figures can be found in the most recent Wiesenberger volume available. These numbers should allow you to pick a fund suited to your needs. If you want to shoot for high returns and can stand large risks, pick a high-volatility (high-beta) fund. But don't forget the lessons of Chapter Seven. Investors who poured their money into the hottest funds of the late 1960s took some bad beatings when the market turned sour. *Larger long-run returns can only be achieved by assuming greater risk.*

Fund Step 3. Buy closed-end funds whenever they are selling well below their average historical discounts. Imagine your surprise if your local bank ran the following advertisement in the newspaper:

> CURRENCY AT A DISCOUNT
> Brand new one-dollar bills, in mint condition, now selling for 75¢. Ten-dollar bills available at $7.50. All denominations available at a 25 percent discount.

Such an ad would seem preposterous. Yet such surprising discounts are often available in the securities markets. Your broker could run an advertisement such as the following in the newspaper *and actually deliver on his promise:*

> COMMON STOCKS AT A DISCOUNT
> Gilt-edge securities, in mint condition, now selling at 25 percent discounts. Shares available in all the blue chips, including IBM, Xerox, Exxon, and many more. Securities available in diversified portfolios selling at 75¢ on the dollar.

Portfolios of blue-chip securities are available at discounts at the present time through closed-end investment companies, more popularly called closed-end funds. Closed-end funds hire professional managers, but their expenses are no higher (and often are actually lower) than ordinary mutual funds. So even if you believe in professional investment management, here is a way to buy it at a discount.

Why should such discounts exist? Many reasons have been offered, but none of them holds up on careful analysis. It's been suggested that some of the closed-end companies have been too conservatively managed and have invested in stable stocks with relatively low average returns. This has been true of some of the companies in the past. Many have had mediocre past records, but others have done quite well, and now the portfolios of most of the closed-end companies are little different from their open-end cousins.

Others have argued that the discounts can be explained by the existence of unrealized capital gains in the funds' portfolios that could affect the timing of an individual's tax liabilities. It is true that funds with larger amounts of unrealized appreciation do tend to sell at bigger discounts. But the tax effect is very small, and funds with no unrealized appreciation at all sell at large discounts.

Another explanation of the discount on some funds has to do with their practice of buying "letter" stock, the sale of which is restricted. Since the shares are generally highly illiquid, the market prices of these stocks are not a fair indication of their value on liquidation. Funds with large amounts of letter stock do, therefore, sell at relatively large discounts from their asset values. Nevertheless, the funds I have labeled as "Diversified Companies" in Appendix Three have almost no restricted stock, and this factor cannot explain the large discounts on these companies.

The real explanation for the discounts on well-diversified investment companies is, I think, a very simple one. Closed-end companies sell at discounts because they must be bought through regular brokers, and brokers don't like to sell them. The problem is that investors usually do not *buy* mutual funds. The public *is sold* fund shares by brokers or by other salesmen. And the name of the game is to sell those types of securities that earn the salesman the largest amount of commission.

If an investor puts $1,000 into a load-type open-end fund, the salesman makes about $45 for himself. (He gets to keep about half of the loading charge.) If an investor puts $1,000 into a closed-end company, the total commission comes to about $25 and the salesman gets to keep only about 30 percent of the total, or $7.50. And since you are unlikely to trade from one closed-end company to another as you might with ordinary stock, the salesman knows his commission is likely to be a one-shot affair. You can see why brokers are unlikely to be enthusiastic advocates of the shares of closed-end companies.

At the current level of discounts, I believe that many closed-end companies represent unusually good value. A sample of funds is shown in the table below:

	Average Discount Past Fifteen Years (Plus Indicates Premium)	*Discount Start of 1974 **
Lehman Corp.	+ 4%	− 16%
Dominick Fund	− 14	− 20
General American Investors	− 5	− 18
International Holdings	− 19	− 30
Madison Fund	+ 9	− 35

* Source: *Wall Street Journal,* December 31, 1973.

Closed-end funds are frequently challenged by the following argument: What good is it to buy closed-end funds at 75¢ on the dollar if the discount is still there when you want to sell? Thus, it is implied, the discount is of no value. The answer is that even if the discount doesn't narrow, the discounted closed-end funds still have a big advantage. For every dollar you put into the fund you will have more than a dollar invested on which dividends can be earned. So even if the fund just equals the market return, as believers in random walk would expect, you will beat the averages.

Think of a $100 savings account paying 5 percent interest. You deposit $100 and earn $5 interest each year. Now suppose you could buy such a savings account at a 50 percent discount; in other words, for $50. You would still get $5 interest (5 percent of $100), but since you only paid $50 for the account, your rate of return is 10 percent (5/50). Note that this increase in yield is not predicated on the discount narrowing at all. Even if you get only $50 back when you cash in, you will still get a big bonus in extra return for as long as you hold the account. The discount on closed-end funds provides a similar bonus. You get your share of dividends from a full dollar of assets, even though you pay only 75¢ for it.

The only real problem would occur if the discount widened in the future. In this case the price of your shares could fall even if the value of the fund's portfolio remained the same. This latter risk is minimized, however, when you can buy the shares at discounts, as you can at this writing, that are about as large as they have ever been historically. These considerations do suggest, however, that closed-end shares may not always be as attractive as they are at the present time. *If the discount closes (and particularly if the shares go to a premium) the shares should be sold and the proceeds invested in open-end companies or other investments.*

In order to help you follow Fund Step 3, Appendix Three to this chapter contains information on historical discounts and premiums for a number of closed-end companies. Current discounts and premiums can be found in a weekly tabulation published in the *Wall Street Journal* on Monday, the *New York Times* on Saturday, and several other newspapers. Information about the relative volatility of closed-end shares to help you select the particular shares that meet your investment objectives can be found in the Wiesenberger "bible." As long as the discounts remain at present levels, I think closed-end shares offer a unique investment opportunity enabling a person to obtain a share in a diversified portfolio at a substantial discount.

They do have a disadvantage compared with the no-load funds, however, for dollar-cost averaging. Small monthly investments will usually incur very high brokerage charges. Thus it is often better to use these funds for investments involving at least several hundred dollars. There are some closed-end companies, however, that offer to pool the small monthly investments of their shareholders so that all may gain the economies in brokerage costs that are available to larger investors.

Fund. Step 4. If you're an aggressive investor and in a high tax bracket, check the dual-purpose funds. At large discounts, capital shares of these funds are an excellent investment for people who can afford high risks. There is another type of closed-end fund, called a dual-purpose fund. These funds originally issued two types of securities, each providing one-half of the beginning assets of the fund. One is a preferred or income share, which is entitled to receive all of the dividend and interest income produced by the assets; the other is a capital share, which is entitled to none of the income but all of the capital gains produced by the fund.

The beauty of the dual-purpose idea is that for every $1 invested you get $2 worth of action. For example, suppose a fund started with $20 million of assets, the capital and income shares each providing $10 million. The income share-owners get all the income produced by the whole $20 million of assets, and thus could reasonably expect about twice the dividend return they might get from a regular mutual fund. Similarly, if the total assets at market value went up from $20 million to $22 million, the entire favorably taxed capital gain would accrue to the capital shareholders and thus produce a percentage return of 20 percent (the $2 million gain expressed as a percentage of $10 million, the original investment). Of course, by the same logic, a 10 percent capital loss on the total portfolio would mean a 20 percent loss for the capital shareholders. It is this leverage that makes the capital shares risky and suitable only for investors able to sustain that risk.

A dual fund operation generally starts with a leverage of 2 to 1. This means that the fund has $2 of total assets for each dollar the capital shareholders contribute. (The other dollar comes from the income shareowners.) As the market prices of the fund's investments change, however, the total value of the assets and the amounts applicable to the capital shares fluctuate as well; thus the leverage ratio varies over time. Current leverage ratios for a sample of dual-purpose funds are shown in the table following.

Like the shares of other closed-end investment companies, the capital shares of the dual-purpose funds have recently been selling at substantial discounts from their net asset value. As this is written these discounts are about as large as they have ever been. The discount, coupled with the leverage feature, provides a particularly attractive investment opportunity for patient long-term investors because of another unusual feature of the dual funds.

All shares of dual funds are redeemable at a specified maturity date; generally this is sometime between 1979 and 1985. Income or preferred shares are redeemed at a predetermined price, typically around the original price the income shareholders paid for their shares. The remaining assets belong to the capital shareholders, who may, if they wish, redeem their shares at full asset value on the maturity date. Thus, unlike the regular closed-end companies, the investor can be confident that the discount will be eliminated in the future. It is this assured payoff at full asset value that gives the duals their greatest edge.

Some representative dual-purpose funds holding diversified portfolios and selling at discounts of at least 30 percent are listed in the following table. It shows recent market prices, corresponding discounts from net asset values, and leverage ratios. The higher the leverage ratio, the larger the potential return in a favorable market environment and the greater the risks.

Fund	Market Price Start of 1974 *	Discount from Net Asset Value Start of 1974 *	Average Discount Since Inception of Fund	Redemption Date	Leverage Ratio Start of 1974
Income and Capital	6⅜	33%	17%	1982	3.05
Gemini	7⅞	30	15	1984	2.89
Putnam Duo Fund	4	42	15	1983	3.85
Scudder Duo-Vest	6¼	36	22	1982	3.16

* Source: *Wall Street Journal,* December 31, 1973.

All the funds listed are now available at bargain-basement prices; however, the discounts are quite volatile and the weekly listings in the newspapers should be checked to insure that the discounts are still large when you are about to make your investment. Remember also that the inherent leverage in these shares makes them a relatively risky investment. A leverage ratio of 3 means that the net assets of the capital shares can be expected to appreciate or depreciate three times as fast as the fund's total portfolio, which presumably will fluctuate with general market conditions. One of the most highly leveraged dual funds lost over 80 percent of its value during the 1969–70 bear market.

Fund Step 5. How to Have Your Cake and Eat It Too.   Suppose you like the assured disappearance of the discount provided by the closed-end funds but dislike the leverage and extra risk that goes along with buying the capital shares. Is there any way you can limit your risk and still benefit from the guaranteed appreciation implied by the elimination of the discount?

The answer is an emphatic yes. Remember that the reason the capital shares are riskier is that the income shares have a prior claim on all the company's earnings. Moreover, the investment company has to pay off the income shareholders at a predetermined price before the capital shareholders get anything. It's a very simple matter, however, to undo the leverage of the capital shares. All you do is buy one income share for every capital share you own.* This, in effect, gives you a direct share in the company's assets. (If you bought all the company's income and capital shares you would own the whole portfolio directly.)

If you in fact did buy up capital and income shares in the proportions in which the shares were outstanding, it would be an easy matter to calculate the total discount of the fund. By total discount I mean the percentage by which the total market value of all the fund's shares is below the worth of the fund's assets.

The following table does the calculation. At the start of 1974 the securities of dual purpose funds were selling for about 75 cents per dollar of the assets held by the funds. Buying up both income and capital shares is the low risk way of

* In the case of the Putnam Duo Fund, you need buy only one-half an income share for each capital share you own. The rule for undoing leverage is to buy income and capital shares in the same ratio that the shares are outstanding.

Total Discounts For Dual-Purpose Funds
Start of 1974

	Year Begun	Number of Capital Shares	Price per Capital Share, Start of 1974	Number of Income Shares	Price per Income Share, Start of 1974	Market Value of Fund's Capital and Income Shares (Dollars)	Value of Net Asset of Fund (Dollars)	Total Discount
American DualVest	1967	1,565,615	5.25	1,565,615	11.75	$26,615,455	$32,878,157	19.05%
Gemini	1967	1,656,155	8	1,656,155	13.25	35,193,294	38,291,554	8.09
Hemisphere	1967	1,404,807	1.375	1,404,807	6.625	11,238,456	17,730,075	36.61
Income & Capital	1967	1,510,011	6.5	1,510,011	11	26,425,193	30,000,081	11.92
Leverage	1967	1,994,744	7.375	1,995,044	12.25	39,150,526	49,790,095	21.37
Putnam	1967	1,505,484	4.25	752,742	16	18,442,179	24,597,460	25.02
Scudder	1967	5,423,565	6.175	5,424,065	7.75	75,255,838	105,101,349	28.40

insuring that you benefit from the disappearance of the discount. Of course, you could still lose if the market went down or if your fund by chance did worse than the averages. Nevertheless, this technique is a useful one to tilt the odds of success a little more in your favor.

Fund Step 6. Investors who want to buy bonds should consider closed-end bond funds when available at substantial discounts. I've already mentioned closed-end bond funds in the previous chapter. They are just like closed-end stock funds except that they hold a portfolio of fixed-income securities rather than stocks.* The argument about the dividend advantage holds with even greater force for the bond funds since their dividend payouts tend to be much larger than those of the stock funds.

You should keep in mind, however, that such funds charge yearly expenses amounting to close to 1 percent of the value of the fund. Consequently, you need a discount of at least 10 percent before you'd do as well with the funds as you would on your own. Let's see why. Suppose bonds were yielding about 10 percent per year. If you bought directly you would earn $10 for every $100 you put in. The bond fund deducts $1 (one percent) in expenses, however, and distributes only $9 per $100 of asset value. Thus you have to buy at a 10 percent discount, i.e., at $90, to earn a 10 percent return. On the other hand, if you can buy at greater than a 10 percent discount, you'll do better through a closed-end bond fund than you could do on your own. Thus, I would recommend that you buy only if such funds are available at discounts greater

* Some closed-end bond funds hold a substantial amount of convertible securities such as convertible bonds. A convertible bond is like a regular I.O.U. except that it is also convertible into common stock at the option of the holder. If the company's stock goes up, it usually becomes worthwhile to convert, so convertibles have important equity features. Because of this advantage, the yield rate on convertibles is generally well below the going yields on similar securities without the convertibility feature.

than 10 percent—15 percent being a good target.

Appendix Four presents a listing of closed-end bond funds, with information about them and their investment policies. If the portfolio contains lower-grade bonds, private placements, bonds with equity features, and if it is leveraged (if it buys some of its securities on margin), you can expect a much riskier (less stable) performance. Information is also given about the fund's policy with respect to portfolio turnover. More turnover means the fund does a good deal of in-and-out trading, and you know how the random walkers feel about that. More up-to-date information about the funds can be found in the weekly listings in your newspaper and in the most recent edition of Wiesenberger's *Investment Companies*.

In Summary

I believe that investment company shares represent the only practical alternative for small investors whereby a diversified portfolio can be obtained for a low dollar investment. I have not stressed the often cited advantage of these funds—namely, that small investors can buy professional investment management with the purchase of fund shares. Random walkers have produced convincing evidence that by and large the funds do no better than randomly selected portfolios with the same risk characteristics. Investment companies do offer convenient diversification and simplied record keeping, however, and even firm converts to the random-walk theory should find them useful instruments.

Nevertheless, investors should *never* buy load-type mutual funds, which typically charge more than 9 percent in commissions. No-load and closed-end funds have done just as well as the typical fund sold by your broker or mutual fund or insurance salesman. But no salesman will come looking for you to sell you a no-load or closed-end company selling at a discount—you will have to use the rules developed in this chapter to go out and find the fund suitable to your objectives.

Appendix One

Information on No-Load Mutual Funds

Name and Address of Fund	Minimum Initial Purchase (Dollars)	Minimum Subsequent Purchase (Dollars)	Net Assets in Millions of Dollars 12/31/73	Expense Ratio in Percent of Net Assets (1972)
Growth: Maximum Capital Gain				
Afuture Fund, 8 Pennell Road, Village of Lima, Pa. 19060	500	30	33.9	1.50
American Investors Fund, Inc. 88 Field Point Road, Greenwich, Conn. 06830	400	10	156.4	0.92
The Barclay Fund Room 2100, 30 Broad Street, New York, N.Y. 10004	1000	100	1.9	1.50
Columbia Growth Fund 6215 W. Morrison, Portland, Ore. 97205	500	50	17.8	1.08
Drexel Equity Fund, Inc. 1500 Walnut Street, Philadelphia, Pa. 19101	250	no 50	16.5	0.98
Edie Special Growth Fund, Inc. 530 Fifth Avenue, New York, N.Y. 10036	1000	no minimum	34.2	0.85
Edie Special Institutional Fund, Inc. 530 Fifth Avenue New York, N.Y. 10036	1000	no minimum	27.8	0.67

Name and Address of Fund	Minimum Initial Purchase (Dollars)	Minimum Subsequent Purchase (Dollars)	Net Assets in Millions of Dollars 12/31/73	Expense Ratio Percent of Net Assets (1972)
Growth: Maximum Capital Gain (continued)				
Fund for Mutual Depositors 200 Park Avenue, New York, N.Y. 10017	200	50	19.3	0.82
Hartwell Leverage Fund 345 Park Avenue New York, N.Y. 10022	5000	50	7.8	1.60
Hedberg and Gordon Fund, Inc. 111 North Broad Street Philadelphia, Pa. 19107	no minimum	no minimum	10.4	1.26
Ivy Fund 441 Stuart Street, Boston, Mass. 02116	500	100	43.8	0.00
Mates Investment Funds, Inc. 237 Madison Avenue, New York, N.Y. 10016	300	50	N.A.	3.94
Mathers Fund One First National Plaza Chicago, Ill. 60670	1000	500	62.7	0.70
Nicholas Strong Fund, Inc. 312 E. Wisconsin Avenue Milwaukee, Wis. 53202	500	200	43.6	1.06

Fund	Address				
Oceanographic Fund, Inc.	15 Exchange Place Jersey City, N.J. 07302	500	no minimum	12.9	2.20
O'Neil Fund	10960 Wilshire Boulevard Los Angeles, Calif. 90024	1000	100	14.0	1.07
Penn Square Mutual Fund	451 Penn Square, Reading, Pa. 19603	100 shares	30 shares	130.9	0.59
Pennsylvania Mutual Fund, Inc.	80 Broad Street, New York, N.Y. 10004	10 shares	50	3.3	2.52
T. Rowe Price New Era Fund, Inc.	One Charles Center Baltimore, Md. 21201	1000	200	230.9	0.74
Scudder Special Fund, Inc.	10 Post Office Square Boston, Mass. 02109	5000	no minimum	123.0	0.69
Dean Sherman Fund, Inc.	140 Broadway, New York, N.Y. 10005	1000	100	3.4	1.15
Smith, Barney Equity Fund, Inc.	1345 Avenue of the Americas New York, N.Y. 10019	10 shares	50	61.7	0.80
Stein Roe and Farnham Capital Opportunities Fund	150 S. Wacker Drive Chicago, Ill. 60606	300	50	26.7	0.69

Growth: Long-Term Growth of Capital and Income

Name and Address of Fund	Minimum Initial Purchase (Dollars)	Minimum Subsequent Purchase (Dollars)	Net Assets in Millions of Dollars 12/31/73	Expense Ratio Percent of Net Assets (1972)
Babson (David L.) Investment Fund 301 W. Eleventh Street Kansas City, Mo. 64105	250	25	142.1	0.81
Consultants Mutual Investments, Inc. 211 S. Broad Street Philadelphia, Pa. 19107	500	50	10.8	1.00
deVegh Mutual Fund, Inc. 20 Exchange Place, New York, N.Y. 10005	500	150	83.6	0.53
Dodge and Cox Stock Fund 3500 Crocker Plaza San Francisco, Calif. 94104	250	no minimum	11.0	0.69
Energy Fund, Inc. 120 Broadway, New York, N.Y. 10005	10 shares	10 shares	139.1	0.76
Growth Industry Shares, Inc. 135 S. LaSalle Street, Chicago, Ill. 60603	200	25	38.8	0.73
The Johnston Mutual Fund, Inc. 460 Park Ave., New York, N.Y. 10022	250	50	297.3	0.62

Mairs and Power Growth Fund, Inc.	W. 2062 First National Bank Bldg., St. Paul, Minn. 55101	500	50	12.6	0.77
The Nassau Fund	P.O. Box 629, Princeton, N.J. 08540	100	25	6.5	1.09
National Industries Fund, Inc.	1880 Century Park East Century City, L.A., Calif. 90067	250	25	13.3	1.02
PRO Fund, Inc.	Valley Forge Colony Bldg. Valley Forge, Pa. 19481	no minimum	no minimum	35.8	0.90
State Farm Growth Fund, Inc.	112 E. Washington Street Bloomington, Ill. 61701	50	25	40.5	0.79
Stein Roe and Farnham Stock Fund	150 S. Wacker Drive, Chicago, Ill. 60606	300	50	171.9	0.56

Current Income and Growth

Farm Bureau Mutual Fund	225 Touhy Avenue, Park Ridge, Ill. 60068	300	200	10.0	0.82
General Securities, Inc.	133 S. Seventh Street, Minneapolis, Minn. 55402	100	10	5.3	1.30
Guardian Mutual Fund, Inc.	120 Broadway, New York, N.Y. 10005	200	50	52.6	0.74

Name and Address of Fund	Minimum Initial Purchase (Dollars)	Minimum Subsequent Purchase (Dollars)	Net Assets in Millions of Dollars 12/31/73	Expense Ratio Percent of Net (1972)
The One William Street Fund, Inc. One William Street, New York, N.Y. 10004	250	50	276.6	0.48
Pine Street Fund 20 Exchange Place, New York, N.Y. 10005	500	no minimum	47.7	0.53
Scudder, Stevens & Clark Common Stock Fund 10 Post Office Square Boston, Mass. 02109	500	500	135.4	0.66
Balanced Funds				
Dodge & Cox Balanced Fund 3500 Crocker Plaza San Francisco, Calif., 94104	250	no minimum	14.2	0.67
Loomis-Sayles Mutual Fund, Inc. 225 Franklin Street, Boston, Mass. 02110	250	50	151.4	0.59
Rittenhouse Fund 1700 Market Street Philadelphia, Pa. 19103	250	50	N.A.	2.65

Scudder, Stevens & Clark Balanced Fund	10 Post Office Square Boston, Mass. 02109	500	500	76.1	0.66
Stein Roe & Farnham Balanced Fund, Inc.	150 S. Wacker Drive Chicago, Ill. 60606	300	50	166.9	0.53

Income Funds

Northeast Investors Trust	50 Congress Street, Boston, Mass. 02109	500	no minimum	68.1	0.66

Growth Funds

(Large Growth Funds—1973 assets over $300,000,000)

Price (T. Rowe) Growth Stock Fund	One Charles Center Baltimore, Maryland 21201	500	50	1,121.0	0.49
Rowe Price New Horizons Fund	One Charles Center Baltimore, Maryland 21201	no minimum	100	328.2	0.59

N.A.—Not available

Source: Wiesenberger Services, Inc., *Investment Companies*

Appendix Two

Risk Estimates for No-Load Mutual Fund Shares

	Beta Estimate Ten-Year Data Jan. 1, 1964– Dec. 31, 1973
Growth Funds	
Large Growth Funds (1972 assets over $300,000,000)	
Price (T. Rowe) Growth Stock Fund	1.04
Rowe Price New Horizons Fund	1.32
Smaller Growth Funds	
Afuture Fund	1.90*
American Investors Fund	1.34
Columbia Growth Fund	1.35
Drexel Equity Fund	1.25
Edie Special Growth Fund	1.10**
Fund for Mutual Depositors	1.11**
Hartwell Leverage Fund	1.28*
Hedberg & Gordon Fund	1.16
Ivy Fund	1.32
Mates Investment Fund	1.78*
Mathers Fund	1.38*
Nicholas Strong Fund	1.72**
Oceanographic Fund	1.11*
O'Neil Fund	.99*
Penn Square Mutual Fund	1.10

* Estimate based on five-year data.
** Estimate based on three-year data.

	Beta Estimate Ten-Year Data Jan. 1, 1964– Dec. 31, 1973
Pennsylvania Mutual Fund	2.35*
Rowe Price New Era Fund	.85**
Scudder Special Fund	1.27
Smith, Barney Equity Fund	1.23*

Growth: *Long-Term Growth of Capital and Income*

Babson (David L.) Investment Fund	.97
deVegh Mutual Fund	1.05
Dodge & Cox Stock Fund	1.04*
Energy Fund	1.06
Growth Industry Shares	1.05
Johnston Mutual Fund	.97
National Industries Fund	1.18
PRO Fund	1.15*
State Farm Growth Fund	.91*
Stein Roe & Farnham Stock Fund	1.06

Current Income and Growth

Farm Bureau Mutual Fund	1.04*
General Securities	1.14
Guardian Mutual Fund	1.06
One William Street Fund	1.03
Pine Street Fund	.96
Scudder, Stevens & Clark Common	1.07

Balanced Fund

Loomis-Sayles Mutual Fund	
Scudder, Stevens & Clark Balanced Fund	.79
Stein Roe & Farnham Balanced Fund	.83

Income Fund   .87

| Northeast Investors Trust | .25 |

* Estimate based on five-year data.
** Estimate based on three-year data.
Source: Wiesenberger Services, Inc., *Mutual Fund Performance Monthly,* year-end edition, January 1974.

Appendix Three

Average Discounts for Closed-End Investment Company Securities

	Average Discount Fifteen Years to 1973
Diversified Companies	
Adams Express	6.8%
Carriers & General	13.1
Consolidated Investment Trust	10.5
Dominick Fund	13.9
General American Investors	4.9
International Holdings	19.2
Lehman Corporation	4.2 (Premium)
Madison Fund	9.3 (Premium)
Niagara Share Corporation	4.4
Surveyor Fund	7.4*
Tri-Continental Corporation	11.1
U.S. & Foreign Securities	17.2
Nondiversified and Specialized Companies	
American–South African	10.0 (Premium)
Central Securities	3.4 (Premium)
Diebold Venture Capital Corp.	35.8**
Inventure Capital Corporation	33.4†
Japan Fund	19.4‡
National Aviation	4.9
New America Fund	37.5§

	Average Discount Fifteen Years to 1973
Petroleum Corporation	2.6
Standard Shares	12.2
United Corporation	12.0
Value Line Development Capital Corporation	28.7**
Average for all companies	14.2

* Data for six years beginning 12/31/67.
** Data for five years beginning 12/31/68.
† Data for three years beginning 12/31/70.
‡ Data for ten years beginning 12/31/63.
§ Data for two years beginning 12/31/71.
Source: Wiesenberger Services, Inc., *Investment Companies.*

Appendix Four

Information on Closed-End Bond Funds

Name of Fund	Market Where Traded	Price	Net Asset Value	Discount or Premium (P)	S&P's 1974 Dividend Estimate	Expected Yield on Market Price	1973 Expense Ratio (expenses as a percentage of net assets)
American General Bond Fund	NYSE	25⅛	24.06	P4.4%	2.03	8.1%	.58%
Drexel Bond-Debenture Trading Fund	NYSE	17	20.97	18.9	1.44	8.5	1.25
Fort Dearborn Income Securities	NYSE	14¾	16.92	12.8	1.37	9.3	.65
Independence Square Income Securities	OTC	23½	21.33	P7.3	1.68	7.1	.96
John Hancock Investors, Inc.	NYSE	23⅜	23.52	0.6	1.88	8.0	.60
Lincoln National Direct Placement Fund	OTC	21¾ *	22.32 *	2.5	1.68	7.7	1.05
MassMutual Corporate Investors	NYSE	17⅜	22.59	23.1	1.56	9.0	1.24
MassMutual Income Investors	NYSE	12⅛	13.46	9.9	1.08	8.9	.91
Mutual of Omaha Interest Shares	NYSE	16	17.50	8.6	1.31	8.2	.76
Paul Revere Investors	OTC	11¾	11.00	P6.8	1.32	11.2	1.19
St. Paul Securities, Inc.	NYSE	11⅛	13.09	15.0	.96	8.6	.66
Transamerica Income Shares	NYSE	19 **	21.99 **	13.7	1.76	9.3	.74
USLife Income Fund	NYSE	10⅜	11.63	10.8	1.00	9.6	.70
Vestaur Securities, Inc.	NYSE	13⅞ **	14.60 **	4.9	1.23	8.6	2.40

* January 31, 1974.
* November 30, 1973.

Name of Fund	Investment Policy
American General Bond Fund	Diversified; 80% high-grade debt securities, 20% other bonds with no equity features; up to 20% private placements; 50% turnover rate per year; leverage up to 5% of net assets.
Drexel Bond-Debenture Trading Fund	Diversified; 75% high-grade debt securities, 25% other bonds, some with equity features, and preferred stock; 300% turnover rate per year; leverage up to 10% of net assets.
Fort Dearborn Income Securities	Diversified; 75% high-grade debt securities, remainder in lower-grade bonds, some with equity features, preferred stock, and private placements; 200% turnover rate per year; leverage up to 20% of net assets.
Interdependence Square Income Securities	Diversified; 60% high-grade debt securities, 20% private placements, 20% lower-grade bonds, some with equity features, and preferred stock; short-term trading is allowed.
John Hancock Investors, Inc.	Diversified; 30% high-grade debt securities, 20% lower-grade bonds, some with equity features, and common and preferred stock; up to 50% private placements; 30% turnover rate per year; leverage up to 10% of net assets.
Lincoln National Direct Placement Fund	Nondiversified; 75% direct placements, some with equity features, remainder in other bonds, short-term notes, and preferred stock; 50% turnover rate per year.
MassMutual Corporate Investors	Nondiversified; 60% private placements, some with equity features, remainder in marketable bonds and short-term notes; no short-term trading; leverage up to 50% of net assets.

MassMutual Income Investors * Diversified; 75% high-grade debt securities, remainder in lower-grade bonds, some with equity features, and preferred stock; 20% turnover rate per year; leverage up to 50% of net assets.

Mutual of Omaha Interest Shares Diversified; 80% high-grade debt securities, 20% lower-grade bonds with no equity features; up to 10% private placements, no short-term trading; leverage up to 5% of net assets.

Paul Revere Investors Nondiversified; 85% long-term direct placements, some with equity features, remainder in convertibles and preferred stock; very little short-term trading.

St. Paul Securities, Inc. Diversified; 75% high-grade debt securities, 25% lower-grade bonds, some with equity features, and preferred stock; up to 25% private placements, 200% turnover rate per year; leverage up to 20% of total assets.

Transamerica Income Shares * Diversified; 50% high-grade debt securities, remainder in lower-grade bonds, 20% of which have equity features; no private placements; 200% turnover rate per year; leverage up to 10% of net assets.

USLife Income Fund Diversified; 50% high-grade debt securities, 50% lower-grade bonds, some with equity features; up to 30% private placements; leverage up to 25% of total assets.

Vestaur Securities, Inc. Diversified; 75% high-grade debt securities, remainder in lower-grade bonds, some with equity features, and preferred stock; up to 25% private placements; 200% turnover rate per year; leverage up to 20% of total assets.

---

* Swap fund—shares in the fund may be bought either with cash or in exchange for bonds of corresponding market value.

CHAPTER TWELVE

Some Personal Reflections

> An optimist sees an opportunity in every calamity; a pessimist sees a calamity in every opportunity.—Anonymous

By now you know that this book is not going to make you rich. What I have done is to lay out the major investment alternatives and indicate how you should choose the types of securities that best suit your needs and temperament. I have also offered a step-by-step guide showing how individual investors, without connections, can make sensible decisions in the stock and bond markets. I even showed how to beat the pros at their own game by purchasing diversified portfolios of stocks and bonds at substantial discounts below their market values.

There is, however, one major question that may continue to trouble any investors who have suffered with equities during the long bear markets of the early 1970s: Why buy stocks at all? I have answered this question in various places in the book, but I think it will be useful to summarize some of that discussion here.

Why Buy Stocks at All?

The Merrill Lynch–University of Chicago study showed that funds put into common stocks for any considerable period since 1925 (including the Great Depression years) have done better than equal funds put into bonds or savings accounts. In general, stocks have earned about 9 to 10 percent a year on average, including both dividends and capital gains. If we start the measurement after sharp bear markets, the rate of return is even higher. Assuming that the future is anything like the past, it does seem reasonable to assume that investors will continue to earn more from stocks than from bonds.

It is also the case that equities have provided protection against inflation over the long pull. True, the relationship has been a very loose one, and during some periods when inflation has been especially rapid, such as in the early 1970s, equities provided no protection at all. Instead, they fell in value as high-interest rates and a fear of a profits squeeze drained money from the stock market. Still, over long periods of time, corporate earnings, dividends, and stock prices have more than kept pace with living costs.

This appeal to the long run may not be satisfactory to everyone—especially to investors who have seen their capital shrink drastically in value. While the broad stock indices, such as the Dow-Jones and Standard and Poor's average, were down in 1974 about 40 percent from their previous highs, the average stock on the New York Stock Exchange had fallen almost twice that much. As Lord Keynes once said, "In the long run we are all dead." The dissatisfaction with equities goes deeper, however, than impatience with the performance over any particular period. Some investors have convinced themselves that "the stock market is dead."

Pessimists about the stock market—and there were many in the mid-1970s—had no trouble finding reasons to be gloomy. Corporate profits (adjusted for inventory revaluations) as a share of U.S. National Income fell considerably during the 1950s and 1960s, and so did rates of return on corporate investment. Many investors could look forward to nothing but more serious trouble, especially since it became very easy for the public to see "high corporate profits" as the clear villain in the inflation drama. "Who can doubt," the pessimists would say, "that the corporation will come under increasingly severe political attack, and with it the profits and dividends that undergird stock prices."

The pessimists could well be right about the gloomier prospects for corporate earnings. But it's well to remember the lessons of the theories we examined in Part Two, which suggested that capital markets are highly efficient. Bad news about corporate earnings and fears about the continued profitability of business investment will not be reflected in stock prices some time in the future—they get reflected in the market immediately. If investors perceive that the risks of investment in common stocks have increased, equities won't fall in the future. Stock prices will have already fallen to provide the higher returns necessary to induce investors to hold them —just as the theory in Chapter Eight holds.

I am suggesting that the prevalence of gloom and doom and recent unfavorable experience with equity investments is no reason to throw in the towel. It is always true that investors are pessimistic when stock prices are falling. Of course, it's possible that more bad news may come out that is not already discounted in equity prices, and the market could fall further. No one can predict for sure what will happen in the future. But it's also possible that investors are far more pessimistic than is warranted by the economic situation, and that the risk in equities has been overly discounted by panic-depressive institutional investors. It is well to remember that for the stock market as a whole Newton's law has always worked in reverse: what goes down must come back up. I firmly believe that reports of the stock market's demise are greatly exaggerated.

A Paradox

I have spent considerable time discussing closed-end funds because I consider them unusually attractive vehicles for investment in stocks at the present time, even for large investors. Nevertheless, I do not anticipate that such favorable discounts will always be available. Indeed, if this book achieves substantial readership and if the public acts on the suggestions I have made, I would anticipate that the discounts would narrow considerably.

This is the fundamental paradox about the usefulness of investment advice concerning specific securities. If the advice reaches enough people and they act on it, knowledge of the advice destroys its usefulness. If everyone knows about a "good buy" and they all rush in to buy, the price of the "good buy" will rise until it is no longer particularly attractive for investment. Indeed, there will be pressure on the price to rise as long as it is still a good buy.

This is the main logical pillar on which the random-walk theory rests. If the spread of news is unimpeded, prices will react quickly so that they reflect all that is known about the particular situation. Thus, I would be very surprised to see the current levels of discount perpetuate themselves indefinitely, and no-load funds may in the future be the only real alternative for small investors.

True believers in the random-walk theory would not be satisfied that the no-load funds provide a fully satisfactory medium for common-stock investors. One problem is that there is an annual investment advisory fee that must be paid to the fund's manager. While this fee is small in relationship to the fund's assets (it typically runs about $\frac{1}{2}$ of 1 percent), it can represent a substantial fraction of the fund's dividend income, and there are also some other expenses as well. Also, the funds tend to trade much more than firm random walkers would like. While this "excessive" trading may reflect an honest but mistaken belief that it will improve performance, there may also be ulterior motives!

Brokers who sell new fund shares are clearly deserving of special reward. More assets produce more management fee income. Funds may therefore be induced to trade so they can reciprocate by funneling commissions to the brokers who sell their shares. Funds that are managed by brokers may also be encouraged to trade more than necessary, since each trade involves earning a full commission for the broker-manager.

I do not mean to imply that all funds trade too much. I know many funds managed by brokers who scrupulously bend over backwards to avoid the possibility of trading that might be considered excessive. And the S.E.C. takes a very dim view of the practice of reciprocal business given to brokers. But there are still tremendous inherent conflicts of interest involved in the investment business, and fund managers are human like everybody else. It is unreasonable to expect that all such conflicts will inevitably be settled in favor of the fund shareholders.

The Author's Suggestion: Two New Investment Instruments

I suggested in the first edition that what we need is a no-load, minimum-management-fee mutual fund that simply buys the hundreds of stocks making up the broad stock-market averages and does no trading from security to security in an attempt to catch the winners. Whenever below-average performance on the part of any mutual fund is noticed, fund spokesmen are quick to point out, "You can't buy the averages." It's time the public could.

If the New York Stock Exchange were genuinely interested in the plight of the small investor, there is no greater service it could provide than to sponsor such a fund and run it on a nonprofit basis. This would give all individuals a chance to ride with the average rather than trying to beat the market. It would also provide a performance yardstick against which the regular mutual funds could be judged.

The fund might also allow individuals to borrow at prime interest rates up to the limits set by margin requirements in order to increase their potential returns as well as their risks. Brokers usually charge small investors at least 2 percent above the prime rate to borrow on margin, even though these loans are perfectly safe and secured by marketable stock. Even if the exchange charged borrowers a service fee sufficient to cover its costs, it would provide small investors with a much-needed investment alternative.

Since the first edition of this book came out, there has been some progress made on an index-fund offering. The Wells Fargo bank attempted to sell to institutions a fund that would buy the Standard and Poor's Index on margin. Unfortunately, the fund ran into both legal difficulties (because it was offered by a bank) and marketing problems (because it came out during a long bear market). There is one index fund, however, that will be available to the general public. American Express is planning a minimum management fee index-type fund. The fund would probably carry a small loading fee, however. While we do not yet have the perfect index alternative available, I am heartened that some progress has been made.

My second suggested innovation is even more important. The earlier discussion of the risks and rewards of various types of securities indicates how difficult it is to combine safety and inflation protection. Indeed, neither stocks nor bonds provided protection during the early 1970s, just when inflation was rapidly accelerating. What is needed is a new investment instrument, a purchasing power (or index-linked) bond that could be issued by the U.S. Treasury.

A purchasing-power bond might work as follows: The value of the bond would be adjusted each year according to the rate of inflation. For example, at an inflation rate of 4 percent, the value of a $1,000 bond would be escalated at the end of the first year to $1,040. At the end of ten years, if the price index stood 50 percent higher than it was during the base year, the bond would be written up in value to $1,500. Thus the principal amount invested would be adjustable to protect the saver against the shrinkage of purchasing power that results from inflation. In exchange for this hedge against inflation, the purchaser might agree to accept a lower interest rate on the principal than is provided by regular bonds. Such a bond would be of enormous benefit to the public.

Some Last Reflections on Our Walk

We are now at the end of our walk. Let's look back for a moment and see where we have been. No one can consistently beat the averages. Neither fundamental analysis of a stock's firm foundation of value nor technical analysis of the market's propensity for building castles in the air can produce superior results. Even the pros must hide their heads in shame in comparison with anyone who picked stocks via the dart board method. The only consistent relationship in the market appears to be that between risk and reward.

Sensible investment policies for individuals must then be developed in two steps. First, it is crucially important to understand the risk-return tradeoffs that are available and to tailor your choice of securities to your temper and requirements. Chapter Nine provided a careful guide for this part of the walk. Next, in Chapter Ten, came a number of warning signals to assure that you avoid the pitfalls of earning inferior returns by such practices as excessive trading, paying higher sales charges than necessary, and avoiding securities like Series E savings bonds and savings deposits where returns are lower than appropriate for their risk level because of gov-

ernment fiat. In addition, I suggested several useful and
tested general rules for stock and bond buying—all consistent with the existence of efficient markets.

I recognize, however, that most investors will not be convinced that the random-walk theory is valid. Telling an investor there is no hope of beating the averages is like telling
a six-year-old there is no Santa Claus. It takes the zing out of
life.

Perhaps these investors will take some comfort from the
strategies outlined in Chapter Eleven for beating the pros at
their own game. Closed-end funds, when available at big discounts, offer an outstanding investment opportunity for individual investors. It's not that I think the managers of these
funds can do any better than average (remember I'm a random walker), but that the very existence of the discount can
permit the individual to gain a higher than average return.*
Even nonbelievers in random walks should find these to be
excellent investments.

For those of you, incurably smitten with the speculative
bug, who insist on picking individual stocks in an attempt to
beat the market, reread the rules in Chapters Five and Ten.
The odds are really stacked against you, but you might just
get lucky and win big.

Investing is a bit like lovemaking. Ultimately it is really
an art requiring a certain talent and the presence of a mysterious force called luck. Indeed, luck may be 99 percent responsible for the success of the very few people who have
beaten the averages. "Although men flatter themselves with
their great actions," La Rochefoucauld wrote, "they are not
so often the result of great design as of chance."

The game of investing is like lovemaking in another important respect, too. It's much too much fun to give up. If

---

* I practice what I preach, too. As income from the first edition of this
book has come in, I've invested it, for the benefit of my son Jonathan,
in some dual-purpose funds selling at 40 percent discounts.

you have the talent to recognize stocks that have good value, and the art to recognize a story that will catch the fancy of others, it's a great feeling to see the market vindicate you. Even if you are not so lucky, my rules will help you limit your risks and avoid much of the pain that is sometimes involved in the playing. If you know you will either win or at least lose not too much, you will be able to play the game with more satisfaction. At the very least, I hope this book makes the game all the more enjoyable.

Bibliography

I have suppressed my academic proclivity for sprinkling each page with footnotes to learned references showing who said what on particular issues. I do hope, however, that this bibliography indicates clearly the sources of the studies I have discussed and provides useful additional readings for those interested in particular points. The references are grouped by chapter, and in some cases (especially for Chapters 6 and 7), notation is made of what the sources contain. Where certain references are cited throughout this book, they are listed only in the first chapter for which they were used.

Part One

CHAPTER ONE

Bernard Baruch, *My Own Story*. Holt, 1957.

Irving Fisher, *The Theory of Interest*. Kelley, 1961.

Benjamin Graham and David L. Dodd, *Security Analysis*. 1st ed. McGraw-Hill, 1934.

Samuel Eliot Guild, *Stock Growth and Discount Tables*. Financial Publishers, 1931.

John M. Keynes, *The General Theory of Employment, Interest and Money*. Harcourt, 1936.

Oskar Morgenstern and Clive William John Granger, *Predictability of Stock Market Prices*. Heath Lexington, 1970.

"Adam Smith," *The Money Game*. Random House, 1968.

John Burr Williams, *The Theory of Investment Value*. Harvard University Press, 1938.

CHAPTER TWO

Frederick L. Allen, *Only Yesterday*. Harper, 1931.

Edward Angly, *Oh Yeah?* Viking, 1931.

Walter Bagehot, *Lombard Street*. London: Murray, 1922.

Bruce Barton, *The Man Nobody Knows*. Bobbs-Merrill, 1925.

John N. Brooks, *Once in Golconda*. Harper & Row, 1969.

———, *The Seven Fat Years*. Harper, 1958.

Lester V. Chandler, *America's Greatest Depression 1929–1941*. Harper & Row, 1970.

William Cobbett, *The Parliamentary History of England*, Volume VII. London: Hansard, 1811.

Cedric B. Cowing, *Populists, Plungers, and Progressives*. Princeton University Press, 1965.

Charles Amos Dice, *New Levels in the Stock Market*. McGraw-Hill, 1929.

John Kenneth Galbraith, *The Great Crash, 1929*. Houghton Mifflin, 1955.

Charles Mackay, *Memoirs of Extraordinary Popular Delusions*, Volume I. Lindsay, 1850.
  (My discussions of the tulip-bulb craze and the South Sea Bubble rely heavily on Mackay's description.)

Cabell Phillips, *The New York Times Chronicle of American Life: From the Crash to the Blitz, 1929–1939*. Macmillan, 1969.

Nicolaas W. Posthumus, *Inquiry into the History of Prices in Holland*. Leiden: Brill, 1964.

Jelle C. Riemersma, *Religious Factors in Early Dutch Capitalism 1550–1650*. The Hague: Mouton, 1967.

Lionel Robbins, *The Great Depression*. London: Macmillan, 1935.

Robert Sobel, *Panic on Wall Street*. Macmillan, 1968.

Dana L. Thomas, *The Plungers and the Peacocks*. Putnam, 1967.

Twentieth Century Fund, *The Security Markets*. 1935.

CHAPTER THREE

Bill Adler, ed., *The Wall Street Reader*. World, 1970.

David L. Babson and Company, Inc., "Wall Street 'Discovers' Investment Quality." *Weekly Staff Letter*, August 6, 1970.

Hurd Baruch, *Wall Street: Security Risk*. Acropolis, 1971.

Murray Teigh Bloom, *Rogues to Riches*. Putnam, 1971.

John Brooks, *Business Adventures*. Weybright and Talley, 1969.

McGeorge Bundy, President's Review in *The Ford Foundation Annual Report 1966.* February 1, 1967.

Christopher Elias, *Fleecing the Lambs.* Regnery, 1971.

John G. Fuller, *The Money Changers.* Dial, 1962.

William W. Helman, *Conglomerates—What Happened?* Smith, Barney & Co., September 24, 1969.

Sidney K. Margolius, *The Innocent Investor and the Shaky Ground Floor.* Trident, 1971.

Martin Mayer, *New Breed on Wall Street.* Macmillan, 1969.

———, *Wall Street: Men and Money.* Harper, 1955.

Securities and Exchange Commission, *Special Study of Securities Market.* House Document No. 95, 88th Congress. U.S. Government Printing Office, 1963.

Robert Sobel, *The Big Board.* Free Press, 1965.

"So Long As It's Electronic," *Forbes,* February 15, 1959.

Andrew Tobias, *The Funny Money Game.* Playboy Press, 1971.

John Wall, "Want to Get Rich Quick?" *Barron's,* February 5, 1968.

CHAPTER FOUR

William W. Helman, *The Economic Outlook for 1973 and 1974.* Smith, Barney & Co., April 1973.

Burton G. Malkiel and John G. Cragg, "Expectations and the Structure of Share Prices." *American Economic Review,* September 1970. (This is a formal empirical study documenting the changing valuation standards of the market over time. It is the study referred to in the text.)

J. Peter Williamson, *Investments.* Praeger, 1971.

Part Two

CHAPTER FIVE

Benjamin Graham, *The Intelligent Investor.* Harper & Row, 1965.

Albert Haas, Jr. and Don D. Jackson, M.D., *Bulls, Bears and Dr. Freud.* World, 1967.

Gerald M. Loeb, *The Battle for Investment Survival.* Simon & Schuster, 1965.

John Magee and Robert Davis Edwards, *Technical Analysis of Stock Trends.* Stock Trend Service, 1954.

Fred Schwed, Jr., *Where Are the Customers' Yachts?* Simon & Schuster, 1940.

Smith, Barney & Co., "The Chemical Industry—The Image Has Changed." *Industry Report,* 1969.

CHAPTER SIX

The following are general works summarizing parts of the academic literature on the efficacy of technical analysis:

Fischer Black, "Implications of the Random Walk Hypothesis for Portfolio Management." *Financial Analysts Journal,* March–April 1971.

(A layman's survey of a number of studies.)

Richard A. Brealey, *An Introduction to Risk and Return from Common Stocks.* M.I.T. Press, 1969.

(Only slightly mathematical.)

——, *Security Prices in a Competitive Market: More About Risk and Return from Common Stocks.* M.I.T. Press, 1971.

(Only slightly mathematical.)

Paul Cootner, ed., *The Random Character of Stock Market Prices.* M.I.T. Press, 1964.

(A compendium of mathematical articles.)

Eugene F. Fama, "Efficient Capital Markets: A Review of Theory and Empirical Work." *Journal of Finance,* May 1970.

(An excellent but highly mathematical summary of empirical research on the random-walk theory.)

James H. Lorie and Mary T. Hamilton, *The Stock Market. Theories and Evidence.* Irwin, 1973.

(Only slightly mathematical.)

Specific studies of technical systems follow:

Sidney S. Alexander, "Price Movements in Speculative Markets: Trends or Random Walks." *Industrial Management Review,* May 1961.

Louis Bachelier, *Théorie de la Spéculation.* Paris: Gauthier-Villars, 1900.

Paul Cootner, "Stock Prices: Random vs. Systematic Changes." *Industrial Management Review,* Spring 1962.

John L. Evans, "The Random Walk Hypothesis, Portfolio Analysis and the Buy-and-Hold Criterion." *Journal of Financial and Quantitative Analysis,* September 1968.

Eugene F. Fama, "Mandelbrot and the Stable Paretian Hypothesis." *Journal of Business,* October 1963.

————, "Tomorrow on the New York Stock Exchange." *Journal of Business,* July 1965.

————, and Marshall E. Blume, "Filter Rules and Stock-Market Trading." *Journal of Business,* January 1966.

————, Lawrence Fisher, Michael C. Jensen, and Richard Roll, "The Adjustment of Stock Prices to New Information." *International Economic Review,* February 1969.

Michael D. Godfrey, C. W. J. Granger, and O. Morgenstern, "The Random-Walk Hypothesis of Stock Market Behavior." *Kyklos,* 1964.

C. W. J. Granger and O. Morgenstern, "Spectral Analysis of New York Stock Market Prices." *Kyklos,* 1963.

F. E. James, Jr., "Monthly Moving Averages—An Effective Investment Tool?" *Journal of Financial and Quantitative Analysis,* September 1968.

Michael C. Jensen, "Random Walks: Reality or Myth—Comment." *Financial Analysts Journal,* November–December 1967.

———— and George A. Benington, "Random Walks and Technical Theories: Some Additional Evidence." *Journal of Finance,* May 1970.

Charles P. Jones and Robert H. Litzenberger, "Quarterly Earnings Reports and Intermediate Stock Price Trends." *Journal of Finance,* March 1970.

Maurice G. Kendall, "The Analysis of Economic Time-Series, Part I: Prices." *Journal of the Royal Statistical Society,* 1953.

Thomas J. Kewley and Richard A. Stevenson, "The Odd-Lot Theory as Revealed by Purchase and Sale Statistics for Individual Stocks." *Financial Analysts Journal,* September–October 1967.

Robert A. Levy, "Random Walks: Reality or Myth." *Financial Analysts Journal,* November–December 1967.

————, "Relative Strength as a Criterion for Investment Selection." *Journal of Finance,* December 1967.

————, "The Predictive Significance of Five-Point Chart Patterns." *Journal of Business,* July 1971.

Benoit Mandelbrot, "Forecasts of Future Prices, Unbiased Markets, and 'Martingale' Models." *Journal of Business,* Special Supplement, January 1966.

———— and Howard M. Taylor, "On the Distribution of Stock Price Differences." *Operations Research,* November–December 1967.

Victor Niederhoffer and M. F. M. Osborne, "Market Making and Reversal on the Stock Exchange." *Journal of the American Statistical Association,* December 1966.

M. F. M. Osborne, "Brownian Motion in the Stock Market." *Operations Research,* March–April 1959.

————, "Periodic Structure in the Brownian Motion of Stock Prices." *Operations Research*, May–June 1962.

Harry V. Roberts, "Stock Market 'Patterns' and Financial Analysis: Methodological Suggestions." *Journal of Finance*, March 1959.

Paul A. Samuelson, "Proof that Properly Anticipated Prices Fluctuate Randomly." *Industrial Management Review*, Spring 1965.

Alan Seelenfreund, George G. C. Parker, and James C. Van Horne, "Stock Price Behavior and Trading." *Journal of Financial and Quantitative Analysis*, September 1968.

Seymour Smidt, "A New Look at the Random Walk Hypothesis." *Journal of Financial and Quantitative Analysis*, September 1968.

H. Theil and C. T. Leenders, "Tomorrow on the Amsterdam Stock Exchange." *Journal of Business*, July 1965.

James C. Van Horne and George G. C. Parker, "The Random-Walk Theory: An Empirical Test." *Financial Analysts Journal*, November–December 1967.

Charles C. Ying, "Stock Market Prices and Volumes of Sales." *Econometrica*, July 1966.

Alan J. Zakon and James C. Pennypacker, "An Analysis of the Advance-Decline Line as a Stock Market Indicator." *Journal of Financial and Quantitative Analysis*, September 1968.

Other works cited:

Ira Cobleigh, *Happiness Is a Stock That Doubles in a Year*. Geis, 1967.

————, "Bull Markets and Bare Knees." In *The Wall Street Reader*, Bill Adler, ed. World, 1970.

Nicholas Darvas, *How I Made Two Million Dollars in the Stock Market*. American Research Council, 1960.

Garfield A. Drew, "The Misunderstood Odd-Lotter." *Barron's*, June 25, 1962.

————, "A Clarification of the Odd Lot Theory." *Financial Analysts Journal*, September–October 1967.

Ralph A. Rotnem, "Measuring Mass Opinion in the Stock Market." *AIC* (American International College) *Journal*, Winter 1972.

John Slatter, "Lambs in the Street." *Barron's*, January 31, 1966.

CHAPTER SEVEN

The following are general works summarizing parts of the academic literature on the efficacy of fundamental analysis:

Irwin Friend, Marshall Blume and Jean Crockett, *Mutual Funds and Other Institutional Investors*. McGraw-Hill, 1970.

(A nonmathematical and very readable report on the performance of mutual funds.)

Michael C. Jensen, "Capital Markets: Theory and Evidence." *Bell Journal of Economics and Management Science,* Autumn 1972.
(An excellent but highly mathematical summary of findings on the broad form of the random walk theory.)

Specific studies of fundamental analysis follow:

Fred D. Arditti, "Another Look at Mutual Fund Performance." *Journal of Financial and Quantitative Analysis,* June 1971.

Marshall E. Blume, "The Measurement of Investment Performance." *Wall Street Transcript,* July 26, 1971.

Robert S. Carlson, "Aggregate Performance of Mutual Funds, 1948–1967." *Journal of Financial and Quantitative Analysis,* March 1970.

Kalman J. Cohen and Jerry A. Pogue, "Some Comments Concerning Mutual Fund Versus Random Portfolio Performance." *Journal of Business,* April 1968.

Irwin Friend, F. E. Brown, Edward S. Herman, and Douglas Vickers, *A Study of Mutual Funds.* 87th Congress, House Report No. 2274. U.S. Government Printing Office, 1962.

Irwin Friend and Douglas Vickers, "Portfolio Selection and Investment Performance." *Journal of Finance,* September 1965.

Ira Horowitz, "The 'Reward-to-Variability' Ratio and Mutual Fund Performance." *Journal of Business,* October 1966.

———, "The Varying (?) Quality of Investment Trust Management." *Journal of the American Statistical Association,* December 1963.

Michael C. Jensen, "The Performance of Mutual Funds in the Period 1945–64." *Journal of Finance,* May 1968.

———, "Risk, the Pricing of Capital Assets, and the Evaluation of Investment Portfolios." *Journal of Business,* April 1969.

Robert A. Levy, "Fund Managers Are Better Than Dart Throwers." *Institutional Investor,* April 1971.

I. M. D. Little, "Higgledy Piggledy Growth." In the *Bulletin of the Oxford University Institute of Economics and Statistics,* November 1962.

Harry Markowitz, *Portfolio Selection: Efficient Diversification of Investments.* Wiley, 1959.

Everett Mattlin, "Are the Days of the Numbers Game Numbered?" *Institutional Investor,* November 1971.

"Portfolio Management: U.S. Senate Style." *Institutional Investor,* October 1967.

D. L. Rosenhan, "On Being Sane in Insane Places." *Science,* January 1973.

Paul A. Samuelson, Statement before *Committee on Banking and Currency,* U.S. Senate, August 2, 1967, re Mutual Fund Legislation of 1967.

William F. Sharpe, "Mutual Fund Performance." *Journal of Business,* Special Supplement, January 1966.

———, *Portfolio Theory and Capital Markets.* McGraw-Hill, 1970.

———, "Risk-Aversion in the Stock Market: Some Empirical Evidence." *Journal of Finance,* September 1965.

John P. Shelton, "The Value Line Contest: A Test of the Predictability of Stock-Price Changes." *Journal of Business,* July 1967.

Jack L. Treynor, "How to Rate Management of Investment Funds." *Harvard Business Review,* January–February 1965.

Oldrich Vasicek and John A. McQuown, "The Efficient Market Model." *Financial Analysts Journal,* September–October 1972.

Henry C. Wallich, "What Really Is the Value of Investment Advice?" *Institutional Investor,* August 1967.

———, "What Does the Random Walk Hypothesis Mean to Security Analysts?" *Financial Analysts Journal,* March–April 1968.

Richard R. West, "Mutual Fund Performance and the Theory of Capital Asset Pricing: Some Comments." *Journal of Business,* April 1968.

CHAPTER EIGHT

The following are general discussions of capital-asset pricing theory arranged in increasing order of difficulty:

James H. Lorie and Mary T. Hamilton, *The Stock Market: Theories and Evidence.* Irwin, 1973, Chapters 10–12.

Franco Modigliani and Gerald A. Pogue, "An Introduction to Risk and Return, I." *Financial Analysts Journal,* March–April 1974.

———, "An Introduction to Risk and Return, II." *Financial Analysts Journal,* May–June 1974.

Michael C. Jensen, "Capital Markets, Theory and Evidence." *Bell Journal of Economics and Management Science,* Autumn 1972.

A number of more specific and technical studies follow:

William J. Baumol, "Mathematical Analysis of Portfolio Selection." *Financial Analysts Journal,* September–October 1966.

Fischer Black, Michael C. Jensen, and Myron Scholes, "The Capital Asset Pricing Model: Some Empirical Tests." In *Studies in the Theory of Capital Markets,* Michael C. Jensen, ed., Praeger, 1972.

Murray T. Bloom, *Rogues to Riches.* Putnam, 1971.

Eugene F. Fama and James D. MacBeth, "Risk, Return and Equilibrium: Empirical Tests." Unpublished Working Paper No. 7237, University of Chicago, Graduate School of Business, August 1972.

William L. Fouse, William W. Jahnke and Barr Rosenberg, "Is Beta Phlogiston?" *Financial Analysts Journal,* January–February 1974.

Gerald D. Levitz, "Market Risk and the Management of Institutional Equity Portfolios." *Financial Analysts Journal,* January–February 1974.

Robert A. Levy, "Beta Coefficients as Predictors of Return." *Financial Analysts Journal,* January–February 1974.

Harry Markowitz, *Portfolio Selection: Efficient Diversification of Investments.* Wiley, 1959.

William F. Sharpe, *Portfolio Theory and Capital Markets.* McGraw-Hill, 1970.

———, "Risk, Market Sensitivity and Diversification." *Financial Analysts Journal,* January–February 1972.

———, and Guy M. Cooper, "Risk-Return Classes of New York Stock Exchange Common Stocks, 1931–1967." *Financial Analysts Journal,* March–April 1972.

"The Strange News About Risk and Return," *Fortune,* June 1973.

Oldrich A. Vasicek and John A. McQuown, "The Efficient Market Model." *Financial Analysts Journal,* September–October 1972.

Chris Welles, "The Beta Revolution: Learning to Live With Risk." *Institutional Investor,* September 1971.

Part Three

CHAPTER NINE

Vladimir P. Chernik, *The Consumer's Guide to Insurance Buying.* Sherbourne, 1970.

Max Fogiel, *How to Pay Lots Less for Life Insurance.* Research and Education Association, 1971.

Pennsylvania Insurance Department, *A Shoppers' Guide to Life Insurance,* 1972.

CHAPTER TEN

David L. Babson and Company, Inc., *Weekly Staff Letter.* March 4, 1971.
George E. Pinches, "The Random Walk Hypothesis and Technical Analysis." *Financial Analysts Journal,* March–April 1970.

CHAPTER ELEVEN

Robert Frank, *Successful Investing Through Mutual Funds.* Hart, 1969.
Eugene Pratt, "Myths Associated with Closed-End Investment Company Discounts." *Financial Analysts Journal,* July–August 1966.
Ralph Lee Smith, *The Grim Truth About Mutual Funds.* Putnam, 1963.
John A. Straley, *What About Mutual Funds?* 2nd rev. ed., Harper & Row, 1967.

CHAPTER TWELVE

Barry Feldman, *An Economic Analysis of Constant Purchasing Power Bonds.* Unpublished Senior Thesis, Princeton University, 1972.
Lawrence Fisher, "Outcomes for 'Random' Investments in Common Stocks Listed on the New York Stock Exchange." *Journal of Business,* April 1965.
——— and James H. Lorie, "Rates of Return on Investments in Common Stocks." *Journal of Business,* January 1964.

Index

305